TEACHINGS FROM THE FLYING A

Gateway to Ancient Voices

Nigel Graddon

Adventures Unlimited Press

Other Books by Nigel Graddon:

ALICE'S WONDERLAND
PYTHAGORAS OF SAMOS
THE GODS IN THE FIELDS
JACK THE RIPPER'S NEW TESTAMENT
THE LANDING LIGHTS OF MAGONIA
U-33: HITLER'S SECRET ENVOY
OTTO RAHN AND THE QUEST FOR THE HOLY GRAIL
CRYSTALS, MOTHER EARTH & THE FORCES OF LIVING NATURE

Other Books of Interest:

VIMANA
ARK OF GOD
THE LOST WORLD OF CHAM
OBELISKS: TOWERS OF POWER
ANCIENT TECHNOLOGY IN PERU & BOLIVIA
THE MYSTERY OF THE OLMECS
PIRATES AND THE LOST TEMPLAR FLEET
TECHNOLOGY OF THE GODS
THE FANTASTIC INVENTIONS OF NIKOLA TESLA
LOST CITIES & ANCIENT MYSTERIES OF THE SOUTHWEST
THE ENIGMA OF CRANIAL DEFORMATION
THE CRYSTAL SKULLS
THE LOST WORLD OF CHAM
ARK OF GOD
OBELISKS: TOWERS OF POWER
ANTARCTICA & THE SECRET SPACE PROGRAM
HAUNEBU: THE SECRET FILES
ANDROMEDA: THE SECRET FILES
VRIL: SECRETS OF THE BLACK SUN

TEACHINGS FROM THE FLYING A

Gateway to Ancient Voices

Adventures Unlimited Press

Teachings From the Flying A: Gateway to Ancient Voices

ISBN 978-1-948803-79-3

Published by:
Adventures Unlimited Press
One Adventure Place
Kempton, Illinois 60946 USA
auphq@frontiernet.net

AdventuresUnlimitedPress.com

TEACHINGS FROM THE FLYING A

Gateway to Ancient Voices

CONTENTS

A Flying A pump that has seen better days!

The person who *always* must know "Why?" usually spends a very boring and mundane life.

—an old Sage

Introduction

In recent books for AUP,[1] I introduced the fictional character of a young Montana man named Brad Pulaski, and his mind-blowing visit in the summer of 1977 to a Flying A gas station. At the time of his adventure, Brad was a twenty-six-year-old lumberjack, a job from which he derived little enjoyment. He got a buzz from working in a nature environment but he regarded the work as boring and repetitive. He wanted more from life but could not put his finger on what it was he was looking for.

The surprisingly clean gas station had ancient pumps, the kind with a crank that when turned filled the top part of the pump so that gasoline drains by gravity into the tank. Brad had cranked up a little less than four gallons, drained it into the tank of his cherished BSA 650 Thunderbolt motorcycle, replaced the cap and had walked over to the attendant's office.

The windows and freshly painted frames were immaculate. An original, colourful old gumball machine sat by the door. Brad had entered and seen that sitting in an oak rocking chair was an elderly gentleman smoking a pipe and reading a large book. The old man had peered over the book and down through his glasses before he spoke. 'Hello, Brad, I think you owe me 90 cents.'

In their ensuing conversation Brad learned that the gas station's proprietor was an "otherworldly" Gatekeeper for a dimension of learning that is available to anyone who possesses an unquenched desire to explore "the other side of things." The Gatekeeper revealed that it was a combination of Brad's abundant intellectual enquiry, spiritual readiness and his no-limits personality that had brought him that day to the Flying A service station. Brad had asked if it was his destiny to find the gas station. The gatekeeper's reply had been a revelation.

'No, Brad, your destiny is solely the product of what you think and do today! You are not born with a destiny. You are born with a karmic purpose, not with a destiny. You are here because of what you thought and did today.'

During those few hours in the Flying A the Gatekeeper introduced

---

[1] *Pythagoras of Samos: Philosopher and Magician of Numbers*, 2021; *Crystals, Mother Earth and the Forces of Living Nature,* 2023;

Brad to metaphysical teachings, the most important of which was to learn how to re-programme the subconscious mind to become a healing force rather than serving as an instrument of control in an increasingly chaotic, mass-conscious world. As that magical day progressed, Brad's higher self absorbed other ancient truths, the fruits of which, he understood, would ripen as his life progressed in the coming years.

Three months later during a visit to Paris, Brad was initiated into the Ancient Mysteries by an elderly figure who stepped from the leaping flames of a bonfire and invited the young man to join him on a special journey. The old man turned out to be none other than the Master of Mysteries, Hermes Mercurius Trismegistus.

Over a three-day journey through the inner worlds, successive teachers imparted to Brad the divine knowledge contained in the books that Hermes had lodged in the Great Library of Alexandria before it was destroyed when Julius Caesar burned his ships during Civil War hostilities in Egypt in 48 BCE.

Under the skilled tutelage of the Hermetic teachers, Brad learned of the intimacies and subtleties of the evolutionary processes within Mother Earth and the corresponding healing faculties that lay deep within his spirit-soul. Especial focus was placed on those six of Hermes' forty-two books that deal specifically with the power of numbers and the arts of healing with herbs and plants, two areas to which Brad felt instinctively drawn.

The Hermetics taught that the mind is always in conflict with its surroundings and that the key to a balanced mind is the ability to magnify, without words, the living energy of the earth. This life force is the *archœus*, the vital substance in Nature upon which all things subsist. To magnify the living energy of the earth is to take time to let the senses relax and listen to what is beyond the façade of the obvious and be open to the unobvious.

At the end of the three-day period Hermes explained to Brad that his initiation would not be concluded until he had applied what he had learned in the "Worlds Within" in his day-to-day life in the "World Without."

We left Brad on the occasion of the Winter Solstice six months after he first entered the magical Flying A gasoline station. The Gatekeeper had asked Brad to return on the 21st of December, when they would speak again and celebrate the Solstice in a special way. On his arrival at the Flying A, Brad, after battling snow and ice on his Thunderbird, was distraught to find that the Flying A was a derelict relic of a bygone time. Inside the ramshackle gas station Brad had found a letter:

'Dear Brad, I'm sorry that we will not be able to keep our appointment at the Flying A on this occasion. The powers-that-be have called me away to help restore order in a Wild West town of my acquaintance. You and I will meet again. Just be patient, live life day to day, laugh a lot, never drink cognac from a paper cup, and never infringe upon any living thing.

'Pythagoras said, "Accept the fate you are given by others and you put on the cloak of a servant." You are beyond that now. It is time to step away from the lumber camp and assume your destiny as a teacher and guide to those who seek life's answers. One last thing—always remember that things are never what they seem.

'Look after yourself, Brad, you are so much more than you think you are. Adieu, your friend now and always, the Gatekeeper.'

Brad eating up the blacktop on his BSA 650 Thunderbolt

Gary Cooper points Brad in the right direction!

Th Flying A Service Station in its Golden Years

An item of classic Flying A signage found by the author at a flea market in South Wales.

Chapter 1

Finley

The air itself is one vast library on whose pages are for ever written all that man has ever said or woman whispered.

—Charles Babbage, 1837

Utterly dejected after reading the Gatekeeper's letter, Brad fired Hermes into life and tore up the blacktop, no particular place to go. He had only ridden for two miles when he slammed on the brakes, nearly skidding off the road on black ice, shouted 'Eureka,' and set off back to the Flying A, an insistent voice in his head repeating over and over, '*restore order in a Wild West town... things are never what they seem.*'

Minutes later Brad re-entered the Flying A. Excitedly, he made his way to the filling station's back room. Lying among dust and debris was a broken picture frame. Behind its splintered glass was a remarkably well-preserved poster for the 1952 movie *High Noon*, "the story of a man who was too proud to run!" When Brad had remarked on the poster back in June, the Gatekeeper, a wry twinkle in his eye, had said it was one of his favourite movies and that each time he watched it he always saw something new and inspirational. Brad had forgotten the remark…until now.

The poster depicts town marshal Gary Cooper standing behind a wooden building. Tensed for action, he is holding a gun while four baddies, guns drawn, make their murderous advance in search for the lawman. Brad recognised the striking similarity between the wooden structure and the rear of the Flying A. He went into the yard behind the filling station and looked in the direction indicated by the marshal's gun barrel.

Adopting Cooper's pose, Brad saw that he was facing an outhouse. On his previous visit Brad had not ventured into this part of the grounds and so was not aware of the small structure. Brad guessed that it must have served as a storage area for tyres, oilcans, vehicle parts and whatnot. Brad pushed open the door of the outhouse, expecting to find a cramped interior filled with clutter and debris but he is amazed to see that the room is impossibly large relative to the dimensions of its tiny construction. Moreover, it is obviously a dining room; its centre table is big enough for maybe twenty diners. Only one place is set. Together with its cutlery, linen napkin, coffee cup and glass of fresh orange juice is a vase with a single stemmed white rose and a place card with copperplate script bearing the name, *Brad Gunther Pulaski.* He could hear the receding sounds of wheels turning at speed, a whip cracking and horses neighing. A stagecoach! Could he have arrived in *High Noon*'s New Mexico town?

'No, we're not in Hadleyville, Brad, but in Finley, your home for the next three days. Welcome to Faith's Boarding House,' said a familiar smiling figure who was coming out of a kitchen with a laden breakfast tray.

'Gatekeeper!' Brad exclaimed delightedly. 'After reading your note I was afraid I wouldn't ever see you again.'

'You did have me going there for a while back then, Brad, thought you might not make it, but I'm pleased to see that your instincts are firing on all cylinders. One could always rely on Gary Cooper to put one onto the right track. Sit, eat!'

Brad didn't need telling twice; he was famished. He sat at the table and dived into his meal. 'Wow, this is tasty, you've lost none of your cooking skills! This crispy bacon is better than ever! Finley, hmm, now that I recall, I heard the place mentioned when I was in Paris a few months ago. While there I met a couple from Brittany, Michel and his wife Monique. Over dinner one night Michel described to me their extensive travels since they had sold their hotel in Lorient. They had been to the States, travelled Route 66 and, being music lovers, had visited Memphis and New Orleans. He then spoke of Finley and said a curious thing. He said it was an unusual town in America's Midwest that many sought but few found. Maybe it was the many glasses of an excellent Chateauneuf du Pape that had made me fuzzy headed that night but for some reason I haven't thought about it since. What is this place? And where is everyone else?'

The Gatekeeper settled in a rocking chair and lit his briar pipe. 'To take your second question first, Brad, there is no one else in Finley. You have the honour of being the last ever visitor from the outside to come to this unusual town, which, to answer your first question, is, like the Flying A, a supportive dimension to your world. Since its creation, Finley has allowed teachers, trainers and friends who have completed their last lifetime in your world but realise they have unfinished business, to come here to help folks with a no-limits attitude to stretch themselves like never before. Michel was here in '55. He was one of our finest students.'

The Gatekeeper puffed on his pipe and sipped some coffee. 'There are many teaching dimensions like Finley. Each has an umbilical cord link with the time and physical space that they work with. Inevitably, that connection is through nature, specifically through water, air, earth or fire.

'Time and space are curious creations made by man so that he can feel he controls his world. Those who live by the ancient esoteric laws know that the only true time is experienced in the movements of the sun, moon, stars and the changing seasons. Within these movements, from time to time a synchronicity of nature allows for doorways to open. Through these doors one finds companion worlds and experiences, which only serve to expand life.

'The ancients called these worlds "Phantom Thresholds." The only barriers within the many worlds that flow in and out of one another are placed there by the human mind. Finley is a place to help you shed those crutches in order that you can really begin to live. You crossed the virgin snow carpeting the earth from the Flying A to its old storeroom and, hey presto, here you are!'

'I'm not sure if I'm quite following you,' said Brad, a little at sixes and sevens.

'Consider it this way, Brad. You can live in a big city and have hundreds of experiences—poverty, wealth, health, illness, success, failure, horror, sadness or any among a whole host of other conditions. One experience or lifestyle will not necessarily interrelate with the other for these are products of the human experience. One comes to Finley to learn to go beyond these limits. It is important to remember that there is one mass consciousness dimension within the earth plane where ninety percent of the population interacts but at the same time there are many other dimensions that exist and function alongside or even within that dimension.'

'I think I'm getting it,' Brad said a little more confidently. 'And I'm also beginning to understand why Finley has such an unassuming name, compared with other legendary dimensions such as Camelot, Narnia or Shangri-La. If an individual, place or thing sounds spiritual or otherworldly, it is almost always a fake. Any person or spiritual organisation that is more interested in their outer image than their inner worth is showing a sure sign of a lack of depth. If you have something distinctive and creative you don't have to sell it, it will sell itself. When a person is unique and has a powerful creativity, they will pull the right people and situations to fulfil their highest potential.'

The Gatekeeper clapped his hands delightedly. 'Your unique

insights, Brad, have brought you to a very important threshold in your continuing journey of self-discovery and metaphysical endeavour. To expand on the answer to your earlier question, the reason why I couldn't keep our Solstice appointment at the Flying A was because I was asked by the powers-that-be to come to Finley to assist in the de-commisioning of this amazing town. In their infinite wisdom, they decided that it had served its purpose and, in future, Don Quixote characters such as you, Brad, will find other otherworldly environments in which to tilt windmills and experience new and unusual adventures. After all, each adventure is only an introduction to a new one.'

The late afternoon sky was now a rainbow of reds, oranges and yellows. Brad had never seen such vibrant colours. He realised he would never see the like on his home world while its atmosphere was becoming so polluted.

He reflected for a while before voicing his next question. 'If Finley is no longer a teaching dimension and you're here to turn out the lights, so to speak, then why am I here?'

The Gatekeeper puffed on his pipe. 'Finley's power to teach and guide the honest truthseeker is not quite over. When we met a few months ago we discussed your passion for all things to do with number and measure. You departed with the understanding that it was in this area, especially in the mystical Pythagorean systems of numerology that your creative and professional future lays. In your recent initiation experience in the company of Hermes and his companions you absorbed powerful insights concerning these areas of esoteric knowledge. You have here in the final hours of Finley's mystical continuance a fantastic opportunity to build on this ancient knowledge. Come, I'll take you to your new classroom.'

Brad walked in step with the Gatekeeper along Finley's main street. They passed by Ellie's Guest House, George's Carpentry Shop, Ginger's Dance Hall and Saloon, Brandon's Bar and Card Room, Teresa's Café, the Sheriff's Office and Jail, Godfrey's Barber Shop and Bath House, the Stage Depot, the Town Hall, Jim's General Store and Ruth's Blacksmith and Livery Stable. Not a soul was to be seen in what Brad imagined must have been until the last few hours a hive of activity in this unusual community of inner learning.

'It's an impressive place. I wish I could have visited while it was still a fully staffed learning centre,' Brad said, laughing.

'Who's to say that it isn't? You and I, at least, are here,' the Gatekeeper answered with a hint of mischief in his tone.

Brad thought he was missing something but by now they had arrived at Ruth's stable, a round building that appeared to be the largest in town. They stepped inside. Brad gasped as he saw that in the centre of the stable was a giant double clear quartz crystal in the form of two pyramids. The upside-down tip of the lower pyramid was sitting on an insulated copper tripod, which sat on the floor of the stable with wires spreading out from it like octopus tentacles.

'Yes, it's an amazing sight, isn't it?' said a female voice.

Brad wheeled round and saw that the speaker was a petite brunette, dressed in jeans, cowboy boots and a blue and white gingham blouse. Her smile filled the large timber stable.

'I kinda hinted we might not be alone, Brad,' said the Gatekeeper. 'Let me introduce you to Ruth, Finley's blacksmith and resident horse whisperer.

'Hi, Ruth, it's a pleasure to meet you,' said Brad delightedly.

'Likewise, Brad, we've been looking forward to seeing you here in Finley before we really and truly shut up shop in just a few hours from now. You are admiring our crystal power generator.'

'Yes, it's mightily impressive,' said Brad.

'The distance from the centre to the top of the crystal pinnacle at ceiling height is twelve feet,' Ruth explained, 'as is the measure from the middle to the point that sits on the copper tripod. Crystal in the form of a double pyramid receives, stores and generates ultra-violet rays. In Finley it serves as a power source to create lighting, produce food and deal with sewage disposal. Additionally, and very importantly for your time here, Brad, it also serves as a gateway from Finley to every other dimension it works with. Access to other dimensions is via one of the nine tile squares that you can see are placed around the double crystal pyramid. Choose one!'

Brad approached the tiles. 'Right now, Ruth, I'm reminded of all the pools of water in the "Wood Between the Worlds" in *The Magician's Nephew*, one of my favourite stories.'

'Clive Lewis was one of our favourite guests here in Finley, a very gifted man with an extraordinary mind. Narnia is a great place to visit. Maybe you'll get the opportunity one day.'

'What, Aslan's creator came here? Wow, and what do you mean, "it's a great place to visit?" Are you saying that Narnia is real?' Brad asked in amazement.

'Why not, if something can be imagined it exists. It worked not just for him but also for Carroll, Barrie, Tolkein and Burnett. Now which tile are you drawn to? Clive didn't hesitate.'

At that moment there was a mighty clap of thunder and the stable shook as if struck by an earthquake. Brad was so startled that he stumbled forward and landed on a tile.

Ruth and the Gatekeeper laughed in unison. 'Mother Nature has decided for you,' said Ruth. 'It's time you continued your education into the "other side of things," Brad. See you soon, we're not done here yet!'

Seconds later, Brad is transferred to a new landscape. He is lying on a grassy slope, eyes entranced by the beauty in the heavens. A pre-dawn sky is embroidered with uncountable beads of stellar sparkle. He is relaxed, at peace and one with the world. Around him is the enchanting perfume of flowers in bloom. Presently, the stars fade and the sun begins its ascent. Brad rises to his feet and sees that he has been lying by a meadow footpath that winds up the slope to a circular temple.

Brad moves off up the path, a fresh breeze cooling his ascent. He passes by two children at play in the meadow, a boy and girl whom he takes to be brother and sister. He has a powerful feeling that he knows them intimately. They wave cheerily, unconcerned by the stranger's appearance. Brad responds.

'*Kalimera, pethia, afto einai mia pragmatika omorfi mera*,'[2] he says, immediately astonished that he is speaking in Greek, a language with which he was wholly unfamiliar.

'*Kalimera se sas, episis, agapite, Brad*,' the girl replied, laughing. '*Kalos ithate sto nao sas, yparchei psomi, to krasi kai tis elies gia to anapsyktiko sas*.'[3]

Brad is equally amazed to discover he can understand the language. The girl had responded in kind and then welcomed him to his temple.

My temple?

Absorbed in thought Brad presses on, suddenly aware that he is hungry. The children's generous gift of bread and olives will make a welcome breakfast. Or is it lunch or dinner? He has no idea of the time, feeling that in this place the concept is meaningless and, frankly, he does not much care anyway.

He picks up his pace and soon reaches the small domed temple. From this vantage point he looks down upon a teal sea that laps onto a sandy cove beyond the meadow and a gently sloping belt of white dunes. A handful of fishermen are on the shore hauling in catches and tending nets. They see the figure on top of the hill and wave cheerily. Brad responds in kind.

---

[2] 'Good morning, children, this is a really beautiful day.'

[3] 'Good morning to you, too, dear Brad. Welcome to your temple, there is bread, wine and olives for your refreshment.'

The temple structure is twenty-five paces in diameter and supported by caryatids. The columns' female figures, representations of the nine Muses, are exquisitely sculpted. Brad steps inside and hears a flute playing an unusual melody. He looks around for the flautist but he is quite alone. The temple's round interior wall is stacked from floor to ceiling with books, parchments and scrolls. It is evidently a library. Understanding comes—*my* temple, *my* library.

In the centre of the temple are a chair and a terra cotta lion's paw tripod table bearing the children's gifts of bread, figs, cheese and olives, a jug of olive oil, a pitcher of cool water and a bronze goblet. Nearby is a *kline*, a wooden sofa adorned with cushions.

Brad sits at the table and pours himself a goblet of water, all the while running his eyes up and down the laden shelves. On one shelf about shoulder height one book among many is standing out proud from its neighbours. Brad reaches for it and makes himself comfortable. Reading its ancient Greek as if he was born to it, Brad takes a sip of water and commences reading Αρχαία Μυστήρια και Μυστικές Εταιρείες.[4]

---

[4] *Archaía Mystíria kai Mystikés Etaireíes* (*Ancient Mysteries and Secret Societies*)

A gleaming Flying A gasoline pump

ANCIENT MYSTERIES
and
SECRET SOCIETIES

Green Man woodcarving, ancient Caerleon, South Wales

Chapter 2

The Druids

Our principal guide through the ancient mysteries and secret societies of the ancient world is Manly P. Hall, the twentieth century's foremost student of esoteric history.[5]

The philosophic-religious doctrines of the pagans were divided to meet the needs of two fundamental groups of human intellect: one philosophic, the other mentally and emotionally incapable of appreciating the deeper mysteries of life. To the discerning few were revealed the esoteric, or spiritual, teachings, while the unqualified majority received only the literal, or exoteric, interpretations.

In order to make simple the great truths of Nature and the abstract principles of natural law the vital forces of the universe were personified, becoming the gods and goddesses of the ancient mythologies. In all cities of the ancient world were temples for public worship and offering. In every community there were also philosophers and mystics, deeply versed in Nature's lore. These individuals were usually banded together, forming exclusive philosophic and religious schools. The more important of these groups were known as the Mysteries, sacred dramas performed at stated periods. Among the most celebrated were those of Isis, Cybele and Eleusis.

Many of the great minds of antiquity were initiated into these secret fraternities by strange and mysterious rites. After being admitted, the initiates were instructed in the secret wisdom which had been preserved for ages. Plato, an initiate of one of these sacred orders, was severely criticized because in his writings he revealed to the public many of the secret philosophic principles of the Mysteries.

Every pagan nation had not only its state religion, but also another into which the philosophic masters gained entrance. Many of these ancient cults vanished without revealing their secrets but a few have survived the test of ages and their mysterious symbols are still preserved.

---

[5] Hall, M., *The Secret Teachings of All Ages*, Philosophical Research Society, 1928

There were literally scores of these ancient cults, with branches in all parts of the Eastern and Western worlds. Some, such as those of Pythagoras and the Hermeticists, show a decided Oriental influence, while the Rosicrucians in Europe gained much of their wisdom from Arabian mystics.

*

There is no common agreement as to the origin of Druidism. Esoteric sources date its origins to the Atlantean era, in which time, Hall explained, they were the continent's Sun-priests. After the destruction of Atlantis Druid alchemists made their way into Europe and Egypt and, over time, established monastic centres. The most prolific among these survivors from the pre-Flood priesthood were the sects in Britain and France. By the use of magical powers, including the deployment of the anti-gravity qualities of sound vibrations these initiates built the stone circles. Fourth century BCE Greek historian, Hecataeus, referred to the gods appearing at Stonehenge:

> On this island [Britain] is a remarkable temple, circular in shape, adorned with many consecrated gifts… It is said that in this island the moon appears very near to the earth, that certain eminences of a terrestrial form are plainly seen on it, that Apollo visits the island once in the course of nineteen years, in which period the stars complete their revolutions and that for this reason the Greeks distinguish the cycle of nineteen years by the name of the "great year." During this season of his appearance the god plays upon the harp and dances every night from the vernal equinox until the rising of the Pleiads, pleased with his own successes.

One line of thinking maintains that British Druid priests secured their information from Tyrian and Phoenician navigators who, thousands of years before the Christian Era, established colonies in Britain and Gaul while searching for tin. Others are of the opinion that the Mysteries as celebrated by the Druids were of Oriental origin, possibly Buddhistic.

Spencer, on the other hand, relates the Druids' emergence in Britain to the "Iberian" or "Mediterranean" race with origins in North-West Africa, perhaps the Sahara region.[6] He notes that there were further influxes of incomers from other parts of Europe, notably the Celts, but

---

[6] Spence, L., *Druids: Their Origins and History*, Barnes & Noble, 1995.

confidently states that it was the Mediterraneans' religious and mystical ideas that dominated in these isles and, thus, Britain was to remain Iberian in the religious sense.

Spencer theorised that when the Celts arrived they found a readily available system of mystical philosophy, Druidism, and so adopted it as their own. Hall referred to the Druids as the Celts' Order of Literati. In their early history the Celts first occupied an area between the upper reaches of the rivers Elbe, Danube and Rhine, spreading into northern Italy around 2,500 years ago. Subsequently, over a 300-year period beginning around 450 BCE the Celts spread rapidly over the European continent; the Romans called them Gauls. During this latter period the Celts sacked Rome (387 BCE), plundered the treasures of Delphi (the "Underworld") in Greece, and populated Spain, Britain and Ireland. Written evidence that could throw light on the development of the Celtic language, spoken today mainly in Brittany in France, Ireland, Scotland, Wales, Cornwall and the Isle of Man, is scarce as the early Celts preferred word-of-mouth communications.

This common lack of a written Celtic language has reinforced the idea held in some quarters of a culture built upon a "secret society" in which its priesthood, the mysterious Druids, played no small part. The Æduan Druid Diviciacus told Julius Caesar that those who 'desire to be perfect adepts of their art make a voyage thither [Britain] to learn it' from the Druids and their seminaries, the most renowned of which was a large college on the Isle of Mona [Anglesey] in Wales.

Caesar said that the Gauls believed that they were descended from Dis, a tradition shared by the Druids. Dis is the Latin form of Hades or Pluto, god of the dead, a term that evokes associations with initiation rites in which students die a symbolic death in order to be reborn as enlightened souls. In Britain, Dis is the Celtic god, Llyr or Bran.

The Celts' primal deity was the earth goddess, the Mother, whom was known by many names according to different sites with which she was associated. One such was Minerva who came to be known in Britain as Brighd or Brigit and who represented the virgin aspect of the Great Goddess. In Aqua Sulis (modern day Bath in the English county of Avon and Somerset) a perpetual fire was maintained in honour of Minerva. Brighd, a goddess of poetry and divine inspiration, was the patroness of the celebrated Druid bard, Taliesin.

Corresponding male gods were also worshipped, Belenos (the Greek Apollo) being held in special reverence. In the British Christian tradition, Belanos became conflated with St. Michael. The forest deity Cernunnos the Horned God, depicted with the antlers of a stag and known also as

Hu or Hesus, was the Celtic god of the underworld, the gatekeeper to the invisible companion dimensions to Earth. Acting as a psychopomp (a guider of souls and spirits), Cernunnos escorted the dead to the afterlife. He also served as a god of fertility, life, animals and wealth. The Horned God is born at the winter solstice, marries the goddess at Beltane, and dies at the summer solstice. The Celts also worshipped totem animals, each associated with an important god or goddess, a fact to recall when we later examine the Glastonbury Zodiac.

The origin of the word Druid is disputed. German scholar Max Müller believed that like the Irish word Drui it means "the men of the oak trees," highlighting his theory by referring to the dryades, the forest gods and tree deities of the Greeks. (In Sanskrit the word dru means "timber.") Others believe it to be of Teutonic origin, others Welsh. A few trace it to the Gaelic druidh, which means "a wise man" or "sorcerer."

At the time of the Roman conquest, the Druids were thoroughly embedded in Britain and Gaul. Such was the respect and reverence with which they were esteemed that opposing foes about to attack each other would lay down their arms on the orders of the white-robed druids. No undertaking of any importance was undertaken without the assistance and blessings of these priests, who stood as mediators between the gods and men and whose understanding of Nature and her laws was unrivalled.

Having appropriated Druidism into their own culture, the Celts in Britain associated their religion with the sanctity of the land and the power of certain key locations within it, usually represented as a natural shape or alignment in the form of a goddess to demonstrate their reverence for nature and its manifestations. Nigel Pennick, one of Britain's foremost authorities on geomancy, sacred geometry and associated topics, underscores the significance of these ancient beliefs when he writes: 'We connect with the "genius loci," the spirit of a place, the mother goddess of the landscape.'[7]

Indeed, the Celtic tradition makes no distinction between mythology and history, religion and daily living; all was one sacred entity. Pennick reminds us that: 'myths are primordial truths expressed at the highest level comprehensible to human beings.'

Some historians have suggested a link between the Celts and the semi-mythical Indo-Europeans ("Aryans"), the peoples of Eastern Europe and Asia Minor. Isabel Hill Elder[8] enlarged on this thinking when

---

[7] Pennick, N., *The Ancient Art of Geomancy*, Thames & Hudson, 1996.

[8] Elder I., *Celt, Druid and Culdee*, The Covenant Publishing Company, England, 1938.

she proposed that the original church of Britain was founded by Judean refugees whom she described as the Culdees ("certain strangers"). Elder believed that the Druids were Culdee priests. In this viewpoint, Elder was partly sharing the earlier opinions of Glastonbury Zodiac re-discoverer, Mrs. Katherine Maltwood, who believed the Culdees (whom she termed Khaldis or Chaldees) to be of Iberian origin.

Maltwood believed that there had to have been many thousands of Chaldee Druids at work in Britain to satisfy the high demand for architect-priest-astrologers during a very lengthy time span for the design and placement of so many earthworks, effigies, dolmens and the like. Spence advanced similar ideas, writing that despite the Romans' efforts to wholly suppress Druidism, the priests continued their religious work under the guise of the Culdees who practised an eccentric style of Christianity.

The Druids' mystery ceremonies were presided over by the goddess Keridwen, her son Avagddu and servant Gwion. These supernatural figures feature heavily in Celtic mystery rites. The Druids, custodians of the Ancient Wisdom and possessed of vast knowledge and understanding, were fundamental in the dissemination of these teachings. They were said to possess extraordinary powers inherited from their ancient mystical forebears: the ability to fly, to raise the dead, to control the weather, to move invisibly, and to travel back and forth in time.

Hall believed that the Druids were initiates of a mystery school that dated back to the Bacchic and Eleusinian rites of Greece and the Egyptian rites of Isis and Osiris. The Eleusinian rites, established by Eumolpos 1400 years before Christ in dedication to Ceres and her daughter Persephone, were the most esteemed of all the ancient religious ceremonies. At the heart of the Eleusinian mysteries is the interpretation of the secrets of Nature.

According to Artemidorus, Ceres and Persephone were worshipped on an island close to Britain with rites and ceremonies similar to those of Samothrace. Its doctrines were taught to students in forests and dark caves. Students were instructed in the creation of the universe, the mysteries of celestial bodies (including the zodiac), the secrets of occult medicine, and the rudiments of magic and sorcery. Initiations took place at the times of the two annual equinoxes and solstices. The birth of the sun god was celebrated on 25th December. They also had a Madonna or Virgin Mother with a Child in her arms who was sacred to their Mysteries. Its deepest teachings are said to have been founded on aspects of Pythagorean philosophy, especially regarding the concepts of reincarnation and metempsychosis.

There is no doubt that the Druidic Pantheon includes a large number of Greek and Roman deities. This greatly amazed Ceasar during his conquest of Britain and Gaul, and caused him to affirm that these tribes adored Mercury, Apollo, Mars and Jupiter in a manner similar to that of the Latin countries. It is almost certain that the Druidic Mysteries were not indigenous to Britain or Gaul, but migrated from one of the more ancient civilizations.

At some remote period the original inhabitants of Britain revived and reformed their national institutes. Their priest had hitherto been simply named Gwydd, but it became necessary to divide this office between the superior priest and another whose influence would be more limited. The former became Der-Wydd (Druid), and the latter Go-Wydd or O-Vydd (Ovate). Both went by the general name of Beirdd (Bards), or teachers of wisdom.

The Druidic Order is deservedly credited with having had a deep understanding of Nature and her laws. The Druids had a fundamental knowledge of medicine, especially the use of herbs and simples. Crude surgical instruments also have been found in England and Ireland. The celebrated transcendentalist, Eliphas Levi, stated:

> The Druids were priests and physicians, curing by magnetism and charging amulets with their fluidic influence. Their universal remedies were mistletoe and serpents' eggs, because these substances attract the astral light in a special manner. The solemnity with which mistletoe was cut down drew upon this plant the popular confidence and rendered it powerfully magnetic. The progress of magnetism will some day reveal to us the absorbing properties of mistletoe.[9]

Not only was the mistletoe sacred as symbolic of the universal medicine, or panacea, but also because of the fact that it grew upon the oak tree. Through the symbol of the oak, the Druids worshipped the Supreme Deity; therefore, anything growing upon that tree was sacred to Him. At certain seasons, according to the positions of the sun, moon, and stars, the Arch-Druid climbed the oak tree and cut the mistletoe with a golden sickle consecrated for that service.

In order to reach the exalted position of Arch-Druid, or spiritual head of the organization, it was necessary for a priest to pass through the six successive degrees of the Druidic Order. (The members of the different degrees were differentiated by the colors of their sashes, for all of them

---

[9] Levi, E., *Dogme et Rituel de la Haute Magie*, Paris, 1854-1856

wore robes of white.) Some writers are of the opinion that the title of Arch-Druid was hereditary, descending from father to son, but it is more probable that the honour was conferred by ballot election. Its recipient was chosen for his virtues and integrity from the most learned members of the higher Druidic degrees.

According to Lomax,[10] there were usually two Arch-Druids in Britain, one residing on the Isle of Anglesea and the other on the Isle of Man. Presumably there were others in Gaul. These dignitaries generally carried golden sceptres and were crowned with wreaths of oak leaves, symbolic of their authority. The younger members of the Druidic Order were clean-shaven and modestly dressed, but the more aged had long gray beards and wore magnificent golden ornaments.

The educational system of the Druids in Britain was superior to that of their colleagues on the Continent, and, consequently, many of the Gallic youths were sent to the Druidic colleges in Britain for their philosophical instruction and training.

The Druids lived in strict abstinence, studied the natural sciences, preserved the deepest secrecy, and admitted new members only after long probationary periods. Many of the priests of the order lived in buildings not unlike the monasteries of the modern world. They were associated in groups like ascetics of the Far East. Although celibacy was not demanded of them, few married. Many of the Druids retired from the world and lived as recluses in caves, in rough-stone houses, or in little shacks built in the depths of a forest. Here they prayed and meditated, emerging only to perform their religious duties.

James Freeman Clarke describes the beliefs of the Druids:[11]

> The Druids believed in three worlds and in transmigration from one to the other: In a world above this, in which happiness predominated; a world below, of misery; and this present state. This transmigration was to punish and reward and also to purify the soul. In the present world, said they, Good and Evil are so exactly balanced that man has the utmost freedom and is able to choose or reject either. The Welsh Triads tell us there are three objects of metempsychosis: to collect into the soul the properties of all being, to acquire knowledge of all things, and to get power to conquer evil. There are also, they say, three kinds of

---

[10] Lomax, T., *A Complete History of the Druids,* 1810

[11] Clarke, J., *Ten Great Religions*, Houghton Mifflin Company, 1881.

knowledge: knowledge of the nature of each thing, of its cause, and of its influence. There are three things which continually grow less: darkness, falsehood and death. There are three which constantly increase: light, life and truth.

Like nearly all schools of the Mysteries, the teachings of the Druids were divided into two distinct sections. The simpler, a moral code, was taught to all the people, while the deeper, esoteric doctrine was given only to initiated priests. To be admitted to the order, a candidate was required to be of good family and of high moral character. No important secrets were entrusted to him until he had been tempted in many ways and his strength of character severely tried. The Druids taught the people of Britain and Gaul concerning the immortality of the soul. They believed in transmigration and in reincarnation.

They borrowed in one life, promising to pay back in the next. They believed in a purgatorial type of hell where they would be cleansed of their sins, afterward passing on to the happiness of unity with the gods. The Druids taught that all men would be saved, but that some must return to earth many times to learn the lessons of human life and to overcome the inherent evil of their own natures.

Before a candidate was entrusted with the secret doctrines of the Druids, he was bound with a vow of secrecy. These doctrines were imparted only in the depths of forests and in the darkness of caves. In these places, far from the haunts of men, the neophyte was instructed concerning the creation of the universe, the personalities of the gods, the laws of Nature, the secrets of occult medicine, the mysteries of the celestial bodies, and the rudiments of magic and sorcery.

The Druids had a great number of feast days. The new and full moon and the sixth day of the moon were sacred periods. It is believed that initiations took place only at the two solstices and the two equinoxes. At dawn of the 25th day of December, the birth of the Sun God was celebrated.

The secret teachings of the Druids are said by some to be tinctured with Pythagorean philosophy, although the Ancient Wisdoms state that it was Druidism which significantly influenced the development of Pythagoras's subsequent teachings. Legend has it that after Pythagoras had spent forty years in a supreme effort to absorb all of the mystical teachings of the known world he was not satisfied that his quest was complete. Accordingly, he headed for the south of France. There he joined a Druid community and was initiated in the traditional dark forests and caves that they had used for centuries. Each Druid initiate was taught about creation, the power of the gods, the laws and strengths of nature and the alignment of the mathematical balance of the heavens. His quest then complete, Pythagoras withdrew to a secret mountaintop nature sanctuary in the South of France and meditated on his next step. After an autumn and winter in self-imposed isolation, Pythagoras decided to create a school in Crotona in southern Italy. The year was approximately 510 BCE.

Both the cross and the serpent were sacred to the Druids, who made the former by cutting off all the branches of an oak tree and fastening one of them to the main trunk in the form of the letter T. This oaken cross became symbolic of their superior Deity. They also worshipped the sun, moon and stars. The moon received their special veneration. Caesar stated that Mercury was one of the chief deities of the Gauls. The Druids are believed to have worshipped Mercury in the presence of a stone cube. They also had great veneration for the Nature spirits, little creatures of the forests and rivers to whom many offerings were made.

Describing the temples of the Druids, Charles Heckethorn, in *The Secret Societies of All Ages & Countries*, says:

> Their temples wherein the sacred fire was preserved were generally situated on eminences and in dense groves of oak, and assumed various forms: circular, because a circle was the emblem of the universe; oval, in allusion to the mundane egg, from which issued, according to the traditions of many nations, the universe, or, according to others, our first parents; serpentine, because a serpent was the symbol of Hu, the Druidic Osiris; cruciform, because a cross is an emblem of regeneration; or winged, to represent the motion of the Divine Spirit. Their chief deities were reducible to two—a male and a female, the great father and mother—Hu and Ceridwen, distinguished by the same characteristics as belong to Osiris and Isis, Bacchus and Ceres, or any other supreme god and goddess representing the two principles of all Being.

Godfrey Higgins states that Hu, the Mighty, regarded as the first settler of Britain, came from a place which the Welsh Triads call the Summer Country, the present site of Constantinople. Albert Pike says that the Lost Word of Masonry is concealed in the name of the Druid god Hu. The information concerning the secret initiations of the Druids indicates a decided similarity between their Mystery school and the schools of Greece and Egypt. Hu, the Sun God, was murdered and, after a number of strange ordeals and mystic rituals, was restored to life.

There were three degrees of the Druidic Mysteries, but few passed them all. The candidate was buried in a coffin, as symbolic of the death of the Sun God. The supreme test, however, was being sent out to sea in an open boat. While undergoing this ordeal, many lost their lives. The few who passed this third degree were said to have been "born again," and were instructed in the secret and hidden truths which the Druid priests had preserved from antiquity. From these initiates were chosen many of the dignitaries of the British religious and political world.

A perfect moonlit night for Druid ritual

The Druid High Priest

Carving of a nature spirit, Caerleon

Chapter 3

The Rites of Mithras

When the Persian Mysteries were brought into Southern Europe, they were quickly assimilated by the Romans. The cult grew rapidly, especially among the Roman military. During the Roman wars of conquest the teachings were carried by the legionaries to nearly all parts of Europe. So powerful did the cult of Mithras become that at least one Roman Emperor was initiated into the Order, which met in caverns under the city of Rome.

Concerning the spread of this Mystery school through different parts of Europe, C.W. King said:[12]

> Mithraic bas-reliefs cut on the faces of rocks or on stone tablets still abound in the countries formerly the western provinces of the Roman Empire; many exist in Germany, still more in France, and in this island [Britain] they have often been discovered on the line of the Picts' Wall and the noted one at Bath.

Mithras is depicted as being born from a rock, emerging from the stone, already in his youth, with a dagger in one hand and a torch in the other. He is nude, standing with his legs together, and wearing a Phrygian cap. In some variations, he is shown coming out of the rock as a child; in one he holds a globe in one hand, sometimes a thunderbolt is seen. There are also depictions in which flames are shooting from the rock and also from Mithras' cap. One statue had its base perforated so that it could serve as a fountain, and the base of another has the mask of a water god.

Sometimes Mithras also has other weapons such as bows and arrows, and there are also animals nearby such as dogs, serpents, dolphins, eagles, lions, crocodiles, lobsters and snails. On some reliefs, there is a bearded figure identified as the water god Oceanus, and on some there are the gods of the four winds.

---

[12] King, C., *Gnostics and Their Remains,* Bell and Dalby, 1864

In these reliefs, the four elements could be invoked together. Sometimes Victoria, Luna, Sol and Saturn also seem to play a role. Saturn in particular is often seen handing over the dagger or short sword to Mithras, used later in the *tauroctony* (depictions, typically in relief or sculpture, of Mithras killing a bull).

Mithras-worship in the Roman Empire was characterised by images of the god slaughtering a bull. In the Mithraic cults the bull represented masculinity, because of its strength and sexual power, as well as lunar and earthly forces, the slaying of the bull representing the triumph of male spirit over his animal nature.

Alexander Wilder[13] stated that Mithras is the Zend title for the sun, and he is supposed to dwell within it. Mithras has a male and a female aspect, though he is not himself androgynous. As Mithras, he is the lord of the sun, powerful and radiant, and most magnificent of the Yazatas (the Genii of the sun). As Mithra, this deity represents the feminine principle, representing Nature as receptive and terrestrial, fruitful only when bathed in the glory of the sun.

The Mithraic cult is a simplification of the more elaborate teachings of Zoroaster, the Persian fire magician. According to the Persians, there co-existed in eternity two principles. The first, Ahura-Mazda, or Ormuzd, was the Spirit of Good. From Ormuzd came forth a number of angels and archangels. The second was Ahriman, initially also a pure and beautiful spirit, but later he rebelled against Ormuzd, being jealous of his power. This did not occur, however, until after Ormuzd had created light, for previously Ahriman had not been conscious of the existence of Ormuzd. Because of his jealousy and rebellion, Ahriman became the Spirit of Evil. From his own self he created a host of destructive creatures to injure Ormuzd.

When Ormuzd created the earth, Ahriman entered into its grosser elements. Whenever Ormuzd did a good deed, Ahriman placed the principle of evil within it. For 3,000 years Ormuzd ruled the celestial worlds with light and goodness. Then he created man and for another 3,000 years he ruled man with wisdom and integrity. Then began the power of Ahriman, who became incarnate in the lower nature of man so that in each personality resided the dual spirits of good and evil. The struggle for the soul of man continues through the next period of 3,000 years. During the fourth period of 3,000 years, the power of Ahriman will be destroyed. Good will return to the world, evil and death will be

[13] Wilder, A., *Philosophy and Ethics of the Zoroaster,* Theosophical Publishing Society, 2005

vanquished, and at last the Spirit of Evil will bow in homage before the throne of Ormuzd. Mithras, God of Intelligence, stands as mediator between the two.

Many authors have noted the similarity between mercury and Mithras. As the chemical mercury acts as a solvent (according to alchemists), so Mithras seeks to harmonize the two celestial opposites.

There are many points of resemblance between Christianity and the cult of Mithras. One of the probable reasons for this is that the Persian mystics invaded Italy during the first century CE and the early history of both cults was closely interwoven. The Encyclopaedia Britannica makes this statement concerning the Mithraic and Christian Mysteries:

> The fraternal and democratic spirit of the first communities, and their humble origin; the identification of the object of adoration with light and the sun; the legends of the shepherds with their gifts and adoration; the flood and the ark; the representation in art of the fiery chariot; the drawing of water from the rock; the use of bell and candle, holy water and the communion; the sanctification of Sunday and of the 25th of December; the insistence on moral conduct; the emphasis placed on abstinence and self-control; the doctrine of heaven and hell; of primitive revelation; of the mediation of the Logos emanating from the divine; the atoning sacrifice; the constant warfare between good and evil and the final triumph of the former; the immortality of the soul; the last judgement; the resurrection of the flesh and the fiery destruction of the universe—[these] are some of the resemblances which, whether real or only apparent, enabled Mithraism to prolong its resistance to Christianity.

The rites of Mithras were performed in caves. Porphyry, in his *Cave of the Nymphs*, states that Zoroaster was the first to consecrate a cave to the worship of God, because a cavern was symbolic of the earth, or the lower world of darkness. Lundy described the cave of Mithras:[14]

> But this cave was adorned with the signs of the zodiac, Cancer and Capricorn. The summer and winter solstices were chiefly conspicuous, as the gates of souls descending into this life, or passing out of it in their ascent to the Gods; Cancer

[14] Lundy, J., *Monumental Christianity,* J.W. Bouton, 1876.

being the gate of descent, and Capricorn of ascent. These are the two avenues of the immortals passing up and down from earth to heaven, and from heaven to earth.

The chair of St. Peter in Rome was believed to have been used in one of the pagan Mysteries, possibly that of Mithras, in whose subterranean grottoes the followers of the Christian religion met in the early days of their faith. In *Anacalypsis*, Godfrey Higgins writes that in 1662, while cleaning this sacred chair of Bar-Jonas, the Twelve Labours of Hercules were discovered upon it, and that later the French discovered upon the same chair the Mohammedan confession of faith, written in Arabic.

Worshippers of Mithras had a complex system of seven grades of initiation and communal ritual meals. Initiates called themselves *syndexioi*, those "united by the handshake." They met in dedicated *mithraea*, underground temples that survive in large numbers.

Initiation into the rites of Mithras, similar to many other ancient schools of philosophy, apparently consisted of three important degrees. Preparation for these degrees consisted of self-purification, the building up of the intellectual powers and the control of the animal nature.

In the first degree the candidate was given a crown upon the point of a sword and instructed in the mysteries of Mithras' hidden powers. He learned that the golden crown represented his own spiritual nature, which must be unfolded before he could comprehend the true power of Mithras; for Mithras was his own soul, standing as mediator between Ormuzd, his spirit, and Ahriman, his animal nature.

In the second degree he was given the power and armour of intelligence and purity, then sent into the darkness of subterranean pits to fight the beasts of lust, passion and degeneracy.

In the third degree he was given a cape, upon which were drawn or woven the signs of the zodiac and other astronomical symbols.

After his initiations were over, he was hailed as one who had risen from the dead, was instructed in the secret teachings of the Persian mystics, and became a full-fledged member of the order.

Candidates who successfully passed the Mithraic initiations were called Lions and were marked upon their foreheads with the Egyptian cross. Mithras himself is often pictured with the head of a lion and two pairs of wings.

Throughout the entire ritual were repeated references to the birth of Mithras as the Sun God, his sacrifice for man, his death that men might have eternal life, and lastly, his resurrection and the saving of all humanity by his intercession before the throne of Ormuzd.

Women were never permitted to enter the Mithraic Order, but children of the male sex were initiates long before they reached maturity.

While the cult of Mithras did not reach the philosophic heights attained by Zoroaster, its effect upon the civilization of the Western world was far-reaching, for at one time nearly all Europe was converted to its doctrines. Rome, in her dealings with other nations, spread her religious principles, and many later institutions exhibited Mithraic culture.

Hall remarked that the references to the "Lion" and the "Grip of the Lion's Paw" in the Master Mason's degree have a strong Mithraic aspect and may easily have originated from this cult. A ladder of seven rungs (some say originally a pyramid of seven steps) appears in the Mithraic initiation. It is possible that the Masonic ladder with seven rungs had its origin in this Mithraic symbol.

This cult is another prime example of those secret societies whose legends are largely symbolic representations of the sun and his journey through the houses of the heavens. Mithras, rising from a stone, is merely the sun rising over the horizon, or, as the ancients supposed, out of the horizon, at the vernal equinox.

Mithras

Chapter 4
The Gnostics

Gnosticism is the belief that human beings contain a piece or divine spark of God within themselves. All physical matter is subject to decay and death. Those bodies and the material world, created according to Gnostic belief by an inferior being, are therefore evil. Trapped in the material world, but ignorant of its status, the pieces of God require knowledge (gnosis) to inform them of their true status. That knowledge must come from outside the material world, and the one who brings it is the saviour or redeemer.

During the first three centuries of Christianity, there was no central authority until after the conversion of Roman emperor Constantine the Great in 312 CE. Christian communities taught many different views. In the 2nd century, some groups, now collectively referred to as Gnostic Christians, claimed to have access to "secret knowledge" about the nature of the universe, the nature of Christ, and what his appearance on earth meant to believers.

The Gnostics were educated in the various schools of philosophy. Many of the schools shared the theories of Plato and his view of the universe. For Plato, "god" (or "the highest good") existed beyond the material universe, was perfect, and so would not have created an imperfect world. He posited the existence of a secondary power, the "Demi-Urge," who created matter, the substance of the physical realm. Most Gnostic systems promoted this view. Gnostic concepts mirror the school of existentialism. Gnostics asked and answered such fundamental questions as: 'Who am I?', 'Where did I come from?', 'What is the meaning of life?', 'Why am I here?', and 'What is my true self?'

However, the entire history of Christian and pagan Gnosticism is shrouded in obscurity. The early members of this faith brought upon themselves the animosity of the early Christian Church, whose leaders, the "Church Fathers" as they became known (Justin Martyr, Irenaeus, Tertullian and others) wrote volumes against these Gnostic Christians. When the mainstream Christian institution reached its position of world power it destroyed all available records of the Gnostic cult.

The name Gnostic means wisdom, or knowledge, and is derived from the Greek. The members of the order claimed to be familiar with the secret doctrines of early Christianity. They interpreted the Christian Mysteries according to pagan symbolism. They concealed their secret information and philosophic beliefs from the profane and taught only to a small group of especially initiated persons.

Simon Magus, the magician of New Testament renown, is often supposed to have been the founder of Gnosticism. Even Simon's enemies conceded that he possessed mysterious and supernatural powers, but they maintained that these were lent to him by the infernal spirits which they claimed were his ever-present companions.

The most interesting legend concerning Simon concerns his theosophic contests with the Apostle Peter while the two were spreading their differing doctrines in Rome. According to the story that the Church Fathers have preserved, Simon was to prove his spiritual superiority by ascending to heaven in a chariot of fire. He was actually picked up and carried many feet into the air by invisible powers. When Peter saw this he cried out in a loud voice, ordering the demons to release their hold upon the magician. The demons were forced to obey. Simon fell a great distance and was killed, which decisively proved the superiority of the Christian powers. This story is undoubtedly apocryphal; it is unlikely that Peter ever came to Rome. That Simon was a philosopher there is no doubt, for wherever his exact words are preserved his esoteric thinking is beautifully expressed. The principles of Gnosticism are well described in his statement, supposedly preserved by Hippolytus:

> To you, therefore, I say what I say, and write what I write. And the writing is this. Of the universal æons [periods, planes, or cycles of creative and created life in substance and space; and also celestial creatures] there are two shoots, without beginning or end, springing from one Root, which is the power invisible, inapprehensible silence [Bythos]. Of these shoots one is manifested from above, which is the Great Power, the Universal Mind ordering all things, male, and the other, [is manifested] from below, the Great Thought, female, producing all things. Hence pairing with each other, they unite and manifest the Middle Distance, incomprehensible Air, without beginning or end. In this is the Father Who sustains all things, and nourishes those things which have a beginning and end.

By this we are to understand that manifestation is the result of a positive and a negative principle, one acting upon the other, which takes place in the middle plane, or point of equilibrium, called the pleroma, a peculiar substance produced out of the blending of the spiritual and material æons. Out of the pleroma was individualized the Demiurgus, the immortal mortal, to whom we are responsible for our physical existence and the suffering we must go through in connection with it.

In the Gnostic system, three pairs of opposites, called *Syzygies*, emanated from the Eternal One. These, with Himself, make the total of seven. The six were described by Simon magus in the *Philosophumena*:

> The first two were Mind [Nous] and Thought [Epinoia]. Then came Voice [Phone] and its opposite, Name [Onoma], and lastly, Reason [Logismos] and Reflection [Enthumesis]. From these primordial six, united with the Eternal Flame, came forth the æons [Angels] who formed the lower worlds through the direction of the Demiurgus.

One group of the Gnostics was of the opinion that the Demiurgus was the cause of all misery and was an evil creature, who, by building this lower world, had separated the souls of men from truth by encasing them in mortal vehicles. The other sect viewed the Demiurgus as being divinely inspired and merely fulfilling the dictates of the invisible Lord. Some Gnostics believed that the Jewish God, Jehovah, was the Demiurgus. This concept, under a slightly different name, apparently influenced medieval Rosicrucianism, which viewed Jehovah as the Lord of the material universe rather than as the Supreme Deity.

This first Gnosticism of Simon Magus and Menander, his disciple, was amplified, and often distorted, by later adherents to the cult. The School of Gnosticism was divided into two major parts, commonly called the Syrian Cult and the Alexandrian Cult. These schools agreed in essentials, but the latter division inclined towards pantheism, while the former was dualistic. While the Syrian cult was largely Simonian, the Alexandrian School was the outgrowth of the philosophical deductions of a clever Egyptian Christian, Basilides, who claimed to have received his instructions from the Apostle Matthew. Like Simon Magus, he was an emanationist,[15] with Neo-Platonic inclinations.

Some assert that Basilides was the true founder of Gnosticism, but there is much evidence to the effect that Simon Magus laid down its fundamental principles in the preceding century. He inculcated Egyptian

---

[15] The philosophical and theological theory that sees all of creation as an unwilled, necessary and spontaneous outflow of beings of descending perfection from an infinite, undiminished, unchanged primary substance.

Hermeticism, Oriental occultism, Chaldean astrology, and Persian philosophy in his followers, and in his doctrines sought to unite the schools of early Christianity with the ancient pagan Mysteries.

To Basilides is attributed the formulation of the concept of the Deity given the name Abraxas. In discussing the original meaning of this word, Godfrey Higgins[16] demonstrated that the numerological powers of the letters forming the word Abraxas when added together result in the sum of 365. The same author also notes that the name Mithras when treated in a similar manner has the same numerical value.

Basilides taught that the powers of the universe were divided into 365 æons, or spiritual cycles, and that the sum of all these together was the Supreme Father, and to Him he gave the Qabalistical appellation Abraxas, as being symbolical, numerologically, of His divine powers, attributes and emanations. Abraxas is usually symbolized as a composite creature, with the body of a human being and the head of a rooster, and with each of his legs ending in a serpent. C.W. King[17] describes the Gnostic philosophy of Basilides, quoting from the writings of the early Christian bishop and martyr, St. Ireneus:

> He asserted that God, the uncreated, eternal Father, had first brought forth Nous, or Mind; this, the Logos, Word; this again Phronesis, Intelligence; from Phronesis sprung Sophia, Wisdom, and Dynamis, Strength.

The Gnostic order claimed to be the only sect to have actual pictures of Jesus. While these were most likely idealistic conceptions based upon existing sculpturings and paintings of the pagan sun gods, they were all that Christianity possessed. To the Gnostics, the Christ was the personification of Nous, the Divine Mind, and emanated from the higher spiritual æons. He descended into the body of Jesus at the baptism and left it again before the crucifixion. The Gnostics declared that the Christ was not crucified, as this Divine Nous could not suffer death, but that Simon, the Cyrenian, offered his life instead and that the Nous, by means of its power, caused Simon to resemble Jesus. Ireneus makes the following statement concerning the cosmic sacrifice of the Christ:

> When the uncreated, unnamed Father saw the corruption of mankind, He sent His firstborn, Nous, into the world, in the form of Christ, for the redemption of all who believe in Him, out of the power of those that have fabricated the world (the

---

[16] Higgins, G., *Celtic Druids,* R. Hunter, London, 1827

[17] Ibid

Demiurgus, and his six sons, the planetary genii). He appeared amongst men as the Man Jesus, and wrought miracles.

The Gnostics divided humanity into three parts: those who, as savages, worshipped only the visible Nature; those who, like the Jews, worshipped the Demiurgus; and lastly, themselves, or others of a similar cult, including certain sects of Christians (including subsequently the Cathar faithful of the Middle Ages), who worshipped Nous (Christ) and the true spiritual light of the higher æons.

After the death of Basilides, Valentinus became the leading inspiration of the Gnostic movement. He still further complicated the system of Gnostic philosophy by adding greatly to the details. He increased the number of emanations from the Great One (the Abyss) to fifteen pairs and also laid much emphasis on the Virgin Sophia, or Wisdom. In the *Books of the Saviou*r—parts of which are commonly known as the Pistis Sophia—may be found much material concerning this doctrine of æons and their strange inhabitants.

Many of the theories of the ancient Gnostics, especially those concerning scientific subjects, have been substantiated by modern research. Several sects branched off from the main stem of Gnosticism, such as the Valentinians, the Ophites (serpent worshippers) and the Adamites. After the third century their power waned, and the Gnostics practically vanished from the philosophic world. An effort was made during the Middle Ages to resurrect Gnostic principles, but owing to the destruction of their records the material necessary was not available.

Sofia—Personification of Wisdom

Chapter 5

The Mysteries of Serapis

The identity of Serapis (known to the Greeks as Serapis and the Egyptians as Asar-Hapi) is shrouded in impenetrable mystery. While this deity was a familiar figure among the symbols of Egyptian initiatory rites, his arcane nature was revealed only to those who had fulfilled the requirements of the Serapic cult. Therefore, excepting the initiated priests, the Egyptians themselves were ignorant of his true character. So far as known, there exists no authentic account of the rites of Serapis, but an analysis of the deity and his symbols reveals their salient points. In an oracle delivered to the King of Cyprus, Serapis described himself:

> A god I am such as I show to thee,
> The Starry Heavens are my head, my trunk the sea,
> Earth forms my feet, mine ears the air supplies,
> The Sun's far-darting, brilliant rays, mine eyes.

Several ancient authors affirmed that Serapis was a name for the Sun because his image so often had a halo of light about its head. In his *Oration Upon the Sovereign Sun*, Julian speaks of the deity in these words: 'One Jove, one Pluto, one Sun is Serapis.' In Hebrew, Serapis is Saraph, meaning "to blaze out" or "to blaze up." For this reason the Jews designated one of their hierarchies of spiritual beings, Seraphim.

The most common theory, however, regarding the origin of the name Serapis is as a derivation from the compound Osiris-Apis. At one time the Egyptians believed that the dead were absorbed into the nature of Osiris, the god of the dead. Hall[18] remarks that while marked similarity exists between Osiris-Apis and Serapis, the theory advanced by Egyptologists that Serapis is merely a name given to the dead Apis, or sacred bull of Egypt, is untenable in view of the transcendent wisdom possessed by the Egyptian priesthood, who used the god to symbolize the soul of the world (the *anima mundi*). The material body of Nature was

---

[18] Ibid

called Api; the soul which escaped from the body at death but was enmeshed with the form during physical life was designated Serapis.

It has been speculated that Serapis is a deity of Brahmanic extraction, the name being the Grecianized form of Ser-adah or Sri-pa, two titles ascribed to Yama, the Hindu god of death. This appears reasonable, especially since there is a legend to the effect that Serapis, in the form of a bull, was brought by Bacchus from India to Egypt. Among other meanings suggested for the word Serapis are: "The Sacred Bull," "The Sun in Taurus," "The Soul of Osiris," "The Sacred Serpent," and "The Retiring of the Bull." The last appellation has reference to the ceremony of drowning the sacred Apis in the waters of the Nile every twenty-five years.

There is considerable evidence that the famous statue of Serapis in the Serapeum at Alexandria was originally worshipped under another name at Sinope in Turkey, from which it was brought to Alexandria. There is also a legend which describes Serapis as a very early king of the Egyptians, to whom they owed the foundation of their philosophical and scientific power. After his death this king was elevated to the estate of a god. Phylarchus declared that the word Serapis means "the power that disposed the universe into its present beautiful order."

In his *Isis and Osiris*, Plutarch gives this account of the origin of the magnificent statue of Serapis which stood in the Serapeum at Alexandria:

> While he was Pharaoh of Egypt, Ptolemy Soter had a strange dream in which he beheld a tremendous statue, which came to life and ordered the Pharaoh to bring it to Alexandria with all possible speed. Ptolemy Soter, not knowing the whereabouts of the statue, was sorely perplexed as to how he could discover it. While the Pharaoh was relating his dream, a great traveller by the name of Sosibius, coming forward, declared that he had seen such an image at Sinope. The Pharaoh immediately dispatched Soteles and Dionysius to negotiate for the removal of the figure to Alexandria. Three years elapsed before the image was finally obtained, the representatives of the Pharaoh finally stealing it and concealing the theft by spreading a story that the statue had come to life and, walking down the street leading from its temple, had boarded the ship prepared for its transportation to Alexandria. Upon its arrival in Egypt, the figure was brought into the presence of two Egyptian Initiates—the Eumolpid Timotheus and Manetho the Sebennite—who immediately pronounced it to be Serapis. The

priests then declared that it was equivalent to Pluto. This was a masterly stroke, for in Serapis the Greeks and Egyptians found a deity in common and thus religious unity was consummated between the two nations.

Several figures of Serapis that stood in his various temples in Egypt and Rome have been described by early authors. Nearly all these showed Grecian rather than Egyptian influence. In some the body of the god was encircled by the coils of a great serpent. Others showed him as a composite of Osiris and Apis.

A description of the god, which Hall regarded as probably accurate, represents him as a tall, powerful figure, conveying the twofold impression of manly strength and womanly grace. His face portrayed a deeply pensive mood, the expression inclining toward sadness. His hair was long and arranged in a somewhat feminine manner, resting in curls upon his breast and shoulders. The face, except for its heavy beard, was also decidedly feminine. The figure of Serapis was usually robed from head to foot in heavy draperies, believed by initiates to conceal the fact that his body was androgynous.

Various substances were used in making the statues of Serapis. Some were carved from stone or marble by skilled craftsmen; others may have been cast from base or precious metals. One colossus of Serapis was composed of plates of various metals fitted together. In a labyrinth sacred to Serapis stood a thirteen-foot statue of him, reputed to have been made from a single emerald. Clement of Alexandria describes a figure of Serapis compounded from the following elements: filings of gold, silver, lead, then all manner of Egyptian stones, including sapphires, hematites, emeralds and topazes; all these being ground down and mixed together with the colouring matter left over from the funeral of Osiris and Apis. The result was a rare and curious figure, indigo in colour. Some of the statues of Serapis must have been formed of extremely hard substances, for when a Christian soldier, carrying out the orders of Theodosius, struck the Alexandrian Serapis with his axe, that instrument was shattered into fragments and sparks flew from it. It is also quite probable that Serapis was worshipped in the form of a serpent, in common with many of the higher deities of the Egyptian and Greek pantheons.

Serapis was called Theon Heptagrammaton, or the god with the name of seven letters (like Abraxas and Mithras). In their hymns to Serapis the priests chanted the seven vowels. Occasionally Serapis is depicted with horns or a coronet of seven rays. These evidently represented the seven divine intelligences manifesting through the solar light.

The Encyclopædia Britannica notes that the earliest authentic mention of Serapis is in connection with the death of Alexander. Such was the prestige of Serapis that he alone of the gods was consulted on behalf of the dying king.

The Egyptian secret school of philosophy was divided into the Lesser and the Greater Mysteries, the former being sacred to Isis and the latter to Serapis and Osiris. Only the priests were permitted to enter the Greater Mysteries. Even the heir to the throne was not eligible until he had been crowned Pharaoh, when, by virtue of his regal office, he automatically became a priest and the temporal head of the state religion.

Much of the information concerning the rituals of the higher degrees of the Egyptian Mysteries has been obtained from an examination of the chambers and passageways in which the initiations were given. Under the temple of Serapis destroyed by Theodosius were found strange mechanical contrivances constructed by the priests in the subterranean crypts and caverns where the nocturnal initiatory rites were celebrated. These machines indicate the severe tests of moral and physical courage undergone by the candidates. After passing through these terrifying rooms and passageways, the neophytes who survived the ordeals were ushered into the presence of Serapis, a noble and awe-inspiring figure illumined by unseen lights.

Labyrinths and mazes were favoured places of initiation among many ancient cults. Remains of these mystic mazes have been found among the American Indians, Hindus, Persians, Egyptians and Greeks. Some of these mazes are merely pathways lined with stones; others are literally miles of gloomy caverns under temples or hollowed from the sides of mountains. The famous labyrinth of Crete, in which roamed the bull-headed Minotaur, was unquestionably a place of initiation into the Cretan Mysteries. Labyrinths were a striking feature in connection with the Rite of Serapis. E.A. Wallis Budge[19] depicts Serapis Minotaur-like with the body of a man and the head of a bull. Labyrinths were symbolic of the involvements and illusions of the lower world through which wanders the soul of man in its search for truth. In the labyrinth dwells the lower animal man with the head of the bull, who seeks to destroy the soul entangled in the maze of worldly ignorance. In this relation Serapis becomes the Adversary who tests the souls of those seeking union with the Immortals. The maze was also designed to represent the solar system,

---

[19] Budge, E., *Gods of the Egyptians,* London: Methuen & Co, 1904.

the Bull-Man representing the sun dwelling in the mystic maze of its planets, moons and asteroids.

The Gnostic Mysteries were acquainted with the arcane meaning of Serapis, and through the medium of Gnosticism this god became inextricably associated with early Christianity. In fact, the Emperor Hadrian, while travelling in Egypt in CE 24, declared in a letter to Servianus that the worshippers of Serapis were Christians and that the Bishops of the church also worshipped at his shrine. He even declared that the Patriarch himself, when in Egypt, was forced to adore Serapis as well as Christ. The importance of Serapis as a prototype of Christ can be best appreciated after a consideration of King's commentary:[20]

> There can be no doubt that the head of Serapis, marked as the face is by a grave and pensive majesty, supplied the first idea for the conventional portraits of the Saviour. The Jewish prejudices of the first converts were so powerful that we may be sure no attempt was made to depict His countenance until some generations after all that had beheld it on earth had passed away.

Serapis gradually usurped the positions previously occupied by the other Egyptian and Greek gods, and became the supreme deity of both religions. His power continued until the occasion in the fourth century when Christian soldiers entered the Serapeum at Alexandria to destroy the image of Serapis which had stood there for centuries. So great was their veneration for the god that they dared not touch the image lest the ground should open at their feet and engulf them. At length, overcoming their fear, they demolished the statue, sacked the building, and finally burned the magnificent library which was housed within the lofty apartments of the Serapeum.

Several writers have recorded the remarkable fact that Christian symbols were found in the ruined foundations of this pagan temple. Socrates, a church historian of the fifth century, declared that after the Christians had razed the Serapeum at Alexandria and scattered the demons that dwelt there under the guise of gods, beneath the foundations was found the monogram of Christ.

[20] Ibid

Bust of Serapis

Serapis of Alexandria, Chiddingstone Castle, Kent

Serapis—the Greco-Roman Deity of the Sun

Chapter 6

Odin

The date of the founding of the Odinic Mysteries is uncertain, some writers declaring that they were established in the first century before Christ; others, the first century after Christ. Robert Macoy, 33°, in his *General History of Freemasonry* described their origin:

> It appears from the northern chronicles that in the first century of the Christian Era, Sigge, the chief of the Aser, an Asiatic tribe, emigrated from the Caspian Sea and the Caucasus into northern Europe. He directed his course northwesterly from the Black sea to Russia, over which, according to tradition, he placed one of his sons as a ruler, as he is said to have done over the Saxons and the Franks. He then advanced through Cimbria to Denmark, which acknowledged his fifth son Skiold as its sovereign, and passed over to Sweden, where Gylf, who did homage to the wonderful stranger, and was initiated into his mysteries, then ruled. He soon made himself master here, built Sigtuna as the capital of his empire, and promulgated a new code of laws, and established the sacred mysteries. He, himself, assumed the name of Odin, founded the priesthood of the twelve Drottars who conducted the secret worship, and the administration of justice, and, as prophets, revealed the future. The secret rites of these mysteries celebrated the death of Balder, the beautiful and lovely, and represented the grief of Gods and men at his death, and his restoration to life.

After his death the historical Odin was deified, his identity being merged into that of the mythological Odin, god of wisdom, whose cult he had spread. Odinism then supplanted the worship of Thor, the thunderer, the supreme deity of the ancient Scandinavian pantheon. The mound where, according to legend, King Odin was buried is still to be seen near the site of his great temple at Upsala. The twelve Drottars who presided over the Odinic Mysteries evidently personified the twelve holy and ineffable names of Odin. The rituals of the Odinic Mysteries were very similar to those of the Greeks, Persians, and Brahmins, after which they were patterned. The Drottars, who symbolized the signs of the zodiac, were the custodians of the arts and sciences, which they revealed to those who passed successfully the ordeals of initiation.

Like many other pagan cults, the Odinic Mysteries, as an institution, were destroyed by Christianity, but the underlying cause of their fall was the corruption of the priesthood. Hall[21] described the sacred drama that formed the basis of the Odinic Mysteries:

> The Supreme, invisible Creator of all things was called All-Father. His regent in Nature was Odin, the one-eyed god. Like Quetzalcoatl, Odin was elevated to the dignity of the Supreme Deity. According to the Drottars, the universe was fashioned from the body of Ymir, the hoarfrost giant. Ymir was formed from the clouds of mist that rose from Ginnungagap, the great cleft in chaos into which the primordial frost giants and flame giants had hurled snow and fire. The three gods—Odin, Vili and Ve—slew Ymir and from him formed the world. From Ymir's various members the different parts of Nature were fashioned.

After Odin had established order, he caused a wonderful palace, called Asgard, to be built on the top of a mountain, and here the twelve gods dwelt together, far above the limitations of mortal men. On this mountain also was Valhalla, the palace of the slain, where those who had heroically died fought and feasted day after day. Each night their wounds were healed and the boar whose flesh they ate renewed itself as rapidly as it was consumed.

Balder the Beautiful, the Scandinavian Christ, was the beloved son of Odin. Balder was not warlike; his kindly and beautiful spirit brought peace and joy to the hearts of the gods, and they all loved him save one. As Jesus had a Judas among His twelve disciples, so one of the twelve gods was false: Loki, the personification of evil. Loki caused Hothr, the blind god of fate, to kill Balder with a mistletoe arrow. With the death of Balder, light and joy vanished from the lives of the other deities. Heartbroken, the gods gathered to find a method whereby they could resurrect this spirit of eternal life and youth. The result was the establishment of the Mysteries.

The Odinic Mysteries were taught in underground crypts or caves, the chambers, nine in number, representing the Nine Worlds of the

[21] Ibid

Mysteries. The candidate seeking admission was assigned the task of raising Balder from the dead. Although he did not realize it, he himself played the part of Balder. He called himself a wanderer; the caverns through which he passed were symbolic of the worlds and spheres of Nature. The priests who initiated him were emblematic of the sun, the moon and the stars. The three supreme initiators—the Sublime, the Equal to the Sublime, and the Highest—were analogous to the Worshipful Master and the junior and Senior Wardens of a Masonic lodge.

After wandering for hours through the intricate passageways, the candidate was ushered into the presence of a statue of Balder the Beautiful, the prototype of all initiates into the Mysteries. This figure stood in the centre of a great room roofed with shields. In the midst of the chamber stood a plant with seven blossoms. In this room, which symbolized the house of the Æsir, or Wisdom, the neophyte took his oath of secrecy and piety upon the naked blade of a sword. He drank the sanctified mead from a bowl made of a human skull and, having passed successfully through all the tortures and trials designed to divert him from the course of wisdom, he was finally permitted to unveil the mystery of Odin—the personification of wisdom. He was presented, in the name of Balder, with the sacred ring of the order; he was hailed as a man reborn; and it was said of him that he had died and had been raised again without passing through the gates of death.

Odin, ruling from Asgard, with his wolves, Geri and Freki, and his ravens, Hugin and Munin that fly all over the world and report on what they see.

Yggdrasil, the Norse Tree of Life, encompassing all the nine worlds of the cosmos

An oak carving of Odin

Chapter 7

The Eleusinian Mysteries

The most famous of the ancient religious Mysteries was the Eleusinian, whose rites were celebrated every five years in the city of Eleusis to honour Demeter, goddess of the harvest (Ceres to the Romans), and her daughter, Persephone.

The initiates of the Eleusinian School were famous throughout Greece for the beauty of their philosophic concepts and the high standards of morality which they demonstrated in their daily lives. Because of their excellence, these Mysteries spread to Rome and Britain. Later the initiations were conducted in both these countries.

The Eleusinian Mysteries, named for the community in Attica where the sacred dramas were first presented, are generally believed to have been founded by Eumolpos in around 1400 BCE. Through the Platonic system of philosophy, their principles have been preserved to modern times. The rites of Eleusis, with their mystical interpretations of the forces of living Nature, overshadowed the civilizations of their time and gradually absorbed many smaller schools, incorporating into their own system whatever valuable information these lesser institutions possessed. Heckethorn[22] suggested in his essay, *Mysteries of Ceres and Bacchus*, that the Eleusinian ceremonies were a metamorphosis of the rites of Isis and Osiris.

The rites were divided into what were called the Lesser and the Greater Mysteries. The Lesser Mysteries were celebrated in the spring, at the time of the vernal equinox, and the Greater in the autumn. It is supposed that the former were given annually and the latter every five years. The rituals were highly involved, and to understand them required a deep study of Greek mythology, which they interpreted esoterically with the aid of their secret keys.

---

[22] Heckethorn, C., *The Secret Societies of All Ages & Countries,* G. Redway, London, 1897.

The Lesser Mysteries were dedicated to Persephone. Thomas Taylor[23] described their purpose: 'The Lesser Mysteries were designed by the ancient theologists, their founders, to signify occultly the condition of the unpurified soul invested with an earthy body, and enveloped in a material and physical nature.'

The legend used in the Lesser rites is that of the abduction of the goddess Persephone, the daughter of Ceres, by Pluto, the lord of the underworld, or Hades. While Persephone is picking flowers in a beautiful meadow, the earth suddenly opens and the lord of death, riding in a magnificent chariot, emerges from its depths and, grasping her in his arms, carries the goddess to his subterranean palace, where he forces her to become his queen.

It is difficult to obtain satisfactory information concerning the Mysteries, for the candidates were bound by oaths never to reveal their inner secrets to the uninitiated. At the beginning of the ceremony of initiation, the candidate stood upon the skins of animals sacrificed for the purpose, and vowed that death should seal his lips before he would divulge the sacred truths which were about to be communicated to him.

Through indirect channels, however, some of their secrets have been preserved. The soul of man—often called Psyche, and in the Eleusinian Mysteries symbolized by Persephone—is essentially a spiritual force. Its true home is in the higher worlds, where, free from the bondage of material form and material concepts, it is said to be truly alive and self-expressive. The human, or physical, nature of man, according to this doctrine, is a tomb, a quagmire, a false and impermanent thing, the source of all sorrow and suffering. Plato describes the body as the sepulchre of the soul; and by this he means not only the human form but also human nature.

The gloom of the Lesser Mysteries represented the agony of the spiritual soul unable to express itself because it has accepted the limitations and illusions of the human condition. The crux of the Eleusinian argument was that man is neither better nor wiser after death than during life. If he does not rise above ignorance during his time here, man goes at death into eternity to wander about forever, making the same mistakes which he made here. If he does not outgrow the desire for material possessions here, he will carry it with him into the next world, where, because he can never gratify the desire, he will continue in endless agony.

---

[23] Taylor, T., *Eleusinian and Bacchic Mysteries: a Dissertation*, Bouton, New York, 1891

Dante's Inferno is symbolically descriptive of the sufferings of those who never freed their spiritual natures from the cravings, habits and limitations of their chthonic personalities. Those who made no endeavour to improve themselves during their physical lives passed at death into Hades, where, lying in rows, they slept through all eternity as they had slept through life.

To the Eleusinian philosophers, birth into the physical world was death in the fullest sense of the word, and the only true birth was that of the spiritual soul of man rising out of the womb of his own physical nature. Longfellows' words: 'The soul is dead that slumbers,' expresses the keynote of the Eleusinian Mysteries. Just as Narcissus, gazing at himself in the water lost his life trying to embrace a reflection, so man, gazing into the mirror of Nature and accepting as his real self the senseless illusory figure that he sees reflected, loses the opportunity afforded by physical life to unfold his immortal, invisible Self.

Teachers in ancient times said that the living are ruled by the dead. Only those conversant with the Eleusinian concept of life could understand that statement. It means that the majority of people are not ruled by their living spirits but by their senseless (hence dead) animal personalities.

Transmigration and reincarnation were taught in these Mysteries, but in a somewhat unusual manner. It was believed that at midnight the invisible worlds were closest to Earth and that souls coming into material existence slipped in during the midnight hour. For this reason many of the Eleusinian ceremonies were performed at midnight. Some of those sleeping spirits who had failed to awaken their higher natures during the earth life and who now floated around in the invisible worlds, surrounded by a darkness of their own making, occasionally slipped through at this hour and assumed the forms of various creatures.

The mystics of Eleusis also laid stress upon the evil of suicide, explaining that there was a profound mystery concerning this crime of which they could not speak, but warning their disciples that a great sorrow comes to all who take their own lives.

As the degree of the Lesser Mysteries dealt largely with the miseries of those who failed to make the best use of their philosophic opportunities, the chambers of initiation were subterranean and the horrors of Hades were vividly depicted in a complicated ritualistic drama.

After passing successfully through the tortuous passageways, with their trials and dangers, the candidate received the honorary title of Mystes. This meant one who saw through a veil or had a clouded vision. It also signified that the candidate had been brought up to the veil, which would be torn away in the higher degree. The modern word mystic, as referring to a seeker after truth in things unseen, is probably derived from this ancient word.

The next step in the candidate's mystical journey, the Greater Mysteries, were sacred to Ceres, the mother of Persephone, and represent her as wandering through the world in search of her abducted daughter. Ceres carried two torches, intuition and reason, to aid her in the quest to find her lost child (the soul). At last she found Persephone not far from Eleusis, and out of gratitude taught the people there to cultivate corn, which is sacred to her. She also founded the Mysteries.

Ceres appeared before Pluto, god of the souls of the dead, and pleaded with him to allow Persephone to return to her home. At first he refused to do so because Persephone had eaten of the pomegranate, the fruit of mortality. At last, he compromised and agreed to permit Persephone to live in the upper world half of the year if she would stay with him in the darkness of Hades for the remaining half.

The Greeks believed that Persephone was a manifestation of the solar energy, which in the winter months lived under the earth with Pluto, but in the summer returned again with the goddess of productiveness. There is a legend that the flowers loved Persephone and that every year when she left for the dark realms of Pluto, the plants and shrubs would die of grief.

The Greater Mysteries revealed to initiates not only the simplest but also the most direct and complete method of liberating their higher natures from the bondage of material ignorance. Like Prometheus chained to the top of Mount Caucasus, Man's higher nature is chained to his inadequate personality.

The nine days of initiation were also symbolic of the nine spheres through which the human soul descends during the process of assuming a terrestrial form. The secret exercises for spiritual unfoldment given to disciples of the higher degrees are unknown, but it is believed that in common with the Serapis rituals they were similar to the Brahmanic Mysteries, since it is known that the Eleusinian ceremonies were closed with the Sanskrit words "Konx Om Pax" (after the mystic Egyptian phrase "Khabs Am Pekht," roughly translating as "Light in Extension").

In considering that part of the allegory referring to the two six-month periods during one of which Persephone must remain with Pluto, while during the other she may revisit the upper world, it is probable that the Eleusinians realized that the soul left the body during steep. Thus Persephone would remain as the queen of Pluto's realm during the waking hours, but would ascend to the spiritual worlds during the periods of sleep. The initiate was taught how to plead with Pluto to permit Persephone (the initiate's soul) to ascend from the darkness of his material nature into the light of understanding. Freed from the shackles of the physical, the initiate was liberated not only for the period of his life but also for all eternity.

In contrast to the idea of Hades as a state of darkness below, the gods were said to inhabit the tops of mountains, a well-known example being Mount Olympus, where the twelve deities of the Greek pantheon were said to dwell together.

During the course of initiation the candidate passed through two gates. The first led downward into the lower worlds and symbolized his birth into ignorance. The second led upward into a room brilliantly lighted by unseen lamps, in which was a brilliantly illumined statue of Ceres and which symbolized the upper world, or the abode of Light and Truth. Here he was instructed in the highest of the secret mysteries of the Eleusis. At the conclusion of this ceremony he was hailed as an Epoptes, which means one who has beheld or seen directly. For this reason, initiation was also termed autopsy. The Epoptes was then given certain sacred books, probably written in cipher, together with tablets of stone on which secret instructions were engraved. Strabo states that the great temple of Eleusis would hold between twenty and thirty thousand people. The caves dedicated by Zoroaster also had these two doors, symbolizing the avenues of birth and death. Porphyry[24] outlined a conception of Eleusinian symbolism:

> God being a luminous principle, residing in the midst of the most subtile fire, he remains for ever invisible to the eyes of those who do not elevate themselves above material life: on this account, the sight of transparent bodies, such as crystal, Parian marble, and even ivory, recalls the idea of divine light; as the sight of gold excites an idea of its purity, for gold cannot he sullied. Some have thought by a black stone was signified the invisibility of the divine essence. To express supreme reason, the Divinity was represented under the human form, and beautiful, for God is the source of beauty; of different ages, and in various attitudes, sitting or upright; of one or the other sex, as a virgin or a young man, a husband or a bride, that all the shades and gradations might be marked. Every thing luminous was subsequently attributed to the gods; the sphere,

[24] Ouvaroff, M., *Essay on the Mysteries of Eleusis,* republished by Forgotten Books, England, 2020

and all that is spherical, to the universe, to the sun and the moon—sometimes to Fortune and to Hope. The circle, and all circular figures, to eternity—to the celestial movements; to the circles and zones of the heavens. The section of circles, to the phases of the moon; and pyramids and obelisks, to the igneous principle, and through that to the gods of Heaven. A cone expresses the sun, a cylinder the earth; the phallus and triangle (a symbol of the matrix) designate generation.

John Weisse[25] described the officials of the Eleusinian Mysteries as consisting of a male and a female hierophant who directed the initiations; a male and a female torchbearer; a male herald; and a male and a female altar attendant. There were also numerous minor officials. According to Porphyry, the hierophant represents Plato's Demiurgus, or Creator of the world; the torchbearer, the Sun; the altar man, the Moon; the herald, Hermes, or Mercury; and the other officials, minor stars.

From the records available, a number of strange and apparently supernatural phenomena accompanied the rituals. Many initiates claim to have actually seen the living gods themselves. Whether this was the result of religious ecstasy or the actual cooperation of invisible powers with the visible priests must remain a mystery.

In the *Golden Ass*, Apuleius describes his initiation into the Eleusinian Mysteries:

> I approached to the confines of death, and having trod on the threshold of Proserpine, I returned from it, being carried through all the elements. At midnight I saw the sun shining with a splendid light; and I manifestly drew near to, the gods beneath, and the gods above, and proximately adored them.

Women and children were admitted to the Eleusinian Mysteries, and at one time there were literally thousands of initiates. The higher teachings were given to only a limited number who, because of superior intellect and receptivity, showed a comprehensive grasp of their underlying philosophical concepts. Socrates refused to be initiated into the Eleusinian Mysteries, for knowing its principles without being a member of the order he realized that membership would seal his tongue.

The garments in which candidates were initiated were preserved for many years and were believed to possess almost sacred properties. Just as the soul can have no covering save wisdom and virtue, so the candidates—being as yet without true knowledge—were presented to the

---

[25] Weisse, *Obelisk in Freemasonry*, J .W. Bouton, New York, 1880

Mysteries unclothed, being first given the skin of an animal and later a consecrated robe to symbolize the philosophical teachings received by the initiate.

According to Heckethorn,[26] the Eleusinian Mysteries survived all others and did not cease to exist as an institution until nearly four hundred years after Christ, when they were finally suppressed by Theodosius, the "Great," who destroyed all who did not accept the Christian faith. Of this greatest of all philosophical institutions Cicero said that it taught men not only how to live but also, most importantly, how to die.

---

[26] Ibid

Demeter, Greek goddess of the harvest

Eleusis

Ceres, Roman goddess of agriculture and fertility

Chapter 8
Orpheus

Orpheus, the Thracian poet, ceased to be known as a man and became a celebrated divinity several centuries before the Christian Era. Thomas Taylor wrote:[27]

> As to Orpheus himself, scarcely a vestige of his life is to be found amongst the immense ruins of time. For who has ever been able to affirm any thing with certainty of his origin, his age, his country, and condition? This alone may be depended on, from general assent, that there formerly lived a person named Orpheus, who was the founder of theology among the Greeks; the institutor of their lives and morals; the first of prophets, and the prince of poets; himself the offspring of a Muse; who taught the Greeks their sacred rites and mysteries, and from whose wisdom, as from a perennial and abundant fountain, the divine muse of Homer and the sublime theology of Pythagoras and Plato flowed.

Orpheus was founder of the Grecian mythological system which he used as the medium for the teaching of his philosophical doctrines. The origin of his philosophy is uncertain. It may be derived from the Brahmins, there being legends that Orpheus received it from the Hindus, his name possibly being derived from the Hindu word for dark.

Orpheus was initiated into the Egyptian Mysteries, from which he secured extensive knowledge of magic, astrology, sorcery and medicine. The Mysteries of the Cabiri at Samothrace were also conferred upon him, and these undoubtedly contributed to his knowledge of medicine and music.

The romance of Orpheus and Eurydice is one of the tragic episodes of Greek mythology and appears to form the outstanding feature of the Orphic Rite. Eurydice, in her attempt to escape from a villain seeking to

---

[27] Taylor, T., *The Mystical Hymns of Orpheus*, 1787

seduce her, died from the venom of a poisonous serpent which stung her in the heel. Orpheus, penetrating to the very heart of the underworld, so charmed Pluto and Persephone with the beauty of his music that they agreed to let Eurydice return to life if Orpheus could lead her back to the sphere of the living without once looking round to see if she were following. So great was his fear, however, that she would become separated from him that he turned his head, and Eurydice was returned into the land of death.

Hearthbroken, Orpheus wandered the earth for a while before dying. Some declare that he was slain by a bolt of lightning; others, that failing to save his beloved Eurydice, he committed suicide. The generally accepted version of his death, however, is that he was torn to pieces by Ciconian women whose advances he had spurned.

In the tenth book of Plato's Republic it is declared that, because of his sad fate at the hands of women, the soul that had once been Orpheus, upon being destined to live again in the physical world, chose to return in the body of a swan rather than be born of woman.

The head of Orpheus, after being torn from his body, was cast with his lyre into the river Hebrus, down which it floated to the sea, where, becoming stuck in the rocks, it gave oracles for many years. The lyre, after being stolen from its shrine and working the destruction of the thief, was picked up by the gods and fashioned into a constellation.

Orpheus has long been sung as the patron of music. On his seven-stringed lyre he played such perfect harmonies that the gods themselves were moved to give thanks for his magical gift. When he touched the strings of his instrument the birds and beasts gathered about him, and as he wandered through the forests his enchanting melodies caused even the ancient trees to draw their roots from out the earth and follow him.

Orpheus is one of the many Immortals said to have sacrificed themselves so that mankind might have the wisdom of the gods. By the symbolism of his music he communicated the divine secrets to humanity, and several authors have declared that the gods, though loving him, feared that he would overthrow their kingdom and therefore reluctantly brought about his destruction.

As time passed on the historical Orpheus became conflated with the doctrine he represented, eventually becoming the symbol of the Greek school of the ancient wisdom. Thus Orpheus was declared to be the son of Apollo, the divine and perfect truth, and Calliope, the Muse of harmony and rhythm. Eurydice is humanity dead from the sting of the serpent of false knowledge and imprisoned in the underworld of ignorance.

In this allegory Orpheus signifies theology, which wins her from the king of the dead but fails to accomplish her resurrection. Hall remarked[28] that the Ciconian women who tore Orpheus limb from limb symbolize the various contending theological factions which destroy the body of Truth. They cannot accomplish this, however, until their inharmonious cries drown out the divine music drawn by Orpheus from his magical lyre.

Hall also explained that the head of Orpheus signifies the esoteric doctrines of his cult. These doctrines continue to live and speak even after his body (the cult) has been destroyed. The lyre is the secret teaching of Orpheus; the seven strings are the seven divine truths which are the keys to universal knowledge. The differing accounts of his death represent the various means used to destroy the secret teachings; wisdom can die in many ways at the same time.

The allegory of Orpheus incarnating in the white swan signifies that the spiritual truths he represented will continue and will be taught by the initiates of all future ages. The swan is the symbol of the initiates of the Mysteries; it is a symbol also of the divine power which is the progenitor of the world.

---

[28] Ibid

Statue of Orpheus, balustrade of the Biblioteca Nazionale Marciana, Venice

Orpheus and Eurydice, Alexandre Charlot de Courcy, 1855.

The Death of Orpheus, Henry Levy, 1832

Chapter 9

Bacchus / Dionysus

In ancient Greek myth, Dionysus is the god of winemaking, orchards and fruit, vegetation, fertility, festivity, insanity, ritual madness, religious ecstasy and theatre. The Greeks also knew him as Bacchus (a name later adopted by the Romans) for a state of frenzy he is said to induce called *baccheia*. For the benefit of simplicity, we shall refer to the god as Dionysus.

As Dionysus Eleutherius ("the liberator"), his wine, music and ecstatic dance free his followers from fear and care, His thyrsus, a fennel-stem sceptre, sometimes wound with ivy and dripping with honey, is both a benevolent wand and a weapon used to destroy those who oppose his cult and the freedoms he represents. Those who participate in his mysteries are believed to become possessed and empowered by the god.

Dionysus's origins are uncertain and his cults took many forms; some are described by ancient sources as Thracian, others as Greek. In Orphism, he was variously a son of Zeus and Persephone; a chthonic or underworld aspect of Zeus; or the twice-born son of Zeus and the mortal Semele.

The Eleusinian Mysteries identify Dionysus with Iacchus, the son or husband of Demeter. Most accounts say he was born in Thrace, travelled abroad, and arrived in Greece as a foreigner. His attribute of "foreignness" as an arriving outsider-god may be inherent and essential to his cults, as he is a god of epiphany, sometimes called "the god who comes."

Wine was a religious focus in the cult of Dionysus and was his earthly incarnation. Wine could ease suffering, bring joy and inspire divine madness. Festivals of Dionysus included the performance of sacred dramas enacting his myths, the initial driving force behind the development of theatre in Western culture.

The cult of Dionysus is also a "cult of the souls"; his *maenads* (female followers) feed the dead through blood-offerings, and he acts as a divine communicant between the living and the dead. He is sometimes categorised as a dying-and-rising god.

Romans identified Dionysus-Bacchus with their own Liber Pater, the "Free Father" of the Liberalia festival, patron of viniculture, wine and male fertility, and guardian of the traditions, rituals and freedoms attached to coming of age and citizenship. The Roman state treated independent, popular festivals of Bacchus (the Bacchanalia) as subversive, partly because their free mixing of classes and genders transgressed traditional social and moral constraints. Celebration of the Bacchanalia was made a capital offence, except in the watered-down forms and greatly diminished congregations approved and supervised by the State. Festivals of Bacchus were merged with those of Liber and Dionysus.

In terms of etymology, the Greek dio- prefix in Διόνυσος (Diónūsos) has been associated since antiquity with Zeus, whose genitive is Dios; the variants of the name seem to point to an original Dios-nysos. The earliest source is the Mycenaean Greek dative form featured on two tablets that had been found at Mycenaean Pylos and dated to the twelfth or thirteenth century BCE. At that time, there could be no certainty on whether this was indeed a *theonym* (a deity's proper name), but the 1989–90 Greek-Swedish Excavations at Kastelli Hill in Chania unearthed four artefacts bearing inscriptions that are thought to confirm Dionysus's early worship.

Hall[29] described the Dionysiac rites. The Rite centres round the allegory of the youthful Dionysus being torn to pieces by the Titans. These giants accomplished this by causing him to become fascinated by his own image in a mirror. After dismembering him, the Titans first boiled the pieces in water and afterwards roasted them. Pallas rescued the heart of the murdered god, and by this precaution Dionysus was renewed in all his former glory.

Jupiter, the Demiurgus, witnessing the crime of the Titans, hurled his thunderbolts and slew them, burning their bodies to ashes with heavenly fire. Out of the ashes of the Titans—which also contained a portion of the flesh of Dionysus, whose body they had partly devoured—the human race was created, thereby ensuring that the worldly life of every man was said to contain a portion of the Dionysiac force. For this reason, the Greek Mysteries warned against suicide. He who attempts to destroy himself raises his hand against the nature of his inner "Dionysus" since man's body is indirectly the tomb of this god and, consequently, must be preserved with the greatest care.

---

[29] Ibid

Dionysus represents the rational soul of the inferior world. He is the chief of the Titans—the makers of the earthly spheres. The Pythagoreans called him the Titanic monad, symbolising the all-inclusive idea of the Titans—the gods of the fragments—serving as the means by which universal substance is fashioned into the pattern of earthly and human form.

The mirror into which Dionysus gazes and which is the cause of his fall is the great sea of illusion—the lower world fashioned by the Titans. Dionysus, the mundane rational soul, seeing his image before him, accepts the image as a likeness of himself and ensouls the likeness. By ensouling the irrational image it implants in it the urge to become like its source, the rational image. Therefore the ancients said that man does not know the gods by logic or by reason but rather by realizing the presence of the gods within himself.

After Dionysus gazed into the mirror and followed his own reflection into matter, the rational soul of the world was broken up and distributed by the Titans throughout the physical world of which it is the essential nature, but the heart, or source of it, they could not scatter.

When Jupiter, the father of Dionysus and the Demiurgus of the universe, saw that the Titans were hopelessly involving the rational or divine idea by scattering its members through the lower worlds, he slew the Titans in order that the divine idea might not be entirely lost. From the ashes of the Titans he formed mankind, whose purpose of existence was to preserve and eventually to release the Dionysiac ideal, or rational soul, from the Titanic fabrication.

Disintegration takes place so that reintegration may follow upon a higher level of form or intelligence. The thunderbolts of Jupiter are emblematic of his disintegrative power, revealing the purpose of death, which is to rescue the rational soul from the devouring power of the irrational nature.

Man is a composite creature, his lower nature consisting of the fragments of the Titans and his higher nature the sacred, immortal flesh, or life, of Dionysus. Therefore man is capable of either a Titanic (irrational) or a Dionysiac (rational) existence.

The Titans, twelve in number, are analogous to the celestial zodiac, whereas the Titans as the murderers of Dionysus represent the zodiacal powers distorted by their involvement in the material world. Thus Dionysus represents the sun who is dismembered by the signs of the zodiac and from whose body the universe is formed. When the terrestrial forms were created from the various parts of his body the sense of wholeness was lost and the sense of separateness established.

The heart of Dionysus, which was saved by Pallas, or Minerva, was lifted out of the four elements symbolized by his dismembered body and placed in the realm of the fifth element, the ether. The heart of Dionysus is the immortal centre of the rational soul.

After the rational soul had been distributed throughout creation and the nature of man, the Dionysiac Mysteries were instituted for the purpose of disentangling it from the irrational Titanic nature. This disentanglement was the process of lifting the soul out of the state of separateness into that of unity. The various parts and members of Dionysus were collected from the different corners of the earth. When all the rational parts are gathered Dionysus is resurrected.

Statues of Dionysus were carried in the Eleusinian Mysteries, especially the lesser degrees. Dionysus, representing the soul of the mundane sphere, was capable of an infinite multiplicity of form and designations. Dionysus apparently was his solar aspect.

The Dionysiac Architects constituted an ancient secret society, in principles and doctrines much like the modern Masonic Order. They were an organization of builders bound together by their secret knowledge of the relationship between the earthly and the divine sciences of architectonics.

They were supposedly employed by King Solomon in the building of his Temple, although they were not Jews, nor did they worship the God of the Jews, being followers of Dionysus. The Dionysiac Architects erected many of the great monuments of antiquity. They possessed a secret language and a system of marking their stones. They had annual convocations and sacred feasts. The exact nature of their doctrines is unknown. It is believed that Hiram Abiff, in mythological sources named as the chief architect of King Solomon's Temple, was an initiate of this society.

Roman statue of Bacchus, Vatican Museum

Carved and guilded wood representation of Bacchus (ca. 1677 CE).
Attributed to Filippo Parodi, (Museo Castello Sforzesco, Milan)

Chapter 10

Tammuz and Ishtar / Dimuzid and Inanna

The myth of Tammuz and Ishtar is one of the earliest examples of the dying-god allegory, probably dating prior to 4000 BCE.[30] The imperfect condition of the tablets upon which the legends are inscribed makes it impossible to gather any more than a fragmentary account of their rites.

Being the esoteric god of the sun, Tammuz did not occupy a position among the first deities venerated by the Babylonians, who for lack of deeper knowledge looked upon him as a god of agriculture or a vegetation spirit. Originally he was described as being one of the guardians of the gates of the underworld. Like many other Saviour-Gods, he is referred to as a "shepherd" or "the lord of the shepherd seat."

Tammuz, known to the Sumerians as Dumuzid the Shepherd and to the Canaanites as Adon, is an ancient Mesopotamian and Levantine deity associated with agriculture and shepherds. Tammuz occupies the unique position of son and husband of Ishtar, the Babylonian and Assyrian Mother-goddess.

Ishtar—to whom Venus was sacred—was the most widely venerated deity of the Babylonian and Assyrian pantheon. In Mesopotamian mythology Ishtar is known as Inanna, the goddess of love, war and fertility. She is also associated with sensuality, procreation, divine law and political power.

The story of Ishtar's descent into the underworld in search for the sacred elixir which could restore Tammuz to life is the key to the ritual of her Mysteries. Tammuz, whose annual festival took place just before the summer solstice, died in midsummer and was mourned with elaborate ceremonies. The manner of his death is unknown but some of the accusations made against Ishtar indicate that she, indirectly at least, had contributed to his death.

---

30 Spence, L., *Myths & Legends of Babylonia & Assyria*, Harrap, 1916.

The resurrection of Tammuz was the occasion of great rejoicing, at which time he was hailed as the "redeemer" of his people. With outspread wings, Ishtar, the daughter of Sin (the Moon), sweeps downward to the gates of death. The house of darkness—-the dwelling of the god Irkalla—is described as "the place of no return." It is without light; the nourishment of those who dwell there is dust and their food is mud. Over the bolts on the door of the house of Irkalla is scattered dust, and the keepers of the house are covered with feathers like birds.

Ishtar demands that the keepers open the gates, declaring that if they do not she will shatter the doorposts, strike the hinges and raise up dead devourers of the living. The guardians of the gates beg her to be patient while they go to the queen of Hades from whom they secure permission to admit Ishtar, but only in the same manner as all others came to this dreary house. Forced to comply, Ishtar descends through the seven gates that lead downward into the depths of the underworld.

At the first gate the great crown is removed from her head; at the second the earrings from her ears, at the third the necklace from her neck; at the fourth the ornaments from her breast; at the fifth the girdle from her waist; at the sixth the bracelets from her hands and feet; and at the seventh gate her cloak. Ishtar remonstrates as each successive item is taken from her, but the guardian tells her that this is the experience of all who enter the sombre domain of death. Enraged upon beholding Ishtar, the Mistress of Hades inflicts upon her all manner of disease and imprisons her in the underworld.

As Ishtar represents the spirit of fertility, her loss prevents the ripening of the crops and the maturing of all life upon the earth. In this respect the story parallels the legend of Persephone.

The gods, realizing that the loss of Ishtar is disorganizing all Nature, send a messenger to the underworld and demand her release. The Mistress of Hades is forced to comply, and the water of life is poured over Ishtar. Cured of the infirmities inflicted on her, she retraces her way up through the seven gates, at each of which she is reclothed with the item which the guardians had removed.

The myth of Ishtar symbolizes the descent of the human spirit through the seven worlds, or spheres of the sacred planets, until finally, deprived of its spiritual adornments, it incarnates in the physical body—Hades—where the mistress of that body heaps every form of sorrow and misery upon the imprisoned consciousness. The waters of life—the secret doctrine—cure the diseases of ignorance; and the spirit, re-ascends to its divine planets.

Another Mystery ritual among the Babylonians and Assyrians was that of Merodach and the Dragon. Merodach, the creator of the inferior universe, slays a horrible monster and out of her body forms the universe. Hall suggested that the legend is the probable source of the allegory of St. George and the Dragon.

The Mysteries of Adonis, or Adoni, were celebrated annually in many parts of Egypt, Phoenicia and Biblos. The name Adonis, or Adoni, means "Lord" and was a designation applied to the sun and later borrowed by the Jews as the exoteric name of their God. Smyrna, mother of Adonis, was turned into a tree by the gods. Afterwards the bark burst open and the infant Saviour came forth. According to one account, he was liberated by a wild boar which split the wood of the tree with its tusks.

Adonis was born at midnight of the 24th of December, and through his unhappy death a Mystery rite was established that led to the salvation of his people. In the Jewish month of Tammuz (another name for Adonis) he was gored to death by a wild boar sent by the god Mars. The Adoniasmos was the ceremony of lamenting the premature death of the murdered god.

In Ezekiel viii. 14, it is written that women were weeping for Tammuz/Adonis at the north gate of the Lord's House in Jerusalem. Frazer[31] cited Jerome: 'He tells us that Bethlehem, the traditional birthplace of the Lord, was shaded by a grove of that still older Syrian Lord, Adonis, and that where the infant Jesus had wept, the lover of Venus was bewailed.' The effigy of a wild boar is said to have been placed over one of the gates of Jerusalem in honour of Adonis, and his rites celebrated in the grotto of the Nativity at Bethlehem.

Adonis was originally an androgynous deity who represented the solar power which was destroyed in the winter by the evil symbol of cold, the boar. After three days (months) in the tomb, Adonis rose triumphant on the 25th day of March.

He was born out of a myrrh tree, myrrh being the symbol of death because of its connection with the process of embalming; and was one of the gifts brought by the three Magi to the manger of Jesus. In the initiation rites of the Mysteries of Adonis the neophyte passed through the symbolic death of the god and, "raised" by the priests, entered into a sublime state of redemption made possible by the sufferings of Adonis.

Nearly all authors believe Adonis to have been originally a vegetation god directly connected with the growth and maturing of flowers and fruits. In support of this viewpoint they describe the "gardens

---

[31] Frazer, J. *The Golden Bough.* Macmillan and Co, 1890

of Adonis," which were small baskets of earth in which seeds were planted and nurtured for a period of eight days. When those plants died for lack of sufficient earth, they were considered emblematic of the murdered Adonis and were usually cast into the sea with images of the god.

In Phrygia there existed a remarkable school of religious philosophy which centred around the life and untimely the fate of another Saviour-God known as Atys, or Attis, considered by many to be synonymous with Adonis. This deity was born at midnight on the 24th day of December. Of his death there are two accounts. In one he was gored to death like Adonis; in the other he emasculated himself under a pine tree and died. His body was taken to a cave by the Great Mother (Cybele), where it remained through the ages without decaying. To the rites of Atys the modern world is indebted for the symbolism of the Christmas tree. Atys imparted his immortality to the tree beneath which he died, and Cybele took the tree with her when she removed the body. Atys remained three days in the tomb, rose upon a date corresponding with Easter morning, and by this resurrection overcame death for all who were initiated into his Mysteries.

The Mysteries of Atys included a sacramental meal during which the neophyte ate out of a drum and drank from a cymbal. After being baptised by the blood of a bull, the new initiate was fed on milk to symbolise that he was still a philosophical infant, having been recently been born out of the sphere of materiality.

In the Attic rituals. Cybele, the Great Mother, signifies the life-giving powers of the universe. Cybele, loving Atys, gives him a starry hat, signifying celestial powers, but Atys (mankind), falls in love with a nymph, thereby forfeiting his divinity and losing his creative powers. In this analogy Atys represents the human condition, his Mysteries concerned with the re-attainment of the starry hat by which one may ultimately attain celestial consciousness.

Towards the end of the epic poem *Inanna's Descent into the Underworld*, Inanna escapes from the Underworld but is pursued by a horde of galla demons, who insist that someone else must take her place. They first come upon Inanna's sukkal (servant) Ninshubur and attempt to take her, but Inanna stops them, insisting that Ninshubur is her loyal servant and that she had rightfully mourned for her while she was in the Underworld. They next come upon Shara, Inanna's beautician, who is still in mourning. The demons attempt to take him, but Inanna insists that they may not, because he had also mourned for her. The third person they come upon is Lulal, who is also in mourning. The demons try to take him, but Inanna stops them once again. Finally, they come upon Dumuzid, who is lavishly clothed and resting beneath a tree, entertained by slave-girls. Inanna, displeased, decrees that the demons shall take him. The demons then drag Dumuzid down to the Underworld.

Inanna later regrets this decision and decrees that Dumuzid will spend half of the year in the Underworld, but the other half of the year with her, while his sister Geshtinanna, the goddess of agriculture, fertility and dream interpretation, stays in the Underworld in his place, thus resulting in the cycle of the seasons.

In the Sumerian poem *Inanna Prefers the Farmer*, Dumuzid competes against the farmer Enkimdu for Inanna's hand in marriage. The poem begins with a rather playful conversation between Inanna and her brother Utu, who reveals to her that it is time for her to marry. Dumuzid comes to court her, along with a farmer named Enkimdu. At first, Inanna prefers the farmer but Utu and Dumuzid gradually persuade her that Dumuzid is the better choice for a husband, arguing that for every gift the farmer can give to her the shepherd can give her something even better. In the end, Inanna marries Dumuzid. The shepherd and the farmer reconcile their differences, offering each other gifts.

In another version of the myth, the poem *The Dream of Dumuzid* begins with Dumuzid telling Geshtinanna about a frightening dream he has had. Then the galla demons arrive to drag Dumuzid down into the Underworld as Inanna's replacement. Dumuzid flees and hides. The galla demons brutally torture Geshtinanna in an attempt to force her to tell them where Dumuzid is hiding. Geshtinanna, however, refuses to tell them where her brother has gone. The demons go to Dumuzid's unnamed "friend," who betrays Dumuzid, telling the galla exactly where Dumuzid is hiding. The galla capture Dumuzid but Utu, the god of the Sun, who is also Inanna's brother, rescues Dumuzid by transforming him into a gazelle. Eventually, the galla recapture Dumuzid and drag him down into the Underworld.

In a subsequent poem, *The Return of Dumuzid*, which begins where *The Dream of Dumuzid* ends, Geshtinanna laments continually for days and nights over Dumuzid's death. She is joined by Inanna, who has apparently experienced a change of heart, and Sirtur, Dumuzid's mother. The three goddesses mourn continually until a fly reveals to Inanna the location of her husband. Together, Inanna and Geshtinanna find him there and Inanna decrees that henceforth Dumuzid will spend half of the year with her sister Ereshkigal in the Underworld and the other half of the year in Heaven with her, while Geshtinanna takes his place in the Underworld.

In addition to being the god of shepherds, Dumuzid was also an agricultural deity associated with the growth of plants. Ancient Near Eastern peoples associated Dumuzid with the springtime, when the land was fertile and abundant but, during the summer months, when the land was dry and barren, it was thought that Dumuzid had "died." During the month of Dumuzid, which fell in the middle of summer, people all across Sumer would mourn over his death. In Lagash, the month of Dumuzid was the sixth month of the year. This month and the holiday associated with it were later transmitted from the Sumerians to Babylonians and other East Semitic peoples, with its name transcribed into those languages as Tammuz. A ritual associated with the Ekur temple in Nippur equates Dumuzid with the snake-god Ištaran, who in that ritual, is described as having died.

Dumuzid was associated with fertility and vegetation and the hot, dry summers of Mesopotamia were believed to be caused by Dumuzid's yearly death. During the month in midsummer bearing his name, people all across Mesopotamia would engage in public ritual mourning for him. The cult of Dumuzid later spread to the Levant and to Greece, where he became known under the name Adonis.

In late nineteenth and early twentieth century scholarship of religion, Tammuz was widely seen as a prime example of the archetypal dying-and-rising god, but the discovery of the full Sumerian text of *Inanna's Descent* in the mid-twentieth century appeared to disprove the previous scholarly assumption that the narrative ended with Dumuzid's resurrection and instead revealed that it ended with Dumuzid's death.

In the Akkadian *Epic of Gilgamesh* Ishtar attempts to seduce the hero Gilgamesh, but he rebuffs her, reminding her that she had struck Tammaz, "the lover of [her] youth," decreeing that he should "keep weeping year after year." Gilgamesh describes Tammaz as a colourful allalu bird (possibly a European or Indian roller), whose wing has been broken and now spends all his time "in the woods crying 'My wing!'" as the love of Ishtar's youth, who was turned into an allalu bird with a broken wing.

The cult of Ishtar and Tammuz continued to thrive until the eleventh century CE and survived in parts of Mesopotamia as late as the eighteenth century. Tammuz is mentioned by name in the Book of Ezekiel.

The consummation of Inanna and Dumuzid

My vulva, the horn,
The Boat of Heaven,
Is full of eagerness like the young moon.
My untilled land lies fallow.
As for me, Inanna,
Who will plow my vulva?
Who will plow my high field?
Who will plow my wet ground?
As for me, the young woman,
Who will plow my vulva?
Who will station the ox there?
Who will plow my vulva?

Make your milk sweet and thick, my bridegroom.
My shepherd, I will drink your fresh milk.
Wild bull, Dumuzi, make your milk sweet and thick.
I will drink your fresh milk.
Let the milk of the goat flow in my sheepfold.
Fill my holy churn with honey cheese.
Lord Dumuzi, I will drink your fresh milk.

Ishtar

Ancient Sumerian depiction of Inanna and Dumuzid

Dumuzid in Hell

Chapter 11

Hermes Trismegistus

THUNDER rolled, lightning flashed, the veil of the Temple was rent from top to bottom. The venerable initiator, in his robes of blue and gold, slowly raised his jeweled wand and pointed with it into the darkness revealed by the tearing of the silken curtain: "Behold the Light of Egypt!" The candidate, in his plain white robe, gazed into the utter blackness framed by the two great Lotus-headed columns between which the veil had hung. As he watched, a luminous haze distributed itself throughout the atmosphere until the air was a mass of shining particles. The face of the neophyte was illumined by the soft glow as he scanned the shimmering cloud for some tangible object. The initiator spoke again: "This Light which ye behold is the secret luminance of the Mysteries. Whence it comes none knoweth, save the 'Master of the Light.' Behold Him!" Suddenly, through the gleaming mist a figure appeared, surrounded by a flickering greenish sheen. The initiator lowered his wand and, bowing his head, placed one hand edgewise against his breast in humble salutation. The neophyte stepped back in awe, partly blinded by the glory of the revealed figure. Gaining courage, the youth gazed again at the Divine One. The Form before him was considerably larger than that of a mortal man. The body seemed partly transparent so that the heart and brain could be seen pulsating and radiant. As the candidate watched, the heart changed into an ibis, and the brain into a flashing emerald. In Its hand this mysterious Being bore a winged rod, entwined with serpents. The aged initiator, raising his wand, cried out in a loud voice: "All hail Thee, Thoth Hermes, Thrice Greatest; all hail Thee, Prince of Men; all hail Thee who standeth upon the head of Typhon!" At the same instant a lurid writhing dragon appeared--a hideous monster, part serpent, part crocodile, and part hog. From its mouth and nostrils poured sheets of flame and horrible sounds echoed through the vaulted chambers. Suddenly Hermes struck the advancing reptile with the serpent-wound staff and with snarling cry the dragon fell over upon its side, while the flames about it slowly died away. Hermes placed His foot upon the skull of the vanquished Typhon. The next instant, with a blaze of unbearable glory that sent the neophyte staggering backward against a pillar, the immortal Hermes, followed by streamers of greenish mist, passed through the chamber and faded into nothingness.

—Manly P. Hall[32]

Iamblichus said that Hermes was the author of twenty thousand books. Manetho increased the number to more than thirty-six thousand, figures which make it evident that one individual, even one driven by divine purpose, could not have accomplished such a monumental feat.

Among the arts and sciences which it is affirmed Hermes revealed to mankind were medicine, chemistry, law, archaeology, astrology, music, rhetoric, Magic, philosophy, geography, mathematics (especially geometry), anatomy and oratory.

In ancient Egypt Hermes was known as Thoth. In his nineteenth century *Biographia Antiquia*,[33] Francis Barrett says of Hermes:

> If God ever appeared in man, he appeared in him, as is evident both from his books and his Pymander; in which works he has communicated the sum of the Abyss, and the divine knowledge to all posterity; by which he has demonstrated himself to have been not only an inspired divine, but also a deep philosopher, obtaining his wisdom from God and heavenly things, and not from man.

Rearchers believe that it was Hermes who was known to the Jews as "Enoch," called by Kenealy the "Second Messenger of God." Hermes was accepted into the mythology of the Greeks, later becoming the Mercury of the Latins. He was revered through the form of the planet Mercury because this body is nearest to the sun. Hermes of all creatures was nearest to God, becoming known as the Messenger of the Gods.

The appellation "Thrice Greatest" was given to Hermes because he was considered the greatest of all philosophers, the greatest of all priests, and the greatest of all kings.

---

[32] Ibid

[33] republished by Kessinger Publishing, 2010

In Egyptian drawings Thoth carries a waxen writing tablet and serves as the recorder during the weighing of the souls of the dead in the judgment Hall of Osiris.

Hermes is of first importance to Freemasonry because he was the author of the Masonic initiatory rituals. Nearly all of the Masonic symbols are Hermetic in character.

Hermes is revered for his reformation of the calendar system. He increased the year from 360 to 365 days, thus establishing a precedent that prevails today.

On the subject of the Hermetic books, James Campbell Brown in his *History of Chemistry* wrote:

> Leaving the Chaldean and earliest Egyptian periods, of which we have remains but no record, and from which no names of either chemists or philosophers have come down to us, we now approach the Historic Period, when books were written, not at first upon parchment or paper, but upon papyrus. A series of early Egyptian books is attributed to Hermes Trismegistus, who may have been a real savant, or may be a personification of a long succession of writers… He is identified by some with the Greek god Hermes, and the Egyptian Thoth or Tuti, who was the moon-god, and is represented in ancient paintings as ibis-headed with the disc and crescent of the moon.
>
> The Egyptians regarded him as the god of wisdom, letters, and the recording of time. It is in consequence of the great respect held for Hermes by the old alchemists that chemical writings were called "hermetic," and that the phrase "hermetically sealed" is still in use to designate the closing of a glass vessel by fusion. We find the same root in the hermetic medicines of Paracelsus, and the hermetic freemasonry of the Middle Ages.

Among the fragmentary writings believed to have come from the stylus of Hermes are two famous works. The first is the *Emerald Table*, and the second is the *Divine Pymander*, or, as it is more commonly called, *The Shepherd of Men*.

An important point in connection with Hermes is that he was one of the few "pagan" philosopher-priests who were not despised by Christians. Some Church Fathers went so far as to declare that Hermes exhibited many symptoms of intelligence, and rued the fact that he had not been born in a more enlightened age.

In his *Stromata*, Clement of Alexandria, one of the few chroniclers of pagan lore whose writings have been preserved, gives practically all the information that is known concerning the original forty-two books of Hermes and the importance with which these books were regarded by both the temporal and spiritual authorities of Egypt. Clement describes one of their ceremonial processions:

> For the Egyptians pursue a philosophy of their own. This is principally shown by their sacred ceremonial. First advances the Singer, bearing some one of the symbols of music. For they say that he must learn two of the books of Hermes, the one of which contains the hymns of the gods, the second the regulations for the king's life. And after the Singer advances the Astrologer, with a horologe in his hand, and a palm, the symbols of astrology. He must have the astrological books of Hermes, which are four in number, always in his mouth. Of these, one is about the order of the fixed stars that are visible, and another about the conjunctions and luminous appearances of the sun and moon; and the rest respecting their risings. Next in order advances the sacred Scribe, with wings on his head, and in his hand a book and rule, in which were writing ink and the reed, with which they write. And he must be acquainted with what are called hieroglyphics, and know about cosmography and geography, the position of the sun and moon, and about the five planets; also the description of Egypt, and the chart of the Nile; and the description of the equipment of the priests and of the place consecrated to them, and about the measures and the things in use in the sacred rites. Then the Stole-keeper follows those previously mentioned, with the cubit of justice and the cup for libations. He is acquainted with all points called Pædeutic [relating to training] and Moschophaltic [sacrificial]. There are also ten books which relate to the honour paid by them to their gods, and containing the Egyptian worship; as that relating to sacrifices, first-fruits, hymns, prayers, processions, festivals, and the like. And behind all walks the Prophet, with the water-vase carried openly in his arms; who is followed by those who carry the issue of loaves. He, as being the governor of the temple, learns the ten books called 'Hieratic'; and they contain all about the laws, and the gods, and the whole of the training of the priests.
>
> For the Prophet is, among the Egyptians, also over the distribution of the revenues. There are then forty-two books of

> Hermes indispensably necessary; of One of the greatest tragedies of the philosophic world was the loss of nearly all of the forty-two books of Hermes mentioned in the foregoing. These books disappeared during the burning of Alexandria, for the Romans—and later the Christians—realized that until these books were eliminated they could never bring the Egyptians into subjection. The volumes which escaped the fire were buried in the desert and their location is now known to only a few initiates of the secret schools.

In his lifetime Hermes entrusted to his chosen successors the sacred Book of Thoth. This work contained the secret processes by which the regeneration of humanity was to be accomplished, and also served as the key to his other writings. Nothing definite is known concerning the contents of the Book of Thoth other than that its pages were covered with strange hieroglyphic figures and symbols, which gave to those acquainted with their use unlimited power over the spirits of the air and the subterranean divinities.

Hall[34] explains that when certain areas of the brain are stimulated by the secret processes of the Mysteries, the consciousness of man is extended and he is permitted to behold the Immortals and enter into the presence of the superior gods. The Book of Thoth described the method whereby this stimulation was accomplished. In truth, therefore, it was the "Key to Immortality."

According to legend, the Book of Thoth was kept in a golden box in the inner sanctuary of the temple. There was but one key and this was in the possession of the "Master of the Mysteries," the highest initiate of the Hermetic Arcanum. He alone knew what was written in the secret book. The Book of Thoth was lost to the ancient world with the decay of the Mysteries, but its faithful initiates carried it sealed in the sacred casket into another land. Hall believed that the book remains in existence.

It has been asserted that the Book of Thoth is, in reality, the mysterious Tarot of the Bohemians—a strange emblematic book of seventy-eight leaves which has been in possession of the gypsies since the time when they were driven from their ancient temple, the Serapeum. (Hall claimed that the gypsies were originally Egyptian priests.)

Thoth Hermes Trismegistus, the founder of Egyptian learning, gave to the priests and philosophers of antiquity the secrets which have been preserved to this day in myth and legend. These allegories and

[34] Ibid

emblematic figures conceal the secret formulae for spiritual, mental, moral and physical regeneration commonly known as the Mystic Chemistry of the Soul (alchemy). These sublime truths were communicated to the initiates of the Mystery Schools but were concealed from the profane. The latter, unable to understand the abstract philosophical tenets, worshipped the concrete sculptured idols which were emblematic of these secret truths.

astrologer Hermes Trismegistos from "*Viridarium chymicum*" by Daniel Stolcius von Stolcenbeerg, 1624

Medieval depiction of Hermes

Hermes Trismegistos Ægypti

Chapter 12

The Pyramid Mysteries

The word pyramid is popularly supposed to be derived from the Greek for fire, πυρ, signifying that it is the symbolic representation of the One Divine Flame. Some authorities believe the word pyramid to mean a "measure of wheat," others that it has a Coptic derivation meaning, "a division into ten."

Initiates of the past accepted the pyramid form as the ideal symbol of both the secret doctrine and those institutions established for its dissemination. Both pyramids and mounds are synonyms for the Holy Mountain, or High Place of God, which was believed to stand in the "midst" of the earth. The Great Pyramid has been associated with the fabled Olympus, further assuming that its subterranean passages correspond to the challenging byways of Hades.

The square base of the Pyramid is a constant reminder that the House of Wisdom is firmly founded upon Nature and her immutable laws. 'The Gnostics,' wrote Albert Pike (*Morals and Dogma*), 'claimed that the whole edifice of their science rested on a square whose angles were: BCDE: Silence, Profundity, Intelligence and Truth.'

The sides of the Great Pyramid face the four cardinal angles, the latter according to Eliphas Levi signifying the extremities of heat and cold (south and north) and the extremities of light and darkness (east and west). The base of the Pyramid further represents the four material elements or substances from the combinations of which the quaternary body of man is formed. From each side of the square there rises a triangle, typifying the threefold divine being enthroned within every quaternary material nature.

Hall stated that if each base line be considered a square from which ascends a threefold spiritual power, then the sum of the lines of the four faces (12) and the four hypothetical squares (16) constituting the base is 28, the sacred number of the lower world. If this is added to the three septenaries composing the sun (21), it equals 49, the square of 7 and the number of the universe.

The twelve signs of the zodiac are symbolized by the twelve lines of the four triangles—the faces of the Pyramid. In the midst of each face is one of the beasts of Ezekiel, and the structure as a whole becomes the Cherubim.

The three main chambers of the Pyramid are related to the heart, the brain and the generative system—the spiritual centres of the human constitution. The triangular form of the Pyramid also is similar to the posture assumed by the body during the ancient meditative exercises. The Mysteries taught that the divine energies from the gods of the original casing stones caused each side of the Pyramid to appear as descended upon the top of the Pyramid, which was likened to an inverted tree with its branches below and its roots at the apex. From this inverted tree the divine wisdom is disseminated by streaming down the diverging sides and radiating throughout the world.

The size of the capstone of the Great Pyramid cannot be accurately determined, for, while most investigators have assumed that it was once in place, no vestige of it remains. There is a curious tendency among the builders of great religious structures to leave their creations unfinished, thereby signifying that God alone is complete. The capstone, if it existed, was itself a miniature pyramid, the apex of which would itself be capped by a smaller block of similar shape, and so on *ad infinitum*. The capstone therefore is the epitome of the entire structure.

Thus, the Pyramid may be likened to the universe and the capstone to man. Following the chain of analogy, the mind is the capstone of man, the spirit the capstone of the mind, and God—the epitome of the whole—the capstone of the spirit. As a rough and unfinished block, man is taken from the quarry and by the secret culture of the Mysteries gradually transformed into a perfect pyramidal capstone. The temple is complete only when the initiate himself becomes the living apex through which the divine power is focused into the diverging structure below.[35]

The Great Pyramid has been called "the House of the Hidden Places," for it represented the inner sanctuary of pre-Egyptian wisdom. The Egyptians associated the Great Pyramid with Hermes, the god of wisdom and letters and the Divine Illuminator worshipped through the planet Mercury. Relating Hermes to the Pyramid doubly emphasises the fact that it was in reality the supreme temple of the Invisible and Supreme Deity.

The Great Pyramid was not a lighthouse, an observatory, or a tomb

---

[35] See appendix for a reproduction of the chapter on the Pyramid's Golden Tip in my 2024 work, *Crystals. Mother Nature and the Forces of Living Nature.*

but the first temple of the Mysteries, the first structure erected as a repository for those secret truths which are the foundation of all arts and sciences. It was the perfect emblem of the microcosm and the macrocosm and, according to the secret teachings, the tomb of Osiris, the black god of the Nile. Osiris represents a manifestation of solar energy, and therefore his house or tomb is emblematic of the universe within which he is entombed and upon the cross of which he is crucified.

Through the mystic passageways and chambers of the Great Pyramid passed the initiated souls of antiquity. They entered its portals as men; they came out as gods. It was the place of the "second birth," the "womb of the Mysteries," and wisdom dwelt in it as God dwells in the hearts of men. Somewhere in the depths of its recesses there resided an unknown being who was called "The Initiator," or "The Illustrious One," robed in blue and gold and bearing in his hand the sevenfold key of Eternity. This was the lion-faced hierophant, the Holy One, the Master of Masters, who never left the House of Wisdom and whom no man ever saw save he who had passed through the gates of preparation and purification. It was in these chambers that Plato came face to face with the wisdom of the ages personified in the Master of the Hidden House.

To the new initiate was revealed the power to know his guardian spirit; the method of disentangling his material body from his divine vehicle was explained. To consummate the ritual, there was revealed the Supreme Deity's Divine Name—by the very knowledge of which man and his God are made consciously one. With the giving of the Name, the new initiate became himself a pyramid, within the chambers of whose soul numberless other human beings might also receive spiritual enlightenment.

In the King's Chamber was enacted the drama of the "second death." Here the candidate, after being crucified upon the cross of the solstices and the equinoxes, was buried in the great coffer. There is a profound mystery to the atmosphere and temperature of the King's Chamber: it is of a peculiar deathlike cold, which cuts to the marrow of the bone. This room was a doorway between the material world and the transcendental spheres of Nature. While his body lay in the coffer, the soul of the neophyte soared as a human-headed hawk through the celestial worlds, there to discover first hand the eternity of Life, Light and Truth, as well as the illusion of Death, Darkness and Sin.

In one sense the Great Pyramid may be likened to a gate through which the ancient priests permitted a few to pass toward the attainment of individual completion. It is also to be noted that if the coffer in the King's Chamber is struck, the sound emitted has no counterpart in any known musical scale. This tonal value may have formed part of that combination of circumstances which rendered the King's Chamber an ideal setting for the conferment of the highest degree of the Mysteries.

One reflects upon the sacred structure, wondering what inspired the herculean labour. Men say of the Great Pyramid that it is the most perfect building in the world, the source of weights and measures, the original Noah's Ark, the origin of languages, alphabets and scales of temperature and humidity. Few realise, Hall reminds us, that it is the gateway to the Eternal.

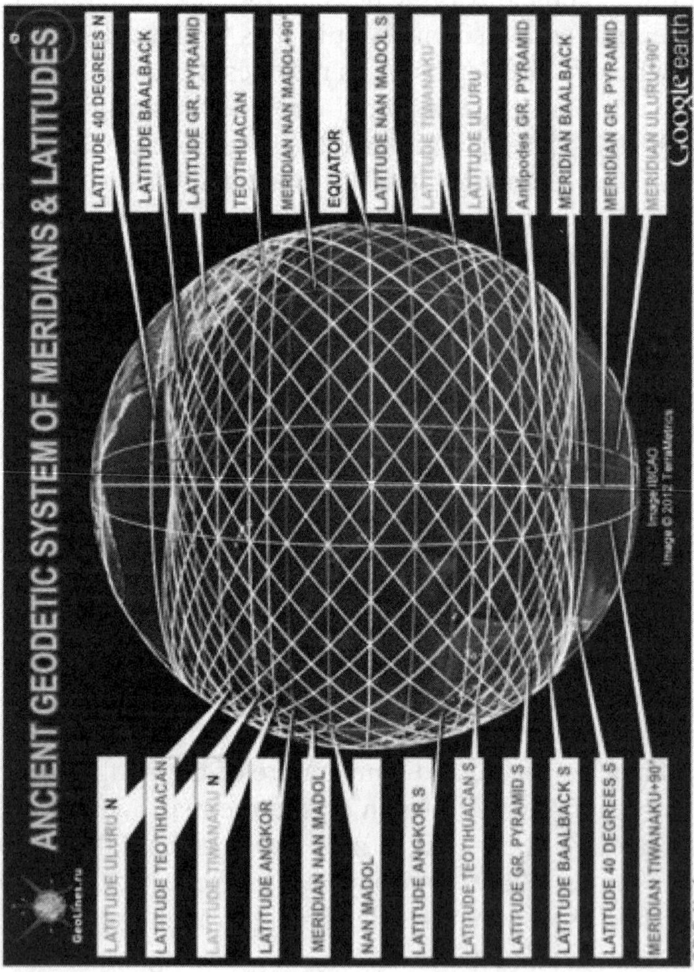

Ancient Geodetic System of Medidians and Latitudes

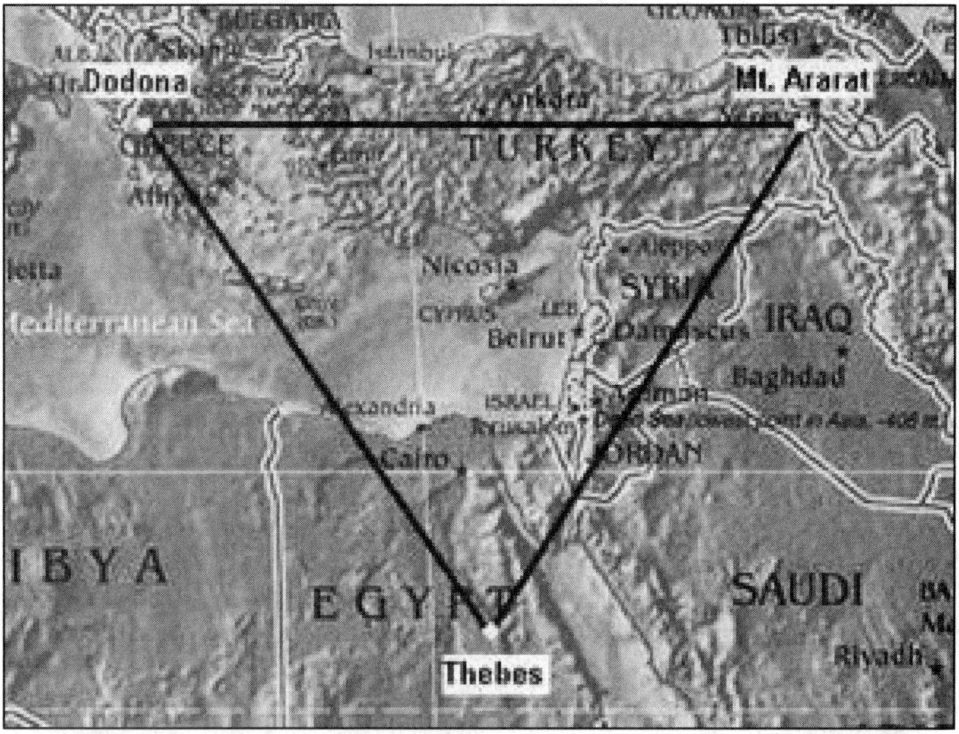

Dodona is the mythological landing place for Deucalion (Greek equivalent of Noah, the son of Prometheus, the creator of humankind) after the Flood, while Ararat is known in Hebraic as the landing place of the Ark for Noah. Apart from this early mythological connection between sites, there is a geographical similarity in that both have ancient oracle centres dedicated to the Earth-Mother placed next to dominant mountains. The distance between them is the same as the distance between Dodona and Thebes, so that the three sites form an almost exact equilateral triangle.

In addition to having been recorded as the first Greek oracle centre, Dodona has a greater and older claim to fame, being located at the foot of Mount Tomaros, which is named in Greek myth as the refuge for Deucalion and his wife, the sole survivors of the Flood. It is within this myth that an older connection can be found in the location of Dodona, for while Mt. Tomaros is the resting place of the Greek ark, the Hebrews record the final resting place of their ark as being on Mount Ararat in Turkey, which both sits on the same latitude as Dodona and happens to be equidistant from Thebes, so that the three locations form an almost perfect equilateral triangle.

Dramatic Nigt Sky over the Giza Plateau

Chapter 13

Isis

I, Isis, am all that has been, that is or shall be; no mortal Man hath ever me unveiled.

Plutarch said that many ancient authors believed the goddess Isis to be the daughter of Hermes; others held the opinion that she was the child of Prometheus. Both of these demigods were noted for their divine wisdom. Plutarch translates the name Isis to mean wisdom. Godfrey Higgins, in his *Anacalypsis,* derives the name of Isis from the Hebrew word for to save. Some authorities believe it to be of Northern extraction, possibly Scandinavian or Gothic. In these languages the name is pronounced Isa, meaning ice, or water in its most passive, crystallized state. Plutarch describes the requisites of a follower of Isis:

> For as 'tis not the length of the beard, or the coarseness of the habit which makes a philosopher, so neither will those frequent shavings, or the mere wearing [of] a linen vestment constitute a votary of Isis; but he alone is a true servant or follower of this Goddess, who after he has heard, and been made acquainted in a proper manner with the history of the actions of these Gods, searches into the hidden truths which he concealed under them, and examines the whole by the dictates of reason and philosophy.

This Egyptian deity appears under many names as the principle of natural fecundity among nearly all the religions of the ancient world. She was known as the goddess with ten thousand appellations and was metamorphosed by Christianity into the Virgin Mary, for Isis, although she gave birth to all living things—chief among them the Sun—still remained a virgin, according to the legendary accounts. Apuleius in the eleventh book of *The Golden Ass* ascribes to the goddess the following statement concerning her powers and attributes:

> Behold, I, moved by thy prayers, am present with thee; I,

> who am Nature, the parent of things, the queen of all the elements, the primordial progeny of ages, the supreme of Divinities, the sovereign of the spirits of the dead, the first of the celestials, and the uniform resemblance of Gods and Goddesses. I, who rule by my nod the luminous summits of the heavens, the salubrious breezes of the sea, and the deplorable silences of the realms beneath, and whose one divinity the whole orb of the earth venerates under a manifold form, by different rites and a variety of appellations. Hence the primogenial Phrygians call me Pessinuntica, the mother of the Gods, the Attic Aborigines, Cecropian Minerva; the floating Cyprians, Paphian Venus; the arrow-bearing Cretans, Diana Dictynna; the three-tongued Sicilians, Stygian Proserpine; and the Eleusinians, the ancient Goddess Ceres. Some also call me Juno, others Bellona, others Hecate, and others Rhamnusia. And those who are illuminated by the incipient rays of that divinity the Sun, when he rises, viz. the Ethiopians, the Arii, and the Egyptians skilled in ancient learning, worshipping me by ceremonies perfectly appropriate, call me by my true name, Queen Isis.

Le Plongeon believed that the Egyptian myth of Isis had a historical basis among the Mayas of Central America, where this goddess was known as Queen Moo. In *Prince Coh* he finds a correspondence to Osiris, the brother-husband of Isis. Le Plongeon's theory is that Mayan civilization was far more ancient than that of Egypt. After the death of Prince Coh, his widow, Queen Moo, fleeing to escape the wrath of his murderers, sought refuge among the Mayan colonies in Egypt, where she was accepted as their queen and was given the name of Isis. Nevertheless, Queen Moo is an insignificant figure when compared with the symbolic World Virgin; and the fact that she appears among so many different races and peoples discredits the theory that she was a historical individual.

According to Sextus Empyricus, the Trojan War was fought over a statue of the moon goddess. Several authors have attempted to prove that Isis, Osiris, Typhon, Nephthys and Aroueris (Horus) were grandchildren of the great Jewish patriarch Noah by his son Ham.

According to English alchemist Robert Fludd (1574–1637), the sun has three properties—life, light, and heat. These three vivify and vitalize the three worlds—spiritual, intellectual and material. Therefore, it is said 'from one light, three lights.' Hall was of the opinion that Osiris represents the third, or material, aspect of solar activity, which revitalizes and enlivens the flora and fauna of the earth. Osiris is not the sun, but the sun is symbolic of the vital principle of Nature, which the ancients knew as Osiris. His symbol, therefore, was an opened eye, in honour of the Great Eye of the universe, the sun

Isis, represented in the Song of Solomon by the dark maid of Jerusalem, is symbolic of receptive Nature—the watery, maternal principle which creates all things out of herself after impregnation has been achieved by the virility of the sun.

In the ancient world the year had 360 days. The five extra days were gathered together to serve as the birthdays of the five gods and goddesses who are called the sons and daughters of Ham. Upon the first of these special days Osiris was born and upon the fourth of them Isis, the number expressing the relation between this goddess and the earth and its elements. Typhon, the Egyptian Demon or Spirit of the Adversary, was born upon the third day. Typhon is often symbolised by a crocodile; sometimes his body is a combination of crocodile and hog. Isis stands for knowledge and wisdom, and, according to Plutarch, the word Typhon means insolence and pride. Egotism, self-centredness, and pride are the deadly enemies of understanding and truth.

After Osiris, here symbolized as the sun, had become King of Egypt and had given to his people the full advantage of his intellectual light, he continued his path through the heavens, visiting the peoples of other nations and converting all with whom he came in contact. Plutarch further asserts that the Greeks recognized in Osiris the same person whom they revered under the names of Dionysus/Bacchus.

While Osiris was away from his country, his brother, Typhon, the Evil One, like the Loki of Scandinavia, plotted against the Sun God to destroy him. Gathering seventy-two individuals as fellow conspirators, he succeeded in his evil plan in a most subtle manner. He had an ornamented box made just the size of the body of Osiris. This he brought into a banquet hall where the gods and goddesses were feasting together. All admired the beautiful chest, and Typhon promised to give it to the one whose body fitted it most perfectly. One after another lay down in the box, but in disappointment rose again, until at last Osiris tried. The moment he was in the chest Typhon and his accomplices nailed the cover down and sealed the cracks with molten lead. They then cast the box into the Nile, down which it floated to the sea. Plutarch declares that the Pans and Satyrs (the Nature spirits and elementals) were the first to discover that Osiris had been murdered. These immediately raised an alarm, and from this incident the word panic, meaning fright or amazement of the multitudes, originated.

Upon receiving the news of her husband's death from children who had seen the murderers making off with the box, Isis robed herself in mourning and made off in quest of him. At length Isis discovered that the chest had floated to the coast of Byblos. There it had lodged in the branches of a tree, which in a short time miraculously grew up around the box. This so amazed the king of that country that he ordered the tree to be cut down and a pillar made from its trunk to support the roof of his palace. Isis recovered the body of her husband but it was again stolen by Typhon, who cut it into fourteen parts, which he scattered all over the earth. In despair, Isis began gathering up the severed remains of her husband but found only thirteen pieces. The fourteenth part (the phallus) she reproduced in gold, for the original had fallen into the river Nile and had been swallowed by a fish. Typhon was later slain in battle by the son of Osiris. Some of the Egyptians believed that the souls of the gods were taken to heaven, where they shone forth as stars. It was supposed that the soul of Isis gleamed from the Dog Star, while Typhon became the constellation of the Bear.

Among the Egyptians, Isis is often represented with a headdress consisting of the empty throne chair of her murdered husband, and this peculiar structure was accepted during certain dynasties as her hieroglyphic. The headdresses of the Egyptians have great symbolic and emblematic importance, for, according to Hall, they represent the auric bodies of the superhuman intelligences, in the same manner that the nimbus, halo and aureole are used in Christian religious art. The robes, insignia, jewels and ornamentations of the ancient hierophants symbolized the spiritual energies radiating from the human body.

Isis is sometimes symbolised by the head of a cow; occasionally the entire animal is her symbol. The first gods of the Scandinavians were licked out of blocks of ice by the Mother Cow (Audhumla), who symbolised the principle of natural nutriment and fecundity because of her milk.

Occasionally, Isis is represented as a bird. She often carries in one hand the crux ansata, the symbol of eternal life, and in the other the flowered sceptre, symbolic of her authority.

The wisdom of Egypt is epitomized in the Sphinx, which has preserved its secrets for a hundred generations. The mysteries of Hermeticism, the great spiritual truths hidden from the world by the ignorance of the world, and the keys of the secret doctrines of the ancient philosophers, are all symbolised by the Virgin Isis. Veiled from head to foot, she reveals her wisdom only to the tried and initiated few who have earned the right to enter her sacred presence, tear from the veiled figure of Nature its shroud of obscurity, and stand face to face with the Mother Goddess.

The statues of Isis were decorated with the sun, moon and stars, and many emblems pertaining to the earth, over which Isis was believed to rule as the Mother Goddess guardian spirit of Nature personified. Isis was generally represented as a partly nude woman, often pregnant, sometimes loosely covered with a garment either of green or black, or of four different shades intermingled black, white, yellow and red. Apuleius describes her:

> A multiform crown, consisting of various flowers, bound the sublime summit of her head. And in the middle of the crown, just on her forehead, there was a smooth orb resembling a mirror, or rather a white refulgent light, which indicated that she was the moon. Vipers rising up after the manner of furrows, environed the crown on the right hand and on the left, and Cerealian ears of corn were also extended from above. Her garment was of many colours, and woven from the finest flax, and was at one time lucid with a white splendour, at another yellow from the flower of crocus, and at another flaming with a rosy redness. But that which most excessively dazzled my sight, was a very black robe, fulgid with a dark splendour, and which, spreading round and passing under her right side, and ascending to her left shoulder, there rose protuberant like the centre of a shield, the dependent part of the robe falling in many folds, and having small knots of fringe, gracefully flowing in its extremities.
>
> Glittering stars were dispersed through the embroidered border of the robe, and through the whole of its surface: and the full moon, shining in the middle of the stars, breathed forth flaming fires. Nevertheless, a crown, wholly consisting of flowers and fruits of every kind, adhered with indivisible connexion to the border of that conspicuous robe, in all its undulating motions. What she carried in her hands also consisted of things of a very different nature. For her right hand, indeed, bore a brazen rattle [sistrum] through the narrow lamina of which bent like a belt, certain rods passing, produced a sharp triple sound, through the vibrating motion of her arm. An oblong vessel, in the shape of a boat, depended from her left hand, on the handle of which, in that part in which it was conspicuous, an asp raised its erect head and largely swelling neck. And shoes woven from the leaves of the victorious palm tree covered her immortal feet.

The green colour symbolises the robe of Mother Nature. The black represents death and corruption as being the way to a new life and generation. White, yellow and red signify the three principal colours of the alchemical medicine after the blackness of its putrefaction is over. Her black drape also signifies that the moon has no light of its own but receives its light and vital force from the sun. Isis was the image or representative of the Great Works of the wise men: the Philosopher's Stone and the Elixir of Life.

The goddess often wore upon her head a hat made of cypress branches to signify mourning for her dead husband, and also for the physical death which she caused every creature to undergo in order to receive a new life in a cycle of resurrection. The head of Isis is sometimes ornamented with a crown of gold or a garland of olive leaves, as marks of her sovereignty as queen of the world and mistress of the entire universe. The gold crown also signifies the spirit essence of the solar and vital fires which she dispenses to every individual by a continual circulation of the elements, this circulation being symbolised by the musical rattle which she carries in her hand.

A serpent interwoven among the olive leaves on her head, devouring its own tail, denotes that the spirit essence was soiled with the venom of terrestrial corruption which surrounded it and must be purified by seven planetary circulations that the alchemists called flying eagles in order to make it medicinal for the restoration of health.

The seven planetary circulations are represented by the circumambulations of the Masonic lodge, by the marching of the Jewish priests seven times around the walls of Jericho, and by the Mohammedan priests making seven revolutions around the Kabba at Mecca. From the crown of gold project three horns of plenty, signifying the abundance of the gifts of Nature proceeding from one root having its origin in the heavens, the head of Isis.

This illustration of Isis represents all the vital powers of the three kingdoms and families of sublunary nature-mineral, plant and the animal kingdom. At one of her ears was the moon and at the other the sun, to indicate that these two were the father and mother principles of all natural objects; and that Isis, Mother Nature, makes use of these to communicate her powers to the whole empire of animals, vegetables and minerals. On the back of her neck were the characters of the planets and the signs of the zodiac which assisted the planets in their functions.

Isis holds in her right hand a small sailing ship with the spindle of a spinning wheel for its mast. From the top of the mast projects a water jug, its handle shaped like a serpent swelled with venom. This indicates that Isis steers the ship of life, full of troubles and miseries, on the stormy ocean of Time. The spindle symbolizes the fact that she spins and cuts the thread of Life.

The serpent throws off its skin annually and is thereby renewed, a process that symbolises the resurrection of the spiritual life from the material nature. This renewal of the earth takes place every spring, when the revivifying spirit of the sun returns to the countries of the Northern Hemisphere,

The symbolic Virgin carries in her left hand a sistrum and a cymbal, or square frame of metal, which when struck gives the key-note of Nature (Fa); sometimes also an olive branch, to indicate the harmony she preserves among natural things with her regenerating power. By the processes of death and corruption she gives life to a number of creatures of diverse forms through periods of perpetual change.

From the right breast of Isis protruded a bunch of grapes and from the left an ear of corn or a sheaf of golden wheat. These indicate that Nature is the source of nutrition for plant, animal, and human life, nourishing all things from herself.

On the girdle surrounding the upper part of the body of the statue appear a number of mysterious emblems. The girdle is joined together in front by four golden plates (the elements), placed in the form of a square. This signified that Isis, Nature, the first matter (an alchemical term), was the essence of the four elements (life, light, heat and force), which, in combination, generated all things. Numerous stars are represented on this girdle, indicating their influence in darkness as well as the influence of the sun in light. Isis is the Virgin immortalised in the constellation of Virgo, where the World Mother is placed with the serpent under her feet and a crown of stars on her head. In her arms she carries a sheaf of grain and sometimes the young Sun God.

The statue of Isis was placed on a pedestal of dark stone ornamented with rams' heads. Her feet trod upon a number of venomous reptiles. The rams' heads indicate that the most auspicious time for the generation of life is during the period when the sun passes through the sign of Aries. The serpents under her feet indicate that Nature is inclined to preserve life and to heal disease by expelling impurities and corruption. In this sense the axioms of the ancient philosophers are verified:

Nature contains Nature,

Nature rejoices in her own nature,

Nature surmounts Nature;

Nature cannot be amended but in her own nature.

From a golden ring on her left arm of Isis a line descends, to the end of which is suspended a deep box filled with flaming coals and incense. Isis, Nature personified, carries with her the sacred fire, kept burning in a special temple by the Vestal Virgins. This fire is the immortal flame of Nature, the Mother of life.

From the right arm of the figure also descends a thread, to the end of which is fastened a pair of scales to denote the exact laws concerning Nature and her provision of universal weights and measures. Isis is often represented as the symbol of justice because Nature is eternally consistent. The World Virgin is sometimes shown standing between two great pillars, demonstrating that understanding is always found at the point of equilibrium

The ancients believed that the universal sperm proceeded from warm vapour, humid but fiery. The veiled Isis, whose very coverings represent vapour, is symbolic of this humidity, which is the carrier or vehicle for the sperm life of the sun, represented by a child in her arms. Because the sun, moon, and stars in setting appear to sink into the sea and also because the water receives their rays into itself, the sea was believed to be the breeding ground for the sperm of living things. This sperm is generated from the combination of the influences of the celestial bodies; hence Isis is sometimes represented as pregnant.

Frequently the statue of Isis was accompanied by the figure of a large black and white ox. The ox represents either Osiris as Taurus, the bull of the zodiac, or Apis, an animal sacred to Osiris because of its peculiar markings and colourings. Among the Egyptians, the bull was a beast of burden. Hence the presence of the animal was a reminder of the ceaseless labours patiently performed by Nature that all creatures may have life and health. Harpocrates, the God of Silence, holding his fingers to his mouth, often accompanies the statue of Isis. He warns all to keep the secrets of the wise from those unfit to know them.

Isis is sometimes used to represent the occult and magical arts, such as necromancy, invocation, sorcery and thaumaturgy. In one of the myths, Isis is said to have conjured the invincible God of Eternities, Ra, to tell her his secret and sacred name, which he did. By means of this Word, a magician can demand obedience from the invisible and superior deities. The priests of Isis became adepts in the use of the unseen forces of Nature. They understood hypnotism, mesmerism and similar practices long before the modem world dreamed of their existence.

The Druids of Britain and Gaul had a deep knowledge concerning the mysteries of Isis and worshipped her under the symbol of the moon. The moon was chosen for Isis because of its dominion over water. The

Druids considered the sun to be the father and the moon the mother of all things. By means of these symbols they worshipped Universal Nature.

During the Middle Ages the troubadours in Europe preserved in song the legends of Isis. They composed sonnets to the most beautiful woman in the entire world. Though few ever discovered her identity, she was Sophia, the Virgin of Wisdom, whom all the philosophers of the world have wooed. Isis represents the mystery of motherhood, which the ancients recognized as the most apparent proof of Nature's limitless wisdom and power.

Isis holding the sistrum of regeneration before Osiris

Isis

Chapter 14

The Rose Cross

The word Rosicrucian derives from Christian Rosencreutz or Rose Cross (or possibly from Ros and Crux—alchemical terms connected with dew as a solvent of gold, and crux as the equivalent of Light). The term Rosicrucian is also said to derive from the Latin "rosa" (rose) and "crux" (cross).

Rosicrucian teachings are a combination of occultism and religious beliefs and practices, including Hermeticism, Jewish mysticism and Christian Gnosticism. The central feature of Rosicrucianism is the belief that its members possess secret wisdom that was handed down to them from ancient times.

The origins and teachings of the Rosicrucians are described in three anonymously published books, which have been attributed to Johann Valentin Andreae (1568–1654), a Lutheran theologian and teacher who wrote the utopian treatise *Christianopolis* (1619). *The Fama Fraternitatis of the Meritorious Order of the Rosy Cross* (abbreviated as the *Fama Fraternitatis*), 1614; *The Confession of the Rosicrucian Fraternity* (abbreviated to the Confessio), 1615; and *The Chymical Marriage of Christian Rosenkreuz* (1616) recount the travels of Christian Rosenkreuz, the putative founder of the group, who is now generally regarded as a fictional character rather than a real person. The Rosicrucian manifestos are set out in the *Fama Fraternitatis* and the *Confessio*. The hero of the manifestos is Father C.R.C. or Christian Rosenkreutz, who is said to have been the founder of an Order or Fraternity and which the manifestos now invite others to join.

Hall[36] described four distinct theories regarding the Rosicrucian enigma. The first proposes that the Order existed historically in accordance with the description of its foundation and subsequent activities published in its manifesto, the *Fama Fraternitatis*. The Fama Fraternitatis begins with a reminder to all the world of God's goodness

---

[36] Ibid

and mercy, and it warns the intelligentsia that their egotism and covetousness cause them to follow after false prophets and to ignore the true knowledge, which God in His goodness has revealed to them. Hence, a reformation is necessary, and God has raised up philosophers and sages for this purpose.

In order to assist in bringing about the reformation, a mysterious person called "The Highly Illuminated Father C.R.C.," a German by birth, descended of a noble family, but himself a poor man, instituted the "Secret Society of the Rose Cross." C.R.C. was placed in a cloister when only five years of age. Later becoming dissatisfied with its educational system, he associated himself with a brother of Holy Orders who was setting forth on a pilgrimage to the Holy Land. They started out together but the brother died at Cyprus and C.R.C. continued alone to Damascus. Poor health prevented him from reaching Jerusalem, so he remained at Damascus, studying with the philosophers who dwelt there.

While pursuing his studies, he heard of a group of mystics and Qabalists in the mystic Arabian city of "Damcar."[37] Giving up his desire to visit Jerusalem, he arranged with the Arabians for his transportation to Damcar. C.R.C. was but sixteen years of age when he arrived there. He was received as one who had been long expected, a comrade and a friend in philosophy, and was instructed in the secrets of the Arabian adepts. While there, C.R.C. learned the Arabic tongue and translated the sacred book *M* into Latin. Upon returning to Europe he brought this important volume with him.

After studying three years in Damcar, C.R.C. departed for the city of Fez, where the Arabian magicians declared further information would be given him. At Fez he was instructed on how to communicate with the Nature spirits and elementals, which disclosed to him many other great secrets of Nature. While the philosophers in Fez were not so great as those in Damcar, the previous experiences of C.R.C. enabled him to distinguish the true from the false and thus add greatly to his store of knowledge.

After two years in Fez, C.R.C. sailed for Spain, carrying with him many treasures, among them rare plants and animals accumulated during his wanderings. He hoped that the learned men of Europe would receive with gratitude the rare intellectual and material treasures which he had brought for their consideration. Instead, he encountered only ridicule, for the so-called wise were afraid to admit their previous ignorance lest their

---

[37] Analysis of the Rosicrucian manifesto suggests that the hitherto unidentified city of Damcar is that of Safed in northern Israel.

prestige be impaired.

Tired, but not discouraged, as the result of the fruitlessness of his efforts, C.R.C. returned to Germany where he built a house in which he could quietly continue his studies. He also manufactured a number of rare scientific instruments for research purposes. While he could have made himself famous had he cared to commercialise his knowledge, he preferred the companionship of God to the esteem of men.

After five years of retirement he decided to renew his struggle for a reformation of the arts and sciences of his day, this time with the aid of a few trusted friends. He sent to the cloister where his early training had been received and called to himself three brethren, whom he bound by an oath to preserve the secrets he should impart and to write down for the sake of posterity the information he should dictate. These four founded the "Fraternity of the Rose Cross." They prepared its secret cipher language and, according to the Fama, a great dictionary in which all forms of wisdom were classified to the glorification of God.

After a while the companions decided to separate and visit the other countries of the earth, not only that their wisdom might be given to others who deserved it but also that they might check and correct any mistakes existing in their own system. Before separating, the brethren prepared six rules, or by-laws, and each bound himself to obey them.

The first rule was that they should take to themselves no other dignity or credit than that they were willing to heal the sick without charge. The second was that from that time on forever they should wear no special robe or garment, but should dress according to the custom of the country wherein they dwelt. The third stated that every year upon a certain day they should meet in the "House of the Holy Spirit," or, if unable to do so, should be represented by an epistle. The fourth decreed that each member should search for a worthy person to succeed him after his death. The fifth stated that the letters "R.C." should be their seal, mark and character from that time onward. The sixth specified that the Fraternity should remain unknown to the world for a period of one hundred years.

After they had sworn to this code five of the Brothers departed to distant lands, and a year later two of the others also went their way, leaving Father C.R.C. alone in the "House of the Holy Spirit." Year after year they met with great joy, for they had quietly and sincerely promulgated their doctrines among the wise of the earth.

When the first of the Order died in England, it was decided that the burial places of the members should be secret. Soon afterward Father C.R.C. called the remaining brothers together, and it is supposed that then he prepared his own symbolic tomb. The Fama records that none of the Brothers alive at the time it was written knew when Father C.R.C. died or where he was buried. His body was accidentally discovered 120 years after his death when one of the Brothers, who possessed considerable architectural skill, decided to make some alterations in the "House of the Holy Spirit." While making his alterations, the Brother discovered a memorial tablet upon which were inscribed the names of the early members of the Order. This he decided to transfer to a more imposing chapel, for at that time no one knew in what country Father C.R.C. had died, this information having been concealed by the original members. In attempting to remove the memorial tablet, which was held in place by a large nail, some stones and plastering were broken from the wall, disclosing a door concealed in the masonry. The members of the Order immediately cleared away the rest of the debris and uncovered the entrance to a vault. Upon the door in large letters were the words: POST CXX ANNOS PATEBO. This, according to the mystic interpretation of the Brethren, meant, "In 120 years I shall come forth."

The following morning the door was opened and the members entered a vault with seven sides and seven corners, each side five feet wide and eight feet high. Although the sun never penetrated this tomb, it was brilliantly illuminated by a mysterious light in the ceiling. In the centre was a circular altar, upon which were brass plates engraved with strange characters. In each of the seven sides was a small door which, upon being opened, revealed a number of boxes filled with books, secret instructions, and the supposedly lost arcanum of the Fraternity.

Upon moving the altar to one side a brass cover was disclosed. Lifting this revealed a body, presumedly that of C.R.C., which, although it had lain there 120 years, was as well preserved as though it had just been interred. It was ornamented and attired in the robes of the Order, and in one hand was clasped a mysterious parchment which, next to the Bible, was the most valued possession of the Society. After thoroughly investigating the contents of the secret chamber, the brass plate and altar were put back in place, the door of the vault was again sealed, and the Brothers went their respective ways. The document ends by saying:

> In accordance with the will of Father C.R.C., the Fama has been prepared and sent forth to the wise and learned of all Europe in five languages, that all may know and understand the secrets of the august Fraternity. All of sincere soul who labour for the glory of God are invited to communicate with the Brethren and are promised that their appeal shall be heard,

regardless of where they are or how the messages are sent. At the same time, those of selfish and ulterior motives are warned that only sorrow and misery will attend any who attempt to discover the Fraternity without a clean heart and a pure mind.

Such, in brief, is the story of the Fama Fraternitatis. Those who accept it literally regard Father C.R.C. as the actual founder of the Brotherhood, which he is believed to have organized in about 1400. The fact that historical corroboration of the important points of the Fama has never been discovered is held against this theory. There is no proof that Father C.R.C. ever approached the learned men of Spain. There is no record that anywhere in Germany existed a place where great numbers of the lame and sick came and were mysteriously healed.

Hall's second theory examines the premise that the Fraternity originated in medieval Europe as an outgrowth of alchemical philosophy. This theory proposes that Johann Valentin Andreae was the true founder, reforming and amplifying a society that had been previously founded by Sir Henry Cornelius Agrippa. Some believed that Rosicrucianism represented the first invasion into Europe of Buddhist and Brahmic culture. Still others held that the society was founded in Egypt and that it also perpetuated the mysteries of ancient Chaldea and Persia.

Whatever its origins the Order, incredibly, was able to retain absolute secrecy for many centuries. A number of very great scholars such as Francis Bacon and Goethe are said to have been affiliated with the Order. Speculators have stated that modern Freemasonry has completely absorbed Rosicrucianism, while others declare that the Rosicrucian Brotherhood still exists, preserving its individuality as the result of having withdrawn from the Masonic Order.

Hall's third theory denies that there ever was such a Rosicrucian Order, which was no more than a satire to ridicule the gullibility of Europe's intelligentsia. Nevertheless, the mystery has resulted in endless controversies and has occupied some of the finest minds in the history of Europe mysticism, scholars such as Michael Maier, Eugenius Philalethes (Thomas Vaughan) and Robert Fludd among them.

Hall's fourth and final proposal has a transcendental premise. It asserts that the Rosicrucians actually did possess all the supernatural powers with which they were credited; that they were literally citizens of two worlds being able to function fully consciously in both a physical and an etheric body, the latter not subject to the laws of time and space. These adepts were conversant with the very highest mysteries that concerned the quest to regenerate, through a process of transmutation, the "base elements" of man's lower nature into the "gold" of intellectual and spiritual realisation. Under this alchemical process Rosicrucian adepts were believed to be able to teach men how to function away from their physical body at will by assisting them to remove the "rose from the cross."

Rosicrucian initiates taught that spiritual nature was attached to the physical form at certain points, symbolised by the three nails of the crucifixion. By three alchemical processes they were able to draw these nails and permit the divine nature of Man to come down from its cross. They concealed the processes by which this was accomplished under three alchemical metaphorical expressions: "The Casting of the Molten Sea," "The Making of the Rose Diamond," and "The Achieving of the Philosopher's Stone." The mystic believes that the true Brethren of the Rosy Cross exist in the inner planes of Nature, and that they can only be reached by those who can transcend the limitations of the material world. To substantiate this view the mystic quotes the *Confessio Fraternitatis*: "...wherefore now no longer are we beheld by human eyes, unless they have received strength borrowed from the eagle." In mysticism the eagle is a symbol of initiation (the spinal Spirit Fire), and by this is explained the inability of the unregenerated world to understand the Secret Order of the Rosy Cross. In this theory of the Fraternity's beginnings the Comte de Saint-Germain was its highest adept and is believed to be the same person as Christian Rosencreutz.

The Tenets of the Rosicrucian Order

What did the Fathers of the Rosicrucian Order desire to achieve by bringing their new philosophy to public attention? Johann Valentin Andrae, putative author of *The Confessio*, proclaimed that:

- ❖ Jehovah, beholding the decadence of civilization, seeks to redeem humanity by revealing to the willing and by thrusting upon the reluctant those secrets which previously He had reserved for His elect.
- ❖ Nature, however, provides a remedy for each new disease that manifests itself, so our Fraternity has provided a remedy for the infirmities of the world's philosophic system.
- ❖ We firmly believe that through deep meditation on the inventions of the human mind and the mysteries of life, through the cooperation of the angels and spirits, and through experience and long observation, our loving Christian Father C.R.C. was so fully

illumined with God's wisdom that were all the books and writings of the world lost and the foundations of science overturned, the Fraternity of R.C. could re-establish the structure of world thought upon the foundation of divine truth and integrity… those who receive this knowledge shall become masters of all arts and crafts; no secret shall be hidden from them; and all good works of the past, present, and future shall be accessible to them. The whole world shall become as one book and the contradictions of science and theology shall be reconciled;

- We declare that God, before the end of the world, shall create a great flood of spiritual light to alleviate the sufferings of humankind. Falsehood and darkness which have crept into the arts, sciences, religions, and governments of humanity--making it difficult for even the wise to discover the path of reality--shall be forever removed and a single standard established, so that all may enjoy the fruitage of truth;
- God has given man two eyes, two nostrils, and two ears, but only one tongue. Whereas the eyes, the nostrils and the ears admit the wisdom of Nature into the mind, the tongue alone may give it forth. In various ages there have been illumined ones who have seen, smelt, tasted or heard the will of God, but it will shortly come to pass that those who have seen, smelt, tasted or heard shall speak and truth shall be revealed;
- We have a magic writing, copied from that divine alphabet with which God writes His will upon the face of celestial and terrestrial Nature. With this new language we read God's will for all His creatures, and just as astronomers predict eclipses so we prognosticate the obscurations of the church and how long they shall last. Our language is like unto that of Adam and Enoch before the Fall;
- … We invite and admit into our Fraternity the worthy of all nations, who thereafter share with us the Light of God: will you not join yourselves with us to the perfection of yourselves, the development of all the arts and the service of the world.

Otto Rahn (1904-1939), a pre-WWII medievalist who, contrary to his philosophical and spiritual beliefs, was pressed by Heinrich Himmler to carry out work for the Nazis for a number of years, closed his second and final published work[38] with the words: "I am going to follow the ancient path of the thief, my eyes constantly fixed on the Great Bear: Arktos, Artur, Arthur, Thor. Thor, the Grand-Father, loved honey. A little bee flies towards the table where I write, and disappears into the evening. Perhaps it will spend the night inside a wild rose. And tomorrow is a new day." Hargrave Jennings described in *The Rosicrucians, Their Rites and Mysteries* an elaborate genealogy of the arms of France in which the bee motif is all-important. Via a complex examination of heraldric devices Hargraves associates these bee-insect motifs with the Lady-Bird which, in the ancient nursery rhyme, is representative of the Virgin Mary (Mary=Mare=the blue and salty bitterness of the sea) and Mother Nature-Isis. In the armorial bearings of the Frankish kings, the Lilies are represented as insects, seeded or spotted upon a blue field. These *scarabaei* were dignified by the Egyptians as the emblems of the "Enlightened." The *scarabaeus* or crab plays a large part in the grand rite of the Mithraic Sacrifice of the Bull. The motto placed under the lilies of the arms of France is "Lilia non laborant, neque nent." (The lily neither toils nor spins.) One recalls the parallel words of Jesus: "Consider the lilies of the field, how they grow; they toil not [like bees], neither do they spin [like spiders]." German peasants believed that bees were the survivors of the Golden Age. Above all other trees, bees love the ash: Yggdrasil, the Tree and the World of Life.

The Cathars of Provence were known as *Tisserands*—weavers. The three Norns wove the threads of Destiny and it was The Norns who sat under one of the three roots of Yggdrasil. The Norns make the laws, weaving and fixing the lives of the sons of men and the destiny of mortals. The three heads of Cerberus and the ancient practice of invocation of Hecate where three roads meet are illustrative of the image of the English broad arrow, representing the Three Nails of the Cross, the Fleur-de-Lis and the Crux Ansata of the Egyptians. The arrow symbolises the sudden directedness of one's inner Living Force. It has to do with projected energy and creative focus, the coming together towards a single goal or purpose of all disassociated forces of thought and of soul.

John Heydon, prominent Rosicrucian thinker, wrote in *The Rosie Cross Uncovered* that the mysterious brethren possessed polymorphous powers, appearing in any desired form at will and had the gift of appearing in more than one place at the same time. Thomas Vaughan corroborated Heydon's claims of the brethren's powers of invisibility,

---

[38] Rahn, O., *Luzifers Hofgesind, Eine Reise zu Europas guten Geistern*, Schwarzhäupter Verlag, Leipzig and Berlin, 1937

saying that they “can move in this white mist. Whosoever would communicate with us must be able to see in this light…”

Brethren were buried in a womb, a glass casket, sometimes called the Philosophical Egg, out of which from time to time they would emerge to function before returning to their shell of glass. *Glas* in German means amber. In his writings Rahn explains that amber is a stone of a very particular kind. These descriptions are mindful of the Arthurian legend in which the Once and Future King is residing in a crystal cave on Avalon, the Island of Apples.

The overall theme of the *Fama* is the re-discovery of an ancient philosophy, primarily alchemical and related to the healing arts, but also concerned with number and geometry, all ingredients underlining the importance of the document as a pathway to illumination of a religious and spiritual nature. The story emphasises the importance of the miraculous discovery in 1604 of the vault housing the body of Brother Rosenkreutz who died in 1484. The allegory of the vault and its everlasting light is a central feature of the Roscicrucian legend. The sun never shines in the vault, which is eternally lit by an inner sun. Geometrical figures adorn the walls. Treasures lie all around, including the works of Paracelsus, magical bells, lamps and “artificial songs.”

A fascinating line of investigation concerns the Bacon-Rosicrucian-Shakespeare enigma. Chapter XII of the Rosicrucian *Confessio Fraternititas* says that one of the philosophers who make light of the Holy Trinity was “a stage player, a man with sufficient ingenuity for imposition.” Hall strongly believed that Andreas’ “stage player” was Francis Bacon (Lord Verulam). The *Anatomy of Melancholy*, 1621, by Democritus Junior, pseudonym for Robert Burton, an intimate of Bacon, contains a short but significant footnote: “Joh. Valent. Andreas, Lord Verulam” indicating Burton’s belief that Andreas and Bacon were one and the same person. Abundant evidence exists to convince many, Manley P. Hall and John Michell among them, that Bacon wrote the works of Shakespeare. Hall states that no one but a Platonist, Qabbalist or Pythagorean could have written *The Tempest, Macbeth, Hamlet* or the *Tragedy of Cymbeline*.

In 1604 a very curious work dedicated to the Duke of Wurttemberg was published in Stuttgart. It was a book of huge length entitled *Naometria* by Simon Studion and its theme focused upon apocalyptic prophecy. It involved a system of numerology based on Biblical descriptions of the Temple of Solomon, leading to prophecies about future events.

Apart from the Andreas-Bacon synthesis, two writers are

acknowledged as the chief protagonists of Rosicrucian philosophy: Robert Fludd in England and Michael Maier in Germany. Maier gave expression to the theme of spiritual alchemy while Fludd gave more focus to the philosophy of macrocosm and microcosm. In his second work, *Viatorum hoc est de Montibus Planetarunt Septem,* Maier sets out his alchemical foundation of beliefs. The theme of the book is the search for the *materia philosophica,* the truth hidden in the arcana of nature, by holding fast, like Theseus, to Ariadne's thread, which will lead one through the labyrinth. In his 1652 work *Themis Aurea* Maier make a description of the R.C Fraternity as both an Order of Chivalry and as an Order of the Golden Fleece.

Dr. Franz Hartmann, in his *Secret Symbols of the Rosicrucians*, believed that the brethren were able to command the elemental spirits and fairy folk and knew the secret of the Philosopher's Stone, a knowledge which rendered its possessor immortal and all-wise.

In general terms Rosicrucianism stood for the individual's quest to undertake private and personal religious experiences by which his total being—body, mind and spirit—was refined and strengthened. As John Dee and Robert Fludd conceived it, the movement was to be inclusive of all religious attitudes. However, especially in Germany, it rapidly encouraged anti-Catholic sentiments as it evolved into a broad evangelical system of belief attractive to all denominations of Protestants. Anti-Catholic Rahn would have experienced little or no internal opposition to embracing these beliefs and expounding Rosicrucian principles *sub-rosa* within his own writings.

The Temple of the Rose Cross
Teophilus Schweighardt Constantiens

Rosicrucian Crucifixion by John Augustus Knapp

Chapter 15

Morrigan: Goddess of Fallen Warriors

Morrígan, also known as Morrígu, is a figure from Irish mythology. Defined by scholarship as a "war goddess," she is associated with terror, confusion, sorcery, prophecy, poetry and doom. Crow on the field of battle, wolf-bitch, naked, screaming, white-haired hag, lovely daughter of a king: in medieval Irish literature, Morrígan is many things. She is often considered a triple goddess, appearances partially due to the Celtic significance of threeness. Sometimes she appears as one of three sisters Morrígan, Badb and Macha. Sometimes the trinity consists of Badb, Macha and Anand, collectively known as the "Morrígna." Occasionally, Nemain or Fea appear in the various combinations. However, Morrígan can also appear alone, and her name is sometimes used interchangeably with Badb.

Morrígan is mainly associated with war and fate, especially with foretelling doom, death, or victory in battle. In this role she often appears as a crow, the badb. She incites warriors to battle and can help bring about victory over their enemies. Morrígan encourages warriors to do brave deeds, strikes fear into their enemies, and in her persona as the "Washerwoman at the Ford" is portrayed laundering the bloodstained clothes of those fated to die. Most frequently seen as a goddess of battle and war, she is also a manifestation of the earth-goddess, chiefly representing her role as guardian of the territory and its people.

There is disagreement over the meaning of Morrígan's name. Mor may derive from an Indo-European root connoting terror and monstrousness, cognate with the Old English maere (which survives in the word "nightmare") and the Scandinavian mara and the Old East Slavic "mara" (also "nightmare"); while rígan translates as "queen." Accordingly, Morrígan is often translated as "Phantom Queen."

The earliest sources for Morrígan are glosses (brief notations or marginalia) in Latin manuscripts. The eighth-century O'Mulconry's

Glossary says that Macha is one of the three morrígna. In a ninth-century manuscript containing the Vulgate version of the Book of Isaiah, the word Lamia is used to translate the Hebrew Lilith. A gloss explains this night hag as "a monster in female form, that is, a morrígan." Cormac's Glossary (also ninth-century) explains the plural word gudemain ("spectres") with the plural form morrígna.

Morrígan's earliest narrative appearances, in which she is depicted as an individual, are in stories of the Ulster Cycle where she has an ambiguous relationship with the hero Cú Chulainn. In the Táin Bó Regamna ("The Cattle Raid of Regamain"), Cú Chulainn encounters Morrígan but does not recognise her as she drives a heifer from his territory. In response to this perceived challenge and his ignorance of her role as a sovereign figure he insults her, but before he can attack her she becomes a black bird on a nearby branch. Cú Chulainn now knows who she is and tells her that had he known they would not have parted in enmity. She notes that whatever he had done would have brought him ill luck. To his response that she cannot harm him, she delivers a series of warnings, foretelling a coming battle in which he will be killed. She tells him, 'It is at the guarding of thy death that I am; and I shall be.'

In the Táin Bó Cúailnge ("The Cattle Raid of Cooley"), Queen Medb of Connacht launches an invasion of Ulster to steal the bull Donn Cuailnge. Morrígan, like Alecto of the Greek Furies, appears to the bull in the form of a crow and warns him to flee. Cú Chulainn defends Ulster by fighting a series of single combats at fords against Medb's champions. In between combats, Morrígan appears to him as a young woman and offers him her love and her aid in the battle but he rejects her offer. In response, she intervenes in his next combat, first in the form of an eel who trips him, then as a wolf who stampedes cattle across the ford, and finally as a white, red-eared heifer leading the stampede, just as she had warned in their previous encounter. However, Cú Chulainn wounds her in each form and defeats his opponent despite her interference. Later, she appears to him as an old woman bearing the same three wounds that her animal forms had sustained. She is milking a cow. She gives Cú Chulainn three drinks of milk. He blesses her with each drink, and her wounds are healed. As the armies gather for the final battle, she prophesises the bloodshed to come.

In one version of Cú Chulainn's death-tale, as he rides to meet his enemies, he encounters Morrígan as a hag washing his bloody armour in a ford, an omen of his death. Later in the story, mortally wounded, Cú Chulainn ties himself to a standing stone with his own entrails so he can die upright, and it is only when a crow lands on his shoulder that his enemies believe he is dead. One of Morrigan's many forms is the *bean nighe*, the "washer woman," an omen of death and a messenger from the Otherworld.

Morrigan is associated, too, with the order of fairies known as the *bean sidhe*, banshees who wash bloody weapons, armour and clothing in a ford of a stream or river. Sometimes she will speak the prophetic words of death to he or she whose belongings she washes. At other times she will say nothing, her appearance alone betokening death. The washer may be a fair young maiden or a loathsome hag.

It is said that *mnathan nighe* (the plural of *bean nighe*) are the spirits of women who died giving birth and are doomed to perform their tasks until the day their lives would have normally ended. It was also believed that this fate could be avoided if all the clothing left by the deceased woman had been washed; otherwise, she would have to finish this task after death

Morrígan also appears in texts of the Mythological Cycle. In a twelfth-century manuscript, the *Lebor Gabála Érenn* ("The Book of the Taking of Ireland"), she is listed among the Tuatha Dé Danann as one of the daughters of Ernmas, granddaughter of Nuada. In addition to Morrigan, Ernmas's other daughters were Ériu, Banba, Fódla, Badb and Macha. A quatrain describes Morrigan, Badb and Macha as wealthy and "springs of craftiness." In Irish myth, the magical Otherworld is a subterranean region invisible to humans except under special circumstance.

Through secret passages and beneath mountains, raths, moats and dolmens the Otherworld was once inhabited by the Partholon, the megalith builders of ancient Ireland. The Parthelon were succeeded by the aristocratic and humanesque Tuatha Dé Danann or Tuath Dé (meaning "the folk of the goddess Danu"). They are often depicted as kings, queens, druids, bards, warriors, heroes, healers and craftsmen who have supernatural powers.

The Tuatha dé Dannan were the tall, beautiful Good People (*Daoine Maithe*), a highly cultured and refined race much like us who lived in the hills, married, bore children, toiled and feasted. They were extremely gifted in the fields of architecture, science, mathematics and engineering. They exercised command over the power of sound to lift and move massive weights. Over time, the Dannan, born from the "waters of heaven or space," a representation of the goddess Anu (later Christianised as Brigit), became known as the fairy folk (later the Sidhe of folklore).

The enemies of the Dannan, the Fomorians, were children of the goddess Domnu, meaning an abyss or deep sea. Legend speaks of the Fomorians as a race of hideous giants (the Nefilim). In a description mindful of a Tolkien tale, the Fomorians were defeated on the Plain of Towers by a cataclysmic Flood generated by the Dagda Mor.

After their defeat by by the Sons of Mil the Tuatha dé Dannan retired into Ireland's emerald hills, together with the leprechauns, pixies, dwarfs and knockers (miners) of the fairy folk. They dwell in the Otherworld but interact with humans and the human world. Prominent members of the Tuath Dé include the Dagda ("the great god"), Morrígan, Lugh, Nuada, Aengus, Brigid, Manannán, Dian Cecht the healer, and Goibniu, a god of metalsmithing and one of the Trí Dé Dána ("three gods of craft").

Morrígan also appears in the Cath Maige Tuired ("The Battle of Magh Tuireadh"). On Samhain (Gaelic festival on 1 November, marking the end of the harvest season), Morrigan keeps a tryst with the Dagda before the battle against the Fomorians. When he meets her, she is washing herself, standing with one foot on either side of the river Unius, near Riverstown in County Sligo. In some sources, she is believed to have created the river. After they have sex, Morrígan promises to summon the magicians of Ireland to cast spells on behalf of the Tuatha Dé, and to destroy Indech, the Fomorian king, taking from him "the blood of his heart and the kidneys of his valour." Later, we are told, she would bring two handfuls of his blood and deposit them in the same river. As battle is about to be joined, the Tuatha Dé leader, Lug, asks each what power they bring to the battle. Morrígan's reply is difficult to interpret, but involves pursuing, destroying and subduing. When she comes to the battlefield, she chants a poem and immediately the battle breaks and the Fomorians are driven into the sea. After the battle, she chants another poem celebrating the victory and prophesying the end of the world.

In another story, she lures away the bull of a woman named Odras. Odras then follows Morrígan to the Otherworld, via the cave of Cruachan, which is said to be her "fit abode." When Odras falls asleep, Morrígan turns her into a pool of water that feeds into the River Shannon. In this story, Morrigan is called the Dagda's envious queen, fierce of mood. She is also called a "shape-shifter" and a cunning raven caller whose pleasure was in mustered hosts.

Morrígan, a goddess intimately associated with war and fate, is said to derive pleasure from murdered hosts. Her role often involves premonitions of a particular warrior's violent death, suggesting a link with the banshee of later folklore. Her role is not only to be a symbol of imminent death, but to also influence the outcome of war. Most often, she does this by appearing as a crow flying overhead, and will either inspire fear or courage in the hearts of the warriors. There are also a few rare accounts where she participates in the battle itself as a warrior and shows her favouritism in a more direct manner.

It has been suggested that Morrigan was closely linked to the fianna, and that these groups may have been in some way dedicated to her. The fianna were bands of youthful warrior-hunters, living on the borders of civilized society and indulging in lawless activities for a time before inheriting property and taking their places as members of settled, landed communities. If true, her worship may have resembled that of Perchta groups in Germanic areas. There is a burnt mound site in County Tipperary known as Fulacht na Mór Ríoghna ("cooking pit of the Mórrígan"). The fulachtaí sites are found in wild areas, and are usually associated with outsiders such as the fianna, as well as with the hunting of deer. There may be a link with the three mythical hags who cook the meal of dogflesh that brings the hero Cú Chulainn to his doom. The Dá Chích na Morrígna ("two breasts of the Mórrígan"), a pair of hills near Brú na Bóinne in County Meath, suggest to some a role as a tutelary goddess, comparable to Anu, who has her own hills, Dá Chích Anann ("the breasts of Anu") in County Kerry. Other goddesses known to have similar hills are Áine and Grian of County Limerick, who, in addition to a tutelary function, also have solar attributes.

There have been attempts by researchers to link Morrígan with the character of Morgan, the latter often being depicted in the legend as a fairy or otherwise supernatural sister of King Arthur. Morgan first appears in literature in Geoffrey of Monmouth's twelfth-century Vita Merlini as a goddess-like figure who takes Arthur to her Otherworld land of Avalon following his mortal wound in a battle. In some Arthurian texts, such as Sir Gawain and the Green Knight, Morgan is portrayed as a hag whose actions set into motion a bloody trail of events that lead the hero into numerous instances of danger. Morgan is also depicted as a seductress, much like the older legends of Morrígan, and has numerous lovers whom she might abduct for this purpose (as in some stories of Lancelot). The character is frequently depicted as wielding power over others to achieve her own purposes, allowing those actions to play out over time, to the benefit or detriment of other characters.

*

Having read this last chapter in the book, Brad shudders and places it back on the shelf. Morrigan was a terrifying entity; Brad sincerely hopes that his continuing education in the ancient mysteries will not entail him coming face to face with the triple… Brad stops himself but it's too late. He should know by now that one can't tempt fate like that and expect to get clean away with it. Hmm…

Brad takes a walk in the meadow to stretch his legs, choosing a path that leads down to the sea. By the time he reaches the shore twenty minutes later, the fishermen Brad saw earlier have gone. He is quite alone. The Gatekeper and Ruth have gifted him a fantastic opportunity to make a journey of discovery that is open to very few individuals. He must make the very best of it and learn all that he could about our world's mythological traditions and the many lessons and signposts concealed within them.

The sun was now almost overhead. Brad is not a sun worshipper and so he makes his way back to the temple for a bite to eat and a long draught of cool water. Sated and refreshed, he reaches for a scroll that has caught his eye. He unties its ribbon, unfurls it and reads its title page—*Sacred Measure, Divine Number*. Great, right up his street, he is really going to enjoy this one!

Morrigan and a Fallen Warrior on the Battlefield

PICTURE GALLERY

Flying A gasoline pumps of yore

Th Flying A Service Station—all gleam and sparkle!

Druid statue, Croome Park
Worcestershire

Mithraic column, Caerleon
Museum

Roman god Attis (Adonis),
Caerleon Museum

Green man carving,
Caerleon

Eleusinian Initiation Ceremony

The death of Orpheus

Thracian Girle carrying head of Orpheus, Gustave Moreau

Orpheus and Eurydice

Old Babylonina erotic terracotta votive plaque of Inanna and Dumuzid

Inanna and Ninshubur

Stylised pyramid scene

One of the oldest photos of Giza

Isis

Rosicrucian symbolism

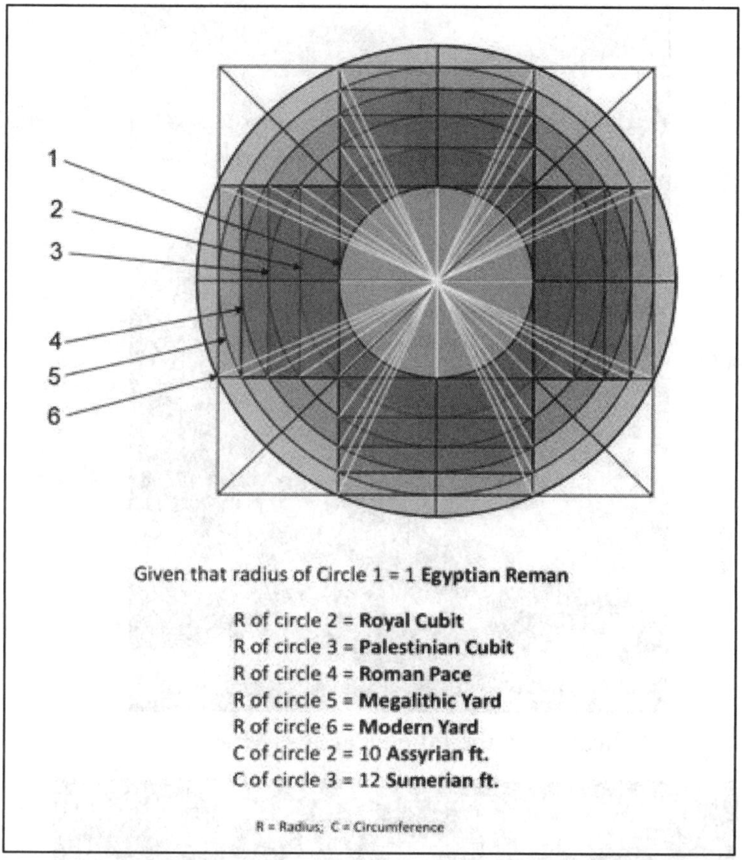

Master diagram of Sacred Geometry

Incorrect triangle measure, Mesopotamia

Ancient Egyptian measures

Dedication to the fallen Cathars, Montsegur

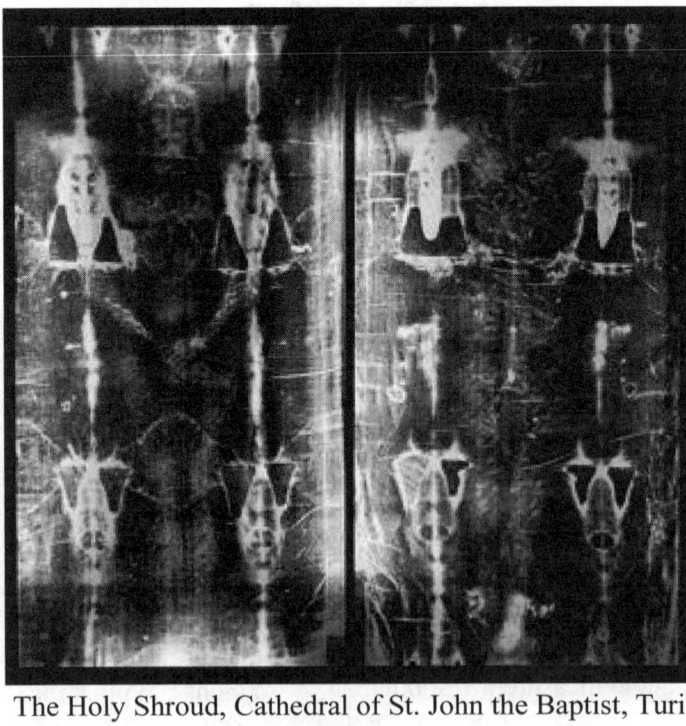

The Holy Shroud, Cathedral of St. John the Baptist, Turin

The Cathar fortress on the pog of Montségur

The Golem and his master

SACRED MEASURE,
DIVINE NUMBER

Everything that can be known has a number; for it is impossible to grasp anything with the mind or to recognize it without this.

—The Pythagorean, Philolaus, *c*.470–*c*.385 BCE

Chapter 16

Ancient Metrology

The principal source for this in-depth review of ancient metrology is John Michell's definitive work,[39] in which the author makes the claim that in some very remote period the earth was scientifically surveyed, and its dimensions were expressed in a unique code of number and measure. Michell proposed that the same code was applied to other ancient sciences, a code that arises naturally from the very structure of arithmetic. His slender volume for the first time in history also precisely indentifies the lengths of certain universal standard units of number and measure and elaborates upon the reasons for the subtle differences between them.

In accordance with Pythagorean thinking, Number existed before anything was created which could be numbered. The principles controlling numbers are the principles of real existence; the elements of numbers are actually the elements of reality. The whole cosmos is a scale and a number. 'Numbers are the sources of Form and Energy in the world,' wrote Platonist mathematican, Theon of Smyrna. Ancient peoples shared this belief, developed it and for the benefit of ensuing generations made sure to encode their knowledge in the dimensions of sacred monuments.

In common with many of his learned peers, Sir Isaac Newton took it for granted that our own civilization stemmed from a greater, now forgotten, culture. He dissected every stanza of the Gematria of the New Testament and the Qabalah of the Old in order to reconstruct the dimensions of the Temple of Jerusalem, which he openly stated was a model of the earth. He did this in an attempt to identify the ancient modules of measurement which he knew were geodetic, in order to complete his *Principia*, which could not be done without an accurate knowledge of the earth's dimensions.

---

[39]Michell, J., *Ancient Metrology*, Pentacle Books, Bristol, 1981

Present day metrologist John Neal remarks[40] that Newton was on the right track because the structure of metrology is sufficient to establish the statistics of the ancient reckoning of the earth's dimensions. The evidence to support these statements is voluminous and unambiguous.

By the beginning of the Christian era these ancient skills of numeracy, geography and metrology had all but disappeared, practised only by a shrinking number of initiates. All that carried it forward through the centuries was its universality and momentum. As Neal points out, whenever one tries to trace its existence back in time there are definite cut-off points invariably instigated by the victors in a situation. The destruction of Gnosticism after the Council of Nicea, which prompted the burning of the Library of Alexandria, the persecution of Confucianism and killing of scholars after the unification of China by the Qin are typical examples of attempts to expunge all cultural traces from vanquished people.

It follows that any attempt to decode the ancient system can only succeed if one is equipped with knowledge of ancient metrology. Naturally, to interpret any set of dimensions it is necessary to establish the lengths of the units of measure in which they were originally framed. Some writers have claimed that the ancient units of measure prove that the size of the earth and other astronomical constants were known in remote antiquity, while others maintain that such claims are patently absurd.

Throughout the world all of its peoples from remote antiquity had used the identical system. This terminology—Egyptian, Greek, Roman, Assyrian, Sumerian, Aztec, Japanese etc.—was redundant. All these national terms were merely those measures the bureaucrats had selected from a wide choice of values to be the national standard for social regulation. It must date from the far mists of time because in the distant past these disparate peoples were not even aware of each other's existence; yet they used the identical measurement systems. Measures of leagues and miles, the intermediary furlongs and stadia, the standard modules of fathoms, paces, yards, cubits and feet right down to the sub-divisions of digits and inches were based on exactly the same methodology.

Michell said of these cultural similarities that the ancient peoples had perfected standardisation of culture, which enabled them to endure for perhaps thousands of years. It was accomplished by reference to the "canon of order" and that this canon governed all of their stylistic

[40] Neal, J., *Ancient Metrology*, vols. I-II, Squeeze Press, 2016-2017

artefacts, architecture and arts.

Knowledge of metrology adds a whole new dimension to archaeology. By his own admission, Michell's greatest discovery was the measurement system that was there since the foundation of the world. The whole subject, because of the necessity for a different mental attitude, is difficult to communicate and it may take a very long time to be acknowledged and generally embraced. But if it is ever accepted, it will be John Michell's lasting memorial and the one that he was proudest of as an accomplishment.

As Michell explained, the whole question is so fraught with political, even religious implications, that it tends to be addressed emotionally rather than rationally. Opinion is generally divided into two camps: those who favour the recent "rise of man" view of history with modern science as the crowning achievement of all preceding ages, and those who see civilisation as a cyclical and transient phenomenon, our own being merely the latest in a series of such universal systems. Since the establishment of the anti-scientific Christian Church, the former belief has gained ascendency in place of the latter.

The origins and values of ancient metrology do not support that viewpoint but rather imply that men of science in very ancient times possessed knowledge of the shape and dimensions of the earth and its planetary neighbours, which is still expressed in ancient monuments, units of measure, systems of numeration and other traditions of the past.

Accurate geodetic surveys were made far earlier than the days of electronics and space satellites, and there is a mystery about how and when ancient civilisation originated and how it became so universally established. There is no question here of a gradual development of knowledge by human endeavours down the ages but of quite the reverse process. The system of interlinked measures, numeration and geodetic standards was evidently the product of a single source or inventor, appearing as if ready-made in its more complete form at some very remote period, leaving its mark in the monuments and cultures of virtually the entire ancient world, and then slowly dissolving until, by the beginning of the Christian era, studies of the tradition were confined to a small number of initiate scholars, who respected them as relics of the higher wisdom of those of the distant past.

The ancient code was of an entirely different quality from our own, for its tenets were designed to be transmitted orally and thereby create the conditions of stability which made it possible for civilisations gone before to preserve the same standards over periods of thousands of years.

The code cannot fail to impress the modern student of the topic. By its application the earth's principal dimensions are not only defined with scientific accuracy but they are related to each other proportionally by number series which develop from the values, expressed in terms of the English foot and mile, of the ancient series of measure. Moreover, these number series which fit the dimensions of our planet are the very same as those which were formerly used for measuring many other classes of natural phenomena.

In ancient times, the patterns of numerical relationships, which occur in the processes of arithmetic and geometry, were regarded as the formative influences behind all nature's productions. The old philosophers were therefore concerned above all with investigating the numerical patterns in the appearances and movements of nature.

There is thus more to the study of metrology than the discovery of the exact lengths of the ancient units of measure and geodetic constants. Behind these is a philosophy of number in which number is used not as a measure of quantities but rather as a means of expressing universal relationships, a process once referred to as "Theoretic Arithmetic," a study of which is calculated to purify, invigorate, enlighten and elevate the mind, rather than practical arithmetic, which, though necessary for day-to-day living, does not in itself raise the quality of the human condition.

Plato's statement in Timaeus that purely mathematical structures are the underlying principle of matter, appeals to modern physicists as providing a much better image of the nature of the atom than was achieved by nineteenth-century scientists with their belief in solid, indivisible particles. It is thus entirely possible that the ancient metrological and geodetic code of number and proportion may once again become a topic of essential study by cosmologists.

Michell took pains to point out that the metre was designed for commercial and general purposes and for the measure of *quantity*, whereas the ancient units were related to each other by *number*. It follows that the proper units for study of ancient metrology are the English foot and mile because their values were constant throughout the ancient world and were designed to bring forward the duodecimal aspect of the ancient metrology.

Gasoline prices of yesteryear!

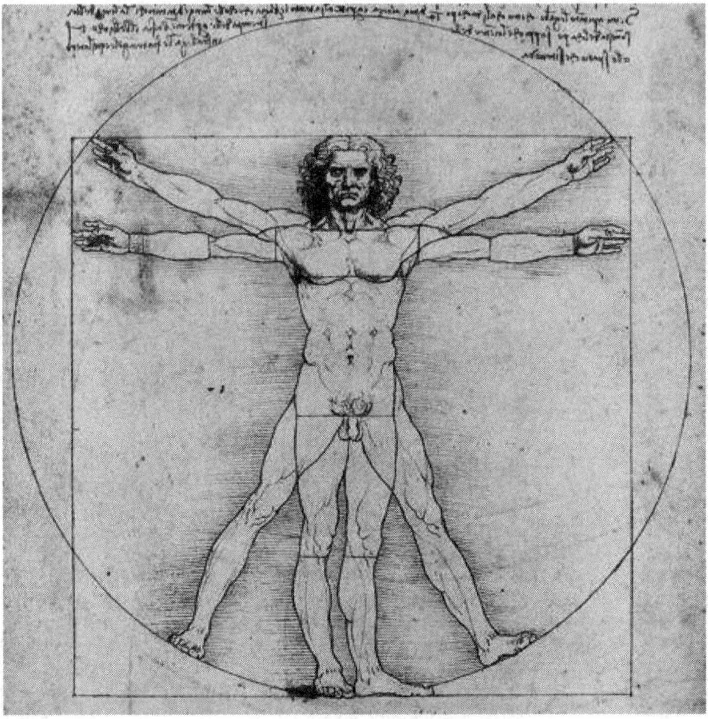

…the measurements of man are in nature distributed in this manner, that is 4 fingers make a palm, 4 palms make a foot, 6 palms make a cubit, 4 cubits make a man, 4 cubits make a footstep, 24 palms make a man and these measures are in his buildings. If you open your legs enough that your head is lowered by 1/14 of your height and raise your arms enough that your extended fingers touch the line of the top of your head, let you know that the center of the ends of the open limbs will be the navel, and the space between the legs will be an equilateral triangle. The length of the outspread arms is equal to the height of the man. From the hairline to the bottom of the chin is one-tenth of the height of the man. From below the chin to the top of the head is one-eighth of the height of the man. From above the chest to the top of the head is one-sixth of the height of the man. From above the chest to the hairline is one-seventh of the height of a man. From the chest to the head is a quarter of the height of the man. The maximum width of the shoulders contains a quarter of the man. From the elbow to the tip of the hand is a quarter of the height of a man; the distance from the elbow to the armpit is one-eighth of the height of the man; the length of the hand is one-tenth of the man. The virile member is at the half height of the man. The foot is one-seventh of the man. From below the foot to below the knee is a quarter of the man. From below the knee to the root of the member is a quarter of the man. The distances from the chin to the nose and the hairline and the eyebrows are equal to the ears and one third of the face.

—Vitruvius the Architect

Chapter 17

Ancient Measures

... the hand of the Lord was upon me... In the visions of God he brought me into the land of Israel, and set me upon a very high mountain, by which was the frame of a city on the south.

And he brought me thither, and behold, there was a man, whose appearance was like the appearance of brass, with a line of flax in his hand, and a measuring reed; and he stood in the gate.

And the man said unto me, Son of man, behold with thine eyes, and hear with thine ears, and set thine heart upon all that I shall shew thee.

—Ezekiel 40: 2 – 4

In that moment of prophetic consciousness, the archetypal pattern of creation is about to be revealed to Ezekiel. The pattern is represented as the frame of a city, oriented toward the south. The city is an architectural metaphor, implying the hand of an architect, and is the holy or heavenly city.

In the Old Testament book of Isaiah, chapter 40, the prophet recognizes God as the great architect, "Who hath measured the waters in the hollow of his hand, and meted out heaven with the span, and comprehended the dust of the earth in a measure, and weighed the mountains in scales, and the hills in a balance," thus conveying the importance of measurement in the creation of the universe.

The text in the nineteenth chapter of Leviticus—"Ye shall do no unrighteousness in judgement, in mete-yard, in weight, or in measure. Just balances, just weights, a just ephah, and a just hin shall ye have..."—reinforces the understanding that a society without a just system of measuring and of establishing due proportion to the substance of the world is a society without justice or virtue.

Ancient man understood that the system by which the world and its constituent parts are measured must be in harmony with the world itself, its dimensions, proportions and patterns. To measure a thing is to render it sensible and functional. It provides the means by which man engages and interacts with the world.

5th century BCE sophist thinker Protagoras of Abdera wrote that "man is the measure of all things." The system of measure by which we create and build our microcosmic world must of necessity serve as the intermediary between the human scale and the macrocosmic scale to achieve universal balance and harmony. There must be resonance between the handiwork of man and the handiwork of God.

A consistent Old Testament theme is the employment of measure as the key to revelation. The key is a universal standard of measure, always presented by a being that is sometimes man, sometimes angel, but simultaneously a geometrician, a builder and, in the original meaning of the word "angel" (malak), a messenger.

> *I lifted up mine eyes again, and looked, and behold a man with a measuring line in his hand. Then said I, Whither goest thou?*
>
> *And he said unto me, to measure Jerusalem, to see what is the breadth thereof, and what is the length thereof.*
>
> —Zechariah 2: 1 – 2

Prior to Michell's discovery, no ancient measuring unit had ever been precisely defined. All had to be expressed between plus or minus parameters. This is because of the variations that they are all subject to, which led historians to regard these as evidence of either slackness in their maintenance or that the ancient systems had been arbitrary. This had led to a general averaging of the units by historians, which further cloaked the astonishing beauty of the complete structure of metrology.

This initial exploration of historical measurement is important on many grounds. It is the first time that related measurements have been grouped into a single classification terminology. Secondly, absolute and exact values are established. Thirdly, John Michell proposed a geodetic, or earth-related, relationship. This means that just as modern standard units were devised through the medium of a detailed survey of the globe, so must the ancient standards have been created.

As absurd as this may sound to modern thought processes, which look upon our ancestors with a patronising attitude, there is nothing outlandish in this statement. All of the instrumentation necessary to conduct just such a survey was available in the very remote past.

In his 48-page book,[41] Michell set out for the first time the exact

[41] Ibid

lengths of the ancient units of measure for Stonehenge and other such monuments as the Parthenon and the Egyptian Pyramids. Modern metrologists have come to believe that these and other ancient linear measures expressed fractions of the earth's dimensions.

Their origin is therefore the same as that of the modern French metre but as Michell took pains to emphasise the metric system, a wholly decimal unit designed for commercial and general purposes and for the measure of *quantity*, is a modern device unrelated to the ancient units of measurement, which were related to each other by *number* and generally based on units of twelve, and that therefore its use in a study of ancient metrology is inappropriate.

From times before recorded history, at least 6,000 years ago, the globe has been divided into 360 degrees of latitude, each degree containing 60 minutes of 3,600 seconds. A journey from the pole to the equator is a distance of 90 degrees or about 6,220 miles, so every degree measures on average some 69 miles, and one-sixtieth part of a degree is one minute of latitude, which is the definition of the nautical mile used by seamen.

For the purposes of latitudinal division the earth was conceived as a perfect sphere. Obviously, this is not the case since it bulges at the equator and flattens towards the poles, having the effect of distorting its divisions so that the distance between each successive degree of latitude increases from about 68.7 miles between the equator and latitude 1° to about 69.4 miles in the north and south Polar Regions.

Because of geographical and cultural factors, the ancient systems of metrology are called Greek, Roman, Egyptian etc., but they are really nothing more than the different divisions of the same standards. For example, the ratio between the Roman and Greek foot is 24:25:

24 Roman digits = 1 Roman cubit (a cubit is 1½ feet), and
25 Roman digits = 1 Greek Cubit = 24 Greek digits

The Roman Foot

John Greaves (1602-1652), a professor of astronomy and geometry at Oxford, suspected that the ancients derived their units of measure from fractions of the earth's dimensions. From investigations he undertook in Egypt and in Rome in the late 1630s, he calculated that the *Pes Statilianus* or longer Roman foot measures 0.972 English feet and that the shorter Roman foot (*Pes Colotianus*) measures 0.967 feet. More recent re-calculations of both measures have resulted in extremely minor changes that to all practical purposes may be regarded as insignificant.

The Greek Foot

John Taylor (1781–1864), author of *The Great Pyramid*, established that in common with the Roman foot there were also two measures of the Greek foot. Measurements made at the Parthenon in 1888 by surveyor F.C. Penrose confirmed Taylor's statement, arriving at 1.01376 feet for the longer Greek foot and a value of 1.008 feet for the shorter Greek foot (the "Ptolomaic" foot), making the ratio between the longer and shorter Greek feet as 176:175, which is also the ratio between the longer and short Roman, Egyptian, Jewish feet and other measures.

Egyptian Measures

From his measurements of the King's Chamber in the Great Pyramid in 1637, John Greaves arrived at a measure for the Egyptian cubit (now termed the "royal" cubit) of 1.719 ft and for the shorter Egyptian foot of 1.146 ft. Isaac Newton dubbed this cubit as the "profane" or Memphis cubit, distinguishing it from the "sacred" cubit at the Temple at Jerusalem which was equal to six fifths of the profane cubit.

Based on more recent surveys of the Great Pyramid, which establish that it measures 440 cubits on each side of its base, or 756 ft., the shorter "royal" Egyptian cubit is re-calculated as 1.718 ft., a 25:22 relationship with the shorter Greek cubit of 1½ Greek feet.

Taylor estimated the length of the longer Egyptian cubit to be 1.728 ft. and the length of the longer Egyptian foot (the royal or Philetaerian foot, as classical writers called it) to be 1.152 feet. The 175:176 ratio between the shorter Egyptian cubit of 1.718 ft. and the longer of 1.728 ft. is the same as between the two versions of each unit in Greek and Roman metrology.

The Sacred Cubit and the Polar Foot

Sir Isaac Newton's interest in ancient metrology was driven by his need to discover the correct dimensions of the earth for testing his ideas on gravitation. He shared the belief in his day that the ancients had possessed accurate knowledge of these dimensions and had framed them in simple fractions of geodetic constants such as the polar diameter. From Greaves's surveys and from measurements in Biblical and Talmudic writings, Newton calculated the mean of the Jewish sacred cubit as 2.06937 ft. (25.57-25.79 inches). Taylor's estimate was 2.0736 ft., a unit that he believed represented a twenty-millionth part of the earth's diameter before the Biblical Flood. According to his theory, Noah's Ark came to land on earth, which, because of the addition at the Flood of the waters of the upper firmament, was of greater dimension than before.

This new-sized earth was found to have a polar diameter of 500,000,000 English inches.

Taylor believed that this inch was used in later building work at the Great Pyramid, the earlier interior work having been carried out in pre-Flood cubits. Taylor's reckoning of the length of the longer sacred cubit was therefore 25 inches plus a small fraction, making the ancient estimate of the earth's polar radius slightly over 20,833.333 ft.

Taylor's theory that the origin of the English inch is a fraction of the earth's diameter has attracted powerful support and is still given credence by some Pyramidologists. Peter Lemesurier[42] claimed that several of the Great Pyramid's inner dimensions reveal the use of a sacred cubit of 2.0855416 ft. (25.02650 inches, a very close correspondence to Taylor's measure), a ten-millionth part of the polar radius of 3,949.89 miles.

John Michell's own findings convinced him that the correct value of the sacred cubit in its longer form is 2.0854491 ft. a 176:175 ratio with its shorter version of 2.0736 ft.

The outer diameter of the circle of lintel stones at Stonehenge is thereby calculated to measure 104.272455 ft., and this contains 50 sacred cubits of 2.0854491 ft. Especially prominent in the Stonehenge dimensions is the Jewish sacred foot, which has the customary 2:3 relationship with its cubit

The longer (or northern) values of ancient units in relationship to the English units

Apart from the English statute mile of 5.280 ft., several other kinds of mile have been known in the British Isles. The Irish mile of 6,720 ft. survived into modern times. In addition, there was a Scottish mile of 5,952 ft., an old Cheshire mile of 7,680 ft., and a Welsh mile of indeterminate length but which Taylor estimated as 5,760 ft.

There is evidence that in pre-Elizabethan times the English mile was sometimes divided like the Greek and Roman into 5,000 feet. That foot would therefore have been equal to 1.056 ft., and at that value it bears the same relationship to the Greek foot as the Greek bears to the Roman, that is 25:24. This is an important clue by which one establishes the precise values of the ancient units of measure, for if 24 English miles are equal to 25 Greek miles, the length of the Greek mile is defined as 5,068.8 ft., and the Greek foot as 1.01376 ft. The lengths of the Roman units are then defined from their known relationship to the Greek:

---

[42] Lemesurier, P., *The Great Pyramid Decoded*, Element Books, U.K., 1977

24 miles of 5,280 ft. = 25 Greek miles of 5,068.8 ft.
25 Greek miles = 25 Roman miles of 4,866.048 ft.

Thus, the length of the Roman foot is 0.9732096 ft., and the same value is given by a 10,000:6,336 ratio between the old 7,680-foot Cheshire mile and the Roman mile.

The same 25:24 ratio between the English furlong, or eighth part of a mile, of 660 ft. and the Greek furlong of 625 Greek or 633.6 English feet also exists between the Greek and Roman furlongs and between the Roman and 600-foot stade.

24 English furlongs = 25 Greek furlongs of 633.6 ft.
24 Greek furlongs = 25 Roman furlongs of 608.256 ft.
24 Roman furlongs = 25 Roman stades of 583.92576 ft.

These figures give the longer value of the Greek and Roman units, and from them can be ascertained the degree of terrestrial latitude to which they relate. 6,000 Greek or 6,250 Roman feet at these values are equal to 6,082.56 ft., and that is virtually the same as the length of a nautical mile or minute of latitude at 50° as given in modern tables. 50° North is the latitude of the southern tip of England, and the longer values of the ancient units, which are related to that latitude, Michell referred to as their northern values.

The following are the amounts and values of the various foot units which are contained in one minute of arc on the meridian, or one nautical mile, at latitude 50°.

6,082.56 ft.
6,250 Roman feet of 0.9732096 ft.
6,125 polar feet of 0.99307102 ft.
6,000 Greek feet of 1.01376 ft.
5,280 Egyptian feet of 1.152 ft.

The shorter or tropical values of the ancient units

The longer or northern values of the old units of measure having been established, it remains to ascertain the shorter values. Michell revealed that one of the clues to that discovery concerns the number 12^4 or 20,736. The corresponding length of a degree of latitude at approximately 10° latitude is 6,048 ft. This nautical mile defines the lengths of the ancient units of measure at their shorter of tropical values in the same way as the nautical mile at 50° defines their northern values. 1 minute of arc or nautical mile at 10° = 6,048 ft.

= 6,250 Roman feet of 0.96768 ft.
= 6,125 polar feet of 0.98742857 ft.
= 6,000 Greek feet of 1.008 ft.
= 5,280 Egyptian feet of 1.1 45… ft.

The difference between the length of one degree of latitude at 50°, which is 364,953.6 ft., and one degree of latitude at 10°, which is 362,880 ft., is 2,073.6 ft. or 1,200 Egyptian cubits at northern value.

That 176:175 is the true ratio between the northern and tropical values of each unit is confirmed by statements made by ancient metrologists that 7 stades of the Egyptian foot are equal to one Roman mile, which shows that 4,200 Egyptian feet are equal to 5,000 Roman feet. From this one can derive the tropical value of a Roman foot as 0.96768 ft., which is 175/176 of its northern value of 0.9732096 ft.

The length of the meridian exemplifying the code of number in all the ancient sciences

Michell emphasised that the study of ancient metrology is inseparable from that of ancient geodesy because the old units were intended to represent fractions of the earth's dimensions. Like all ancient sciences that involved measure and number, geodesy, by which were established the definitive measurements of the globe, was governed by a code of number and proportion.

By this code certain key numbers were emphasised and brought into relationship with others to provide formulas that could easily be committed to memory. In his *Laws* Plato refers to this sacred canon of proportion, which the Egyptian priesthood insisted should be used by artists and craftsmen. In that way, the manner and style of Egyptian civilisation remained unchanged over thousands of years.

The old geometers' cosmological diagramatic schemes of number reflected the Pythagorean idea that number preceded Creation. From this principle arose the mystical practice of stereometry, referred to by Plato in *Epinomis*, which was the art of finding correpondences between different orders of natural phenomena through the structure of proportion and number that underlies them all.

Certain numbers are prominent in arithmetic as linking different systems of numeration, for example 5,040, which equals 1 x 2 x 3 x 4 x 5 x 6 x 7 x 8 x 9 x 10, or as forming part of a series as in 12, 12^2, 12^3, 12^4 etc. Such numbers are also prominent in the system of numeration used in the ancient arts and sciences, including metrology, astronomy, timekeeping, architecture and musical harmony. They were expressed by means of the appropriate units of measure in the principal dimensions of the earth.

In the old cosmologies, the earth in the centre of the geometer's diagram was represented by the circle of its meridian with the equator as diameter. The meridian, described by St. John in Revelation as the "wall" of the terrestrial paradise, was therefore an important measure.

> *And he that talked with me, had a golden reed to measure the city, and the gates thereof, and the wall thereof. And the city lieth foursquare, and the length is as large as the breadth: and he measured the city with the reed, twelve thousand furlongs.*
>
> *The length, and the breadth, and the height of it are equal. And he measured the wall thereof, an hundred and forty and four cubits, according to the measure of a man, that is, of the angel.*
>
> —Revelation 21: 15 – 17

Taking the old estimate of the length of a minute of arc on the meridian as the average length of one minute of latitude, and multiplying it by 21,600, the number of minutes in a circle, produces a figure for the length of the earth's meridian circumference of 24,883.2 miles, or a tenth part of 12 x 12 x 12 x 12 x 12 x 12 miles.

This exemplifies the system of duodecimal numeration based on the power and multiples of the number 12, by which the intervals of ancient metrology, geodesy, astronomy and systems for measuring time were reckoned.

This is illustrated, for example, in that 25,920 is the number of years in the "great year" during which the sun completes its journey through the zodiac, being made up of of 12 "Platonic" months each of 2,160 years. 2,160 is also the measure of the diameter of the moon in miles. In St. John's account of New Jerusalem, the microcosm of the ideal earth (Revelation 21), 12^5 or 248,832 is the measure of the circumference of the earth on a scale of one foot to 100 miles.

Other units of length and measure

Sumerian Shusi

Determined from studies of Gudea's tablet, found in 1881 by Ernest de Sarzec while excavating the ruins of Lagash. The tablet contains the ground plan of a temple accompanied by a graduated rule with sixteen equal subdivisions.

Additional tablets displayed the same graduated rule. From the tablets, now in the Louvre, the length of the Sumerian foot and digits were determined. The digit, called a shusi in the cuneiform texts, was determined to be equal in length to 0.66 inches.

Sumerian Foot

Two versions of the Sumerian foot have been determined, a long and a short version. The shorter foot is taken to be equal in length to the graduated rule found on Gudea's and other tablets, that is sixteen shusi. The longer version is known from references in the cuneiform tablets to be equal to 20 shusi.

Sumerian Cubit

Equal in length to 30 shusi.

Digit

The basic unit of Egyptian linear measure, considered by A.E. Berriman to be equal to 0.729 inches.

Reman

An Egyptian unit of linear measure, analyzed by F.H. Griffith in 1892, as well as by Petrie and Berriman. Considered to be equal to 20 digits or 14.58 inches. In his work *Historical Metrology* Berriman refined the length of the reman to 1.2165 feet.

Assyrian Foot

Measurements made of Babylonian ruins by linguist Jules Oppert in 1853 revealed a unit of length equal to 1.08 modern feet.

Span

The distance between the tip of the thumb and the tip of the little finger when the hand is fully extended, generally taken as 9 inches or ½ of the standard Hebrew Cubit. The Chinese had an equivalent measure of 9 inches called the ch'ih.

Reed

A Hebrew unit of length from the Bible equal to 6 cubits, usually assumed to be Hebrew cubits of 18 inches length.

Palestinian Cubit

Knowledge of the Palestinian Cubit survives in the writings of Epiphanius, a Bishop of Constantia in Cyprus, who wrote a treatise on weights and measures in 392 CE. It conforms to the cubit of the altar as mentioned in Ezekial 43:13, that is, the cubit and a handbreadth. The Palestinian cubit is generally taken as 25.284 inches or 2.107 feet.

Stade

An ancient Greek unit equivalent to the length of a Greek foot-racing course, usually semi-circular. From this root word comes the English term stadium. John Michell states that its length is equal to a tenth part of a nautical mile or minute of latitude and made up of 600 Greek feet or 625 Roman feet. These ancient feet were each divided into 16 digits of finger's breadths, the Roman digit being equal to one part in 100,000 of one minute of latitude.

Roman Pace

1/1000th of the Roman mile equal to 8 stades of 607.5 feet, hence equal to 4.86 feet. This would make the half pace, or stride, equal to 2.43 feet.

Megalithic Yard (MY)

Discovered by the Scottish engineer, Alexander Thom, who in the 1960's and 70's surveyed and analyzed over 500 megalithic remains and stone circles throughout the British Isles. The megalithic yard was determined by Thom to be equal to 2.72 feet ± 0.003 feet.

Megalithic Mile (MY)

Deduced by scholar J.F. Neal from an extensive analysis of the intervals between megalithic sites in Great Britain. Because it bore virtually the same relation to the statute miles as the Megalithic Yard bore to the foot, Neal called the unit a Megalithic Mile. John Michell noted that Neal's Megalithic Mile was identical to the Indo-Chinese Pu, identified in Jackson's *Modern Metrology* as being equal to 2.727272 statute miles. Neal observed that the distance from Stonehenge to Silbury Hill is precisely 6 Megalithic Miles.

Egyptian Aurora

A unit of square land measuring 100 Royal Cubits on each side.

Roman Jugerum

Equal to 165 feet on a side, totaling 1652 or 27,225 square feet.

Nivartana

An ancient Hindu unit of land measure equal to 20 x 20 "bamboo poles."

A bamboo pole was equal to 10 cubits of 18 inches, the same as the modern Hebrew cubit, making the Nivartana 300 feet on a side.

Hide

An old English measure of land considered being adequate to support one family and dependents, usually taken as 120 English acres.

English Acre

The English acre is the same acre that is presently used in the U.S. to measure land area. The size of an acre has varied somewhat but has been standardized at 1/640 of a square mile. The term "acre" goes back to a Greek word meaning "open land" or "ploughed field." Ultimately this standard for land measure was considered to be the amount of land a yoke of oxen might plough in one day.

Biblical Measures

An **omer** is 1/10th of an ephah.

An **ephah** is equal to 72 logs

The **log** is equal to the Sumerian mina

The **mina** is equal to 60 shekels and is 1/60th of a maris

A **talent** is equal to 60 mina. The Egyptian, Sumerian, Greek and Hebrew talents were equal.

1 **hin** is a liquid measure equal to 12 logs

12 minas = 1 **hin**

Ancient Units of Measure and their two values (in English feet). Numbers followed by ellipses indicate recurring decimals. (Source: *Ancient Metrology*, John Michell)			
		Tropical values	**Northern values**
Roman	digit	0.06048	0.0608256
	foot	0.96768	0.9732096
	remen (20 digits)	1.2096	1.216512
	cubit	1.45152	1.4598144
	stade	483.84	486.6048
	stade (600 feet)	580.608	583.92576
	furlong (625 feet)	604.08	608.256
	mile	4,838.4	4,866.048
Greek	digit	0.063	0.06336
	foot	1.008	1.01376
	cubit	1.512	1.52064
	stade (500 feet)	504	506.88
	stade (600 feet)	604.8	608.256
	furlong (625 feet)	630	633.6
	mile	5,040	5,068.8
Egyptian	foot	1.1 45…	1.152
	cubit	1.718	1.728
	stade (500 feet)	572.72…	576
	stade (600 feet)	687.27…	691.2
	furlong (625 feet)	715.90	720
	mile	5,727.27…	5,760
Polar	foot	0.98742857	0.99307102
	cubit	1.48114286	1.4896665
	stade (500 feet)	493.714286	496.53551
	stade (600 feet)	592.45714	595.84261
	furlong (625 feet)	617.142857	620.66938
	mile	4,937.14286	4,965.3551
Jewish or Sacred	cubit	2.0736	2.08544914
	foot	1.3824	1.3902994

Chapter 18

Ancient Geodesy

In the diagrams of traditional astronomy, as described by Theon of Smyrna, the movement of the sunrise point throughout the year was figured as a circle divided into 365¼ parts. These parts were put into four slightly uneven groups according to the various number of days in which the sun travels between the solstices and the equinox. In that case, taking the length of the equator to be 131,490,000 ft. or 24,903.4 miles, each of the 365¼ degrees of equatorial longitude contains 360,000 English feet, each minute 6,000 ft. and each second 100 ft.

Remarkably, this ancient figure of 131,490,000 ft. for the measure round the equator exceeds by less than two miles the modern estimate of 131,479,713, a very close correspondence that makes plain the geodetic significance of the duodecimal-based English foot in ancient metrology.

Now that two of the measurements that the ancients attributed to the earth's dimensions—the meridian circumference of 24,883.2 miles and the equatorial measure of 24,903.4 miles—have been identified, one must establish the remaining three measures necessary to complete the earth's size and shape: the lengths of the polar radius, the mean radius and the equatorial radius.

Polar radius

The Jewish sacred cubit, if the ancient metrological tradition is sound, provides the key to the length of the polar radius, of which it is reputed to measure one ten-millionth part. The sacred cubit is the "cubit and a handsbreadth" referred to by Ezekiel, containing six of the handbreadths of which five make up the Egyptian royal cubit. As listed in the preceding table, the greater length of the Egyptian cubit is 1.728 ft., and the value of the sacred cubit or six-fifths of the length is therefore 2.0736 ft.

Multiplying 2.0736 ft. by ten million produces a figure of 3,927.27 miles, a figure that is too short by more than 20 miles according to the modern estimates. The appropriate geodetic unit is not therefore the sacred cubit but is its longer form, relating to it in the same way as the longer and shorter forms of the other units relate by the ratio 176:175. Applying this ratio provides a measure for the longer sacred cubit of 2.0854491 ft, of which ten million make up the polar radius of 3,949.7142 miles.

The earth's polar radius of 3,949.7142 miles relates precisely to the meridian circumference of 24,883.2 miles by the ratio 10:63, which accords to the canon of numbers and simple ratios in which the ancients expressed the earth's dimensions and the derived units of measure.

Mean radius

The mean radius of the earth, as estimated in ancient geodesy, is obtained by dividing the meridian circumference of 24,883.2 miles by 44/7. This provides a radius of 3,958.6909 miles, an amazing figure that is as good as identical with the number given in the *Encyclopaedia Britannica* at the time Michell was writing *Ancient Metrology.* The ancient significance of this figure is expressed in the calculation that 3,958.6909 miles is exactly equal to 20,736,000 or 1000 x 12^4 Greek feet and 21,600,000 Roman feet at tropical values.

The difference between the earth's mean radius and its polar radius expressed in these values is 47,396.58 ft., which is equal to 96 polar stades or 48,000 polar feet at their shorter value

Equatorial radius

The above formula, by which 96 polar stades added to the polar radius gives the length of the mean radius, suggests a similar procedure for discovering the ancient standard length of the equatorial radius. The most accurate figure is obtained by adding 120 Roman furlongs or 120 Greek stades of 600 Greek feet to the length of the polar radius, giving a result of 3,963.5382 miles. Alternatively, in terms of the shorter value of the Roman furlong, the measure of the equatorial radius is 3,963.4596 miles.

As Michell pointed out, an extraordinary conclusion arises from these calculations. If it is true that the ancient estimate of the earth's equatorial radius was indeed 3,963.4989 miles, its relationship with the corresponding equatorial circumference should be 2π. The value of π corrected to 6 decimal places is 3.141593. If the equatorial radius of 3,963.4989 miles is multiplied by twice 3.141593, the product is 24.903.4 miles—which is the exact figure given above as the ancient estimate of the measure of the equator.

Amazingly, it would appear that whoever first established these canonical figures for the earth's dimensions in the distant past knew the value of π to a greater accuracy that five places of decimals. And the corresponding geodetic measurements in which this is demonstrated are not only accurate in themselves but are brought together under one system of proportion and number, thus revealing a mindblowing cosmological mathematical mindset wholly alien to the prosaic attitudes of modern science.

Pliny on the dimensions of the earth

At the end of the second volume of his *Natural History*, written in the first century CE, Pliny discusses geography, the distances between the cities throughout the known world, and the various estimates of the earth's dimensions. He reports that Eratosthenes had measured the length of the earth's circumference and stated it to be 252,000 stades, an odd result because it exceeds the true measure by exactly one seventh. In the earth's circumference of 24,883.2 miles there are not 252,000 but 216,000 Roman furlongs or stades.

From what follows it seems evident that Eratosthenes, like Pliny, was privy to the traditional canon of earth's measurements but since it was unlawful to disclose publicly this esoteric knowledge he presented them in incomplete form. In the final passage Pliny accepts Eratosthene's measure of 252,000 stades but by deploying a seemingly childish fable that describes his receiving a letter from the centre of the earth from "celebrated geometrician" Dionysodorus of Melos, he subtlely provides the information required to calculate the earth's true measures. As was the custom of writers and commentators in his time, Pliny employed childish allegories when referring to knowledge that was supposed to be limited to initiated scholars.

It required a skilled and learned geometer to decode Pliny's fable. One had to possess a detailed knowledge of units of measure, principally of Greek, Roman and polar stades, hexagonal geometry and the measure of π, and, not least, an understanding of the esoteric canon of numerical ratios and harmonics which codified all the ancient arts and sciences.

Considering how easy it could have been for knowledge of these ancient canonical measures and units to be lost to mankind during the two millennia after Pliny, it is nothing short of remarkable that John Michell, a precociously gifted thinker, should have emerged in the twentieth century with the skill and insights to crack the code.

By applying the various essential factors of knowledge and understanding that Pliny hid in his allegory, Michell arrived at the true solution for the earth's circumference: a measure that is indeed 24,883.2 miles but derived from a figure obtained by adding 252,000 polar stades of 493.71427 ft. and 12,000 Roman stades of 580.608 ft., both at tropical values. Smart Pliny, and, equally smart Michell!

Chapter 19

Gematria

Gematria is a Qabalistic method of interpreting the Hebrew Scriptures by computing the numerical value of words, based on the values of their constituent letters. According to Aristotle (384–322 BCE), *isopsephy*, the practice of adding up the number values of the letters in a word to form a single number, was part of the Pythagorean tradition.

It is a fundamental axiom of the ancient wisdom which underpins the development and deployment of Gematria, that there is an inner determination for all appearances and outer form. Nowhere more than in the scriptures of the world's religions is one more likely to find this principle of inner and outer better exemplied.

Not only are there layers of meaning to each of the scriptures in moral and philosophical dimensions but there is also the inner interpretation of the science of mathematics, the latter being a cosmological expression of the universal ideas on which our world depends. This science of mathematics is both qualitative and quantitative and points towards the hidden numerical and geometrical basis of the cosmos. Wisdom can be revealed at many levels. The knowledge that there are even further extensions of meaning to the words within sacred texts serves only to increase their value to laymen and scholars alike.

The first evidence of use of Hebrew letters as numbers dates to 78 BCE. Similar systems have been used in other languages and cultures, derived from or inspired by either Greek isopsephy or Hebrew gematria and include Arabic abjad numerals.

The development in the fifth and sixth centuries BCE of this system is marked by the extension of the Greek alphabet in order to have sufficient symbols to accommodate the Denary (base-ten) system of numeration.

The Greek alphabet was perfected about 400 BCE, when several signs were added and older compound letters superseded; other signs were retained as numerals.

The Greek alphabet and corresponding values for Gematria purposes[43]								
Αα	Ββ	Γγ	Δδ	Εε	F*	Ζζ	Ηη	Θθ
1	2	3	4	5	6	7	8	9
Ιι	Κκ	Λλ	Μμ	Νν	Ξξ	Οο	Ππ	Ϙ**
10	20	30	40	50	60	70	80	90
Ρρ	Σσ	Ττ	Υυ	Φφ	Χχ	Ψψ	Ωω	ϡ***
100	200	300	400	500	600	700	800	900

Frederick Bligh Bond F.R.I.B.A, director of excavations at Glastonbury Abbey between 1908 and 1921, and his colleague Dr. Thomas Simcox Lea, Vicar of Saint Austell, believing that there exists an esoteric teaching dating from great antiquity and finding expression in a harmonised scheme of symbolism in which geometrical and mathematical truths play an important part, with a numerical key concealed in language, set out to explore its origins.

In about the fifth century BCE there began to appear in the Syro-Phoenician centre east of the Meditteranean, traces of a mode of writing in which the letters of the alphabet served also as numerals. Though coming from this area, Bond and Lea were of the opinion that the origin of this method had arisen further east.

From this parent influence two systems arose: the Greek and the Hebrew, both systems attaining a high degree of development by about the third century BCE. Both languages are constructed with great skill, evidently by adepts inspired by a clear purpose. Their alphabets, which also show numerals, exhibit unexplained features. The two scholars believed that the application of the mystical science of Gematria might offer insights into the esoteric laws that govern the unexplored regions in which life, growth and the dynamic phenomena of nature have their origin.

In this respect, the human mind may be attesting subconsciously its recognition of truths that it has been unable to formulate by ordinary mental process or to prove by use of ordinary human language. Bond and Lea claimed that Gematria might provide a pathway to explore the æonial realities of these mystical correspondences, a fact with which the early Gnostics, who sought knowledge concerning the higher dimensions of space, were acquainted.

---

[43] * The digamma, an obsolete letter corresponding to the Hebrew Vav. In sound like a a W, and retained as a numerical sign.

** and *** Koppa and Sampi respectively—obsolete, used for numerals only.

Gradually, Bond and Lea learned that formerly a great deal of secret information of a political, commercial or esoteric nature was distributed under cover of the code of ΓΕΜΑΤΡΙΑ (Gematria), the word being a recognized variant of ΓΕΩΜΕΤΡΙΑ (Geometry). Further, the best elements of this teaching, constituting divine Knowledge (ΓΝΩΣΙΣ—Gnosis) were incorporated into the Scriptures to record and memorise geometrical formula.

They realised that Geometry is independent of matter: that it is eternal and by its aid the human mind can reach transcendental space. It is because of Geometry's divine nature that the higher powers of the mind claim kinship with it and choose it instinctively as their interpreter for the expression of their ideal conceptions. In this way, Geometry provides a pathway to awareness of the greater realities beyond human knowledge and understanding.

In 1917 Bond and Lea published the outcome of their studies,[44] in which they brought to public attention the ancient teachings which reveal that each letter of the alphabet in Gematria possesses a number that helps to establish a numerical link between one apparently different word or phrase and another, and this with a third, and so on. They demonstrated that when a body of such associations has been linked together, the strength of the link itself could be transformed into a kiln for firing into being further and deper dimensions of meaning.

They observed that in addition to the Christian Gospel narrative there exists a more inward revelation. They referred to Jesus as having trained as a Carpenter or Builder (ΤΕΚΤΩΝ), a suggestion that behind this outward fact there lies a mystery, that He was the Builder of the Æons (Heb. i. 2), and that the knowledge He gave His Church was the knowledge of those principles by which the worlds were made (Heb. Xi. 3).

In the New Testament there are several references to the Knowledge and the Mysteries (as in Cor. xiii.), which the faithful might learn, as well as powers that they might exercise. Some of these mysteries concern names. For example, it is probable that the number of the Beast, 666, is that of Emperor Nero. In the Hebrew נרון קסר (NRVN QSR) = 666. It was a cipher or code whose usage prevailed both in Hebrew and in Greek.

---

[44] Bond, F., and Lea, T., *Gematria, A Preliminary Investigation of the Cabala contained in the Coptic Gnostic Books and of a similar Gematria in the Greek text of the New Testament*, 1917

Examples of Gematria in Biblical Scripture

- Α Ω and ΠΕΡΙΣΤΕΡΑ each enumerate to 801, thereby identifying the First and the Last with the Dove. 801 is three times 267, the number of the Kingdom (Η ΒΑΣΙΛΕΙΑ).
- Ten times 801 is 2670 = ΚΥΡΙΟΣ ΦΩΤΟΣ (Lord of Light) and, as applied to Christ, ΤΟ ΦΩΣ ΚΟΣΜΟΥ (The Light of the World), who is also 'Η ΔΥΝΑΜΙΣ ΜΕΓΑΛΗ ΦΩΤΟΣ (The Great Power of Light). It is also the number of the Church of Jesus Christ ('Η ΕΚΚΛΗΣΙΑ ΙΗΣΟΥΣ ΧΡΙΣΤΟΥ)
- The geometrical word ΚΗΦΑΣ symbolises the perfect ashlar, cubic stone, since ΚΗΦΑΣ = 729 or 9x9x9.
- ΤΟ ΘΥΣΙΑΣΤΗΡΙΟΝ, literally "the Sacrifice," but also the word regularly employed in Scripture to designate the Altar, = 1728 or 12x12x12.
- The Holy of Holies, the Debir, is 6x6x6.
- The Greek Sanctuary, the ΑΓΙΑΣΜΑ, is 256 or 4x4x4, embodying in addition to the Cube a transcendental fourth measure.
- The New Jerusalem of the Apocalypse—visualised as a foursquare City—Η ΚΑΙΝΗ ΙΕΡΟΥΣΑΛΗΜ = Ο ΟΥΡΑΝΟΣ (Heaven), has the number 961 or the square of 31.
- ΟΥΡΑΝΟΣ, symbolising Heaven conceived as a circle, is 891 or 11 times the square of Nine. The Circle is generated from the Diameter, by convention equal to 284, number of ΘΕΟΣ—GOD, by whom the heavens were made. The perimeter of the square that encloses the Circle, which is 1136, is the number of ΜΕΣΟΥΡΑΝΟΣ, the Mid-Heaven.
- ΙΗΣΟΥΣ (Jesus) = 888. The number EIGHT, often called the Dominical number, is found throughout the Scriptures as exemplifying the ideas of salvation, regenerating and perfected humanity.
- ΘΕΟΤΗΣ (Divinity) = 592, added to the 888 of ΗΣΟΥΣ, gives 1480 = ΧΡΙΣΤΟΣ (Christ). 888 + 592 + 1480 = 2960, 'ΥΙΟΣ ΤΟΥ ΑΝΘΡΩΠΟΥ (Son of Man)
- ΚΥΡΙΟΣ (Lord) = 800, the antithesis to 600 = ΚΟΣΜΟΣ (World)
- The number of Light (ΦΩΣ) = 1500, also the Gematria for ΕΝΔΥΜΑ ΚΥΡΙΟΥ (the Robe of the Lord).

The Cube of Light

Φωσ (light)

- 3375,000,000 = $(1500)^3$
- 3375 is 15^3 (15 x 15x 15), and by Gematria represents the cube of 1500 (φωσ), since only the first four significant digits are of consequence, and the cyphers are written off.
- 3375 is related geometrically to 2683, the number of the First Precept. In Gematria 3375 is the name of:
    - IEOY as Bishop of Light (Επικοκοσ τον φωτοσ),
    - the Descent of Light (Καταβασισ τον φωτοσ),
    - thus, creating the Division of Light from Darkness of Genesis i.4(Το μεσον φωτοσ), resulting in the First Sphere of Light, Σφαιρα α' φωτοσ), which = 2683
- But the connection with IEOY is also a geometrical one as the area of one face of the cube 33750 is very nearly 4850, or 10 x 485 = IEOY
- ΦΩΣ – Light, = 1500, and ΑΥΧΝΟΣ - Lamp = 1500, whilst ΑΥΧΝΟΝ, another form, is 1200. These three words are therefore arithmetically related in Gematria as:
    - ΦΩΣ = 1500 (150 x 10);
    - ΑΥΧΝΟΣ 1350 (150 x 9);
    - ΑΥΧΝΟΝ = 1200 (150 x 8).
- Together, these three words represent the harmonic proportionals 8, 9 and 10 apparent in physical law. And the first two are related geometrically, since 1350, Αυχνοσ, is the surface of the cube of 15.00 or 3375. For each face of the cube is 15^2 or 225, and all six faces are 225 x 6 or 1350.
- The number of the exterior or surface cubes in the block of 3375 cubes is 1178 = ΜΥΣΤΗΡΙΟΝ (Mystery), and the metacube, or total number visible to sight, is 631—ΘΑΝΑΤΟΣ = Death. The Gnosis therefore tells us that Death is but a part of the great Mystery.

THE BIBLE - ALPHABETS AND NUMERICAL VALUES															
	Hebrew						Syr	Greek							
OV		ARL	TNR	NV	P	Name			ARL		TNR		NV	P	Name
1	𐤀	א	א	1	(a)	Alef	ܐ	Α	Α	α	Α	α	1	A	Alpha
2	𐤁	ב	ב	2	B, V	Bet	ܒ	Β	Β	β	Β	β	2	B, V	Beta
3	𐤂	ג	ג	3	G	Gimel	ܓ	Γ	Γ	γ	Γ	γ	3	G	Gamma
4	𐤃	ד	ד	4	D	Dalet	ܕ	Δ	Δ	δ	Δ	δ	4	D	Delta
5	𐤄	ה	ה	5	H	He	ܗ	Є	Ε	ε	Ε	ε	5	E	Epsilon
6	𐤅	ו	ו	6	W, V	Vav	ܘ		F, Ϛ	F, ς	F, Ϛ	F, ς	6	W	Digamma*
7	𐤆	ז	ז	7	Z	Zayin	ܙ	Ζ	Ζ	ζ	Ζ	ζ	7	Z	Zeta
8	𐤇	ח	ח	8	H, X	Chet	ܚ	Η	Η	η	Η	η	8	E	Eta
9	𐤈	ט	ט	9	T	Tet	ܛ	Θ	Θ	θ	Θ	θ	9	Th	Theta
10	𐤉	י	י	10	J, I, Y	Yod	ܝ	Ι	Ι	ι	Ι	ι	10	I, J	Iota
11	𐤊	כ ך	כ ך	20	K, X	Kaph	ܟ	Κ	Κ	κ	Κ	κ	20	K, C	Kappa
12	𐤋	ל	ל	30	L	Lamed	ܠ	Λ	Λ	λ	Λ	λ	30	L	Lambda
13	𐤌	מ ם	מ ם	40	M	Mem	ܡ	Μ	Μ	μ	Μ	μ	40	M	Mu
14	𐤍	נ ן	נ ן	50	N	Nun	ܢ	Ν	Ν	ν	Ν	ν	50	N	Nu
15	𐤎	ס	ס	60	S	Samekh	ܣ	Ξ	Ξ	ξ	Ξ	ξ	60	Ks	Xi
16	𐤏	ע	ע	70	(o)	Ayin	ܥ	Ο	Ο	ο	Ο	ο	70	O	Omicron
17	𐤐	פ ף	פ ף	80	P, F	Pe	ܦ	Π	Π	π	Π	π	80	P	Pi
18	𐤑	צ ץ	צ ץ	90	Ts	Tsade	ܨ		Ϙ, ϟ	ϙ, ϟ	Ϙ, ϟ	ϙ, ϟ	90	K, Q	Qoppa
19	𐤒	ק	ק	100	K, Q	Qoph	ܩ	Ρ	Ρ	ρ	Ρ	ρ	100	R	Rho
20	𐤓	ר	ר	200	R	Resh	ܪ	C	Σ	σ, ς	Σ	σ, ς	200	S	Sigma
21	𐤔	ש	ש	300	S, Sh	Shin	ܫ	Τ	Τ	τ	Τ	τ	300	T	Tau
22	𐤕	ת	ת	400	T	Tav	ܬ	Υ	Υ	υ	Υ	υ	400	U, Y	Upsilon
23								Φ	Φ	φ	Φ	φ	500	Ph	Phi
24								Χ	Χ	χ	Χ	χ	600	Kh	Chi
25								Ψ	Ψ	ψ	Ψ	ψ	700	Ps	Psi
26								ω	Ω	ω	Ω	ω	800	O	Omega
27									Ͳ, ϡ	Ͳ, ϡ	Ͳ, ϡ	Ͳ, ϡ	900	Ts	Sampi

The Bible – Hebrew and Greek alphabets and numerical values

Chapter 20

The Numbers of Stonehenge

The imposing features in what remains of Stonehenge: the seventeen 13½-ft.-tall upright pillars of sarson rock that still support six curved stone lintels—all that survive of the completed circle of 30 lintels over 30 uprights—are enough to establish the dimensions of the original circle to within a fraction of an inch.

A staggering achievement, Stonehenge's builders constructed a circle that was one of the most precise and symmetrical works of architecture ever created. That they fully intended to create a structure of such unparalelled symmetry is evidenced in the particulars of its build.

Such precision strongly suggests that the design was metrologically conceived. This is correct. An examination of the circle's dimensions reveals that the original architectural standards employed by the builders were based on ancient measures and systems of numeration.

Excavations show that several different arrangements of stones have been made in the construction at different times. The structure's ruinous state does not permit unequivocal interpretation of its dimensions, although Thom's archaeo-astronomical work conducted at more than 500 megalithic sites is helpful in efforts to determine the setting of Stonehenge's great sarson stone trilithons.

Professor Alexander Thom (1894-1985) was a Scottish engineer most famous for his theory of the Megalithic Yard,[45] categorisation of stone circles and his studies of Stonehenge and other archaeological sites. While professor and chair of engineering science at Brasenose College at Oxford, Thom became interested in the methods that prehistoric peoples used to build megalithic monuments. In 1955 he first suggested the MY as a standardised prehistoric measurement. Six years later he retired from academia to spend the rest of his life devoted to this area of

---

[45] Thom proposed that the MY is equal to about 2.72 ft. He also proposed the megalithic rod of 2.5 megalithic yards and the megalithic inch, one hundred of which comprise a megalithic rod and forty a megalithic yard.

research. From studies measuring and analysing the data created at over five hundred megalithic sites, he suggested that several were built as astronomical complexes to predict eclipses via nineteen-year cycles. Thom went on to identify numerous solar and stellar alignments at stone circles, providing the foundations for the scientific discipline of archaeo-astronomy. He further suggested that the prehistoric peoples of Britain must have used a solar method of keeping calendar. Based on statistical histograms of declinations at horizon marks between 2100 and 1600 BCE, Thom suggested a year based on sixteen months: four with twenty-two days, eleven with twenty-three and one with twenty-four. Thom's suggested megalithic solar year was divided by midsummer, midwinter and the two equinoxes into four, and then subdivided into eight by early versions of the modern Christian festivals of Whitsun, Lammas, Martinmas and Candlemas.

Michell explained that Stonehenge's sarsen circle with its lintels provides three sets of dimensions: those of the circles formed by the inner and outer rims of the lintels, and those of the circle passing through the lintels' centres. The inner faces of the circle's upright pillars are smoothed and polished, whereas their outer faces are rough hewn and considerably different in width, making it clear that they were not intended to serve as indicators of the circle's outer dimensions.

Metrology of the Stonehenge dimensions

Inner diameter	= 97.32096 ft.
	= 1,600 digits of 0.0608256 ft.
	= 100 Roman feet of 0.9732096 ft.
	= 98 polar feet of 0.99307102 ft.
	= 96 Greek feet of 1.01376 ft.
	= 80 remens of 1.216512 ft.
	= 64 Greek cubits of 1.52064 ft.
	= 46⅔ sacred cubits of 2.0854491 ft.
	= 70 sacred feet of 1.3902994 ft.
Outer diameter	= 104.272455 ft.
	= 105 polar feet
	= 50 sacred cubits
	= 75 sacred feet.
Width of lintels	= 3.4757485 ft.
	= 3½ polar feet

$=1\frac{2}{3}$ sacred cubits

$= 2\frac{1}{2}$ sacred feet or 1 sacred rod

The distances from the outer and inner rims of the lintels determine the measures of the two semi-diameters or radii of the lintel circle. These are found to represent simple fractions of the earth's dimensions according to the ancient reckoning: -

Outer radius x 400,000 = 20,854,491 ft. = earth's polar radius

Outer radius x 2,520,000 = 131,383,296 ft. = earth's meridian circumference

Inner radius x $^{3\,000\,000}/_{7}$ = 20,854,491 ft. = earth's polar radius

Inner radius x 2,700,000 = 131,383,296 ft. = earth's meridian circumference

Width of lintels x 6,000,000 = 20,854,491 ft. = earth's polar radius

In reviewing these figures, Michell was stunned by the evident fact that four to five thousand years ago the Stonehenge architect, guided by reference to a canon of harmonies and numerical ratios, designed two concentric circles whose diameters are both whole number multiples of the standard units of measure and also simple fractions of the earth's principal dimensions. The finished product was a magnificent structure that symbolised the order of the universe, the most perfect expression, such as the Pythagoreans conceived it, of the monad or number one, which contains and generates all other numbers. Such an extraordinary achievement points to Stonehenge having been built as a global cosmic temple, which would have been the foremost power centre for all the world's ancient civilisations of the time.

Among the supporting functions of the Temple, such as known from those at Jerusalem and Heliopolis, was its role to preserve standards and measures and to serve as a microcosmic representation of the whole world. Additionally, it also served as a celestial observatory, a monumental record of astronomic data, an instrument for measuring time, the seasons and planetary cycles, and as a centre for yearly rituals by which the order of society was regulated.

The striking feature of the universe in that it combines and harmonizes all the irreconcilable and incommensurate elements that comprise it is repeated microcosmically in the ancient ideal of the Temple, of which Stonehenge is the most striking of the surviving examples. Within the simple construction of its two circles, the outer diameter of which is equal to 1 part in 400,000 of the earth's polar axis, is a synthesis of ancient units of measure, systems of numeration and geodetic standards. Michell highlighted the striking symbolism of the numbers 1008 and 31680 in the Stonehenge circle: -

Mean diameter = 100.8 ft. = 100 Greek feet of 1.008 ft. (tropical value)
= 88 Egyptian feet of 1.1 45… ft. (tropical value)
= 87.5 Egyptian feet of 1.152 ft. (northern value)

Earth's mean radius = 100.8 x 207,360 = 20,901,888 ft.

One minute of latitude at 10° = 100.8 x 60 ft.

Mean circumference = 316.8 ft. = $^{6}/_{100}$ miles
= 312.5 Greek feet or half a Greek furlong at northern value

Earth's meridian circumference = 316.8 x 207,360 x 2= 131,383,296 ft.

These two power numbers are also ideal for expressing the 7:22 (π) diameter : circumference ratio in terms of duodecimal number. This is demonstrated as: 1,008 = 7 x 12^2 and 3,168 = 22 x 12^2. The same numbers also express 7:22, in that a circumference of 31,680 ft. has a radius of 1 x 2 x 3 x 4 x 5 x 6 x 7 = 5,040 ft, while a quadrant of that circle measures 8 x 9 x 10 x 11 = 7,920 ft. Moreover, using $^{22}/_{7}$ as π, the area of a semi-circle with diameter 10,080 ft. and circumference of 31,680 ft. is 39,916,800 square ft., or the product of 1 x 2 x 3 x 4 x 5 x 6 x 7 x 8 x 9 x 10 x 11.

In light of this beautiful symmetry, Michell was of the belief that the Stonehenge architect knew precisely what they were doing when they designed a circle with circumference of 316.8 ft., thereby clearly proclaiming the intrinsic nature of the whole Stonehenge design as a cosmological structure that expresses the dimensions of the earth and its proportional relationship with our moon. 3168 is referenced in many ancient sources as the symbolic measure of the universal circumference:

- In his *Natural History*, Pliny implies that 3,168,000 miles is the measure round earth.
- The New Jerusalem envisioned by St. John in Revelations, 21, measures 12,000 furlongs on each of its four sides. The English furlong is the same measure as the old Sumerian stade, 660 ft., and in terms of that unit the perimeter of the New Jerusalem is 31,680,000 ft.
- In his *Republic*, Plato describes his ideal city as a circle divided

laterally into 12 parts and its radius divided into 5,040 units. 31,680 of these units is therefore the measure of the circumference of the city.

- The mythic history of the Celtic sanctuary at Glastonbury portrays it as an enclosure of area 12 hides. A hide of land is 120 acres. 12 hides are 1,440 acres and this area laid out as a square has a side of 7,920 ft. and a perimeter 7,920 x 4 = 31,680 ft.

The Number 353 at Stonehenge

Michell[46] describes the striking fact that Stonehenge's dimensions systematically incorporate the "Hermetic" number 353, and its alternative value 352 (applying the Greeks' Colel Rule of gematria that allows values to be rounded up or down by one unit). The units that underline the many appearances of this number are the foot, the MY and the mile, which is equal to 5280 or 352 x 15 feet.

Beginning with the lintels of the sarsen stone circle, it is evident from engineer E.H. Stone's measurements[47] that they were designed in units of 3.52 feet. The average length of each lintel stone is 10.56 feet or 3.52 yards; the measured width, 3½ feet, is doubtless intended to be 3.52 feet, a third of the length. The average interval between the pillars is 3.52 feet, and the pillars themselves are each 7.04 feet (3.52 x 2) wide. The thickness of the pillars varies considerably, but the average is about 4 feet. The lintels formed an accurate circle of mean circumference 316.8 feet (3.52 x 90), which, if the width of the pillars is taken to be about 4 feet, is equal to three times the extreme outer diameter of the sarsen circle, 105.6 feet.

Professor Thom's researches show that the megalithic builders practised geometrical methods of shortening the circumference of a circle in order that it should be three times the diameter. The same result is achieved at Stonehenge by allowing for the thickness of the stones. Moreover, 1056 feet or 353 yards is one fifth of a mile, and it is also equal to 353 + 35.3 MY. The mean diameter of the sarsen circle, 100.8 feet, is the exact mean between 96 feet (35.3 MY) and 105.6 feet (35.3 + 3.53 MY).

As Michell remarked, there is little value in attaching any prominence to the prevalence of 353 and 352 in the Stonehenge measurements, unless it can be shown to have a corresponding

---

[46] Michell, J., *The City of Revelation*, Abacus, 1973

[47] Stone, E., *The Stones of Stonehenge*, Robert Scott, London, 1924

numerological significance. In fact, they are Hermetic numbers.

353, the Hermetic Number

The number 353 was very important in cabalistic numerology. Its chief significance is that 353 is the value of *Ἑρμῆς*, Hermes, the hermaphrodite messenger of the gods, who, as the inspiration of human inventiveness, serves as a link between the divine powers and our own world of phenomena. Similarly, in the language of numerology, 353 provides a link between the supreme solar number 666 and the lunar principle represented by 1080, as evidenced in these examples:

666 and 353

A circle of radius 1059 (353 x 3) has a circumference of 666o. 35,200 feet is 6.666 miles, and this is the circumference of the circle that contains the square of the New Jerusalem measuring 6 miles round its perimeter.

1080 and 353

The Stonehenge sarsen circle, mean circumference 316.8 (35.2 x 9) feet, contains an area of 1080 square MY.

A circle with diameter 352 feet has an area of 10,800 square yards.

A rhombus contained in a vesica of width 353 feet has an area of 108,000 square feet.

Hermes, 353, the Roman Mercurius, is the principle that may be considered as a universal magnetic field, within which the action of cosmic forces becomes apparent. In this sense, Hermes is the creator of all that is manifest, this being apparent in the gematria of his name. The ruler of this world is *κοσμόκρατωρ*, 1791, the cosmo-krater, and 1791 is also the number of *Ἑρμῆς Τριςμέγιστος*, thrice-greatest Hermes. This spirit is now often referred to as the life-essence, the medium that binds and unifies all nature, known in the East as the kundalini or serpent current, which energises the nervous centres of the body, and corresponds in the macrocosm to the intergalactic flow of cosmic energy.

The value of *ό μόνος* αληθινός θεός, the only true God, is 1162; Jesus Christ, *Ιησούς Χριστός*, is 2368, so the sum of the two phrases is 3530, a reference to Hermes, god of the Mysteries.

Michell notes that the Greek Hermes my be compared with the British Emrys, whose name is preserved at Stonehenge in the name of its legendary builder, Ambrosius, and of the neighbouring town, Amesbury. In Greek, Hermes and Emrys share the same letters and therefore the same gematria value of 353.

Mercury is behind every type of energy flux or motion, in currents, lines of communication, and along roads. The number of *ή οδος*, the Way, is 352. The Greeks dedicated paths and crossroads to Hermes. *Τριοτριοδίτίς,* goddess of the three ways, has number 1004, and this is also the number of *Διονύσιος,* Dionysus the "mad god," who represents the wild, ecstatic side of Mercury's character. The same spirit enters the body at baptism, for which the Greek is *Το βάπτισμα*, 1004.

1059 and 353

The Stonehenge sarsen circle consists of thirty lintels set on thirty pillars, and its extreme diameter is some 105.9 feet. The number of aeons in the gnostic pleroma (the totality of divine powers) was 30 and the number by gematria of *πλερώμα*, Pleroma, is 1059, so the numerical symbolism in this part of the temple is evident.

The number 1059 (353 x 3) represents the triple Hermes, keeper of the mysteries, and the word *μυστήρια*, mysteries, has the same value, 1059. There are gnostic references to the secret of initiation as the "treasure," and *ό θησαυρός*, the treasure, has the number 1058.

105.8½ is the diameter of a circle with area 888o, ten times the number of *ό παράκλητος*, the Comforter, and a circle with radius 105.9 has a circumference of 666.

Snow covered Stonehenge, 3 January 2025

Sunrise at Stonehenge

Shooting stars over Stonehenge

Chapter 21
Pythagorean Number

The substance of this chapter is drawn from the author's recent work for AUP on Pythagoras.[48]

Arithmetic is the mother of the mathematical sciences. This is proved by the fact that geometry, music and astronomy are dependent upon it but it is not dependent upon them. Thus geometry may be removed but arithmetic will remain; if arithmetic is removed, geometry is eliminated. Similarly, music depends upon arithmetic but the elimination of music affects arithmetic only by limiting one of its expressions.

Arithmetic is prior to astronomy for the latter is dependent upon both geometry and music. The size, form and motion of the celestial bodies are determined by the use of geometry, their harmony and rhythm by the use of music. If astronomy is removed neither geometry nor music is injured; but if geometry and music are eliminated astronomy is destroyed. The priority of both geometry and music to astronomy is therefore established. Arithmetic, however, is prior to all; it is primary and fundamental.

The Pythagoreans maintained that the only geometry deserving of study is one where each new theorem sets up a platform by which we may ascend, thus lifting one's soul on high and freeing it from subservience to the common needs of this mortal life.

Number

Pythagoras believed that the essence of being can be found in the form of numbers and can be perceived through the study of mathematics. For instance, he believed that matters like health rely on a stable proportion of elements, with too much or too little of one thing causing an imbalance that makes a person unhealthy. Manly P. Hall remarks on this, writing that: 'The Pythagoreans declared arithmetic to be the mother of the

---

[48] Ibid

mathematical sciences. This is proved by the fact that geometry, music and astronomy are dependent upon it but it is not dependent upon them. The Pythagoreans also demonstrated arithmetic to be prior to astronomy for the latter is dependent upon both geometry and music. The size, form and motion of the celestial bodies is determined by the use of geometry; their harmony and rhythm by the use of music.'

Hall added that the secret significance of numbers died on Pythagoras' death. Since the day when the Master died by fire in his library at Crotona, philosophers all over the world have attempted to unravel the mysteries but none has claimed complete success.

Number

1 (Monad)

Pythagoras defined number to be the extension of the generative energies contained in the monad: the "One that is Everything." The monad is the Supreme Mind distributed throughout all parts of the Universe. It is the Cause of all things, the Intelligence of all things, and the Power within all things.

The monad was the God of Pythagoras and was represented by a circle. The Pythagoreans called the monad the "noble number, Sire of Gods and men." The monad also signifies the sum of any combination of numbers considered as a whole. Thus, the universe is considered as a monad but its individual parts (such as the planets and elements) are also monads in relation to the parts of which they themselves are composed, though they, in turn, are parts of the greater monad formed of their sum.

The monad may also be likened to the seed of a tree, which, when it has grown, has many branches (the numbers). In other words, the numbers are to the monad what the branches of the tree are to the seed of the tree. The monad is so called because it remains always in the same condition: separate from multitude. It is called mind because the mind is stable and has pre-eminence; hermaphrodism because it is both male and female; odd and even, for being added to the even it makes odd, and to the odd, even; God, because it is the beginning and end of all but itself has neither beginning nor end; good for such is the nature of God; the receptacle of matter, because it produces the duad, which is essentially material.

Other names given to it were: Apollo because of its relation to the sun; Prometheus because he brought man light; Pyralios, one who exists in fire; germinal reason because it is the origin of all the thoughts in the universe; Vesta, the home-fire, because it is located in the midst of the universe and remains there inclining to no side as a dot in a circle; form because it circumscribes, comprehends and terminates; love, concord, and piety because it is indivisible; geniture because without it no number can exist; substance because substance is primary; cause of truth; and constitution of symphony—all these because the monad is the primordial One.

Pythagoreans also likened monad to chaos, obscurity and chasm, Tartarus, Styx, abyss, Lethe, Atlas, Axis, Morpho (a name for Venus), ship, chariot, Proteus (a god capable of changing his form), Mnemosyne and Polyonymous (having many names). Between greater and lesser the monad is equal; between intention and remission it is middle; in multitude it is mean; and in time it is now because eternity knows neither past nor future.

The Platonists drew an important distinction between the number one and the monad. They defined the former as "the summit of the many." The one differs from the monad in that the term monad is used to designate the sum of the parts considered as a unit, whereas the one is the term applied to each of its integral parts.

2 (Duad)

Because the duad has been divided and is two rather than one (and when there are two, each is opposed to the other), the following are among the symbolic names ascribed to it: genius, evil, darkness, inequality, instability, movability, boldness, fortitude, contention, matter, dissimilarity, partition between multitude and monad, defect, shapelessness, indefiniteness, indeterminateness, harmony, tolerance, root, top, Phanes, opinion, fallacy, alterity, diffidence, impulse, death, motion, generation, mutation, division, longitude, augmentation, composition, communion, misfortune, sustentation, imposition, marriage, soul and science.

In his book, *Numbers*, W. Wynn Westcott says of the duad: 'It was called "Audacity," from its being the earliest number to separate itself from the Divine One; from the "Adytum of God-nourished Silence," as the Chaldean oracles say.'

Paraphrasing the early sources, Hall wrote: "As the monad is the father, so the duad is the mother; therefore, the duad has certain points in common with the goddesses Isis, Rhea (Jove's mother), Phrygia, Lydia, Dindymene and Ceres; Erato, Diana because the moon is forked; Dictynna, Venus, Dione, Cytherea; Juno because she is both wife and sister of Jupiter; and Maia, the mother of Mercury. While the monad is the symbol of wisdom, the duad is the symbol of ignorance for in it exists the sense of separateness, the beginning of ignorance. The duad is also the mother of wisdom because ignorance—out of the nature of itself—gives birth to wisdom.

The Pythagoreans revered the monad but despised the duad, because it was the symbol of polarity. By the power of the duad the deep was created in contradistinction to the heavens. The deep mirrored the heavens and became the symbol of illusion, for the below was a reflection of the above.

The below was called maya, the illusion, the sea, the Great Void, and, to symbolise it, the Magi of Persia carried mirrors. From the duad arose disputes and contentions, until by bringing the monad between the duad, equilibrium was re-established by the Saviour-God, who took upon Himself the form of a number and was crucified between two thieves for the sins of men."

3 (Triad)

The triad is the first number actually odd (monad not being considered a number). It is the first equilibrium of unities, Pythagoras illustrating this principle in his observation that the prophetess of Apollo at Delphi gave oracles from a tripod and advised offer of libation three times. The keywords to the qualities of the triad are friendship, peace, justice, prudence, piety, temperance and virtue.

The deities that partake of its principles are: Saturn (ruler of time), Latona, Cornucopi, Ophion (the great serpent), Thetis, Hecate, Polyhymnia (a Muse), Pluto, Bacchus, Mars, Triton, President of the Sea, Tritogenia, Achelous and the Faces, Furies and Graces. The number 3 is called wisdom because men organise the present, foresee the future and benefit by the experiences of the past.

The triad is the number of knowledge, music, geometry and astronomy and of the terrestrial and celestial sciences. Pythagoras taught that the cube of this number—27—has the power of the lunar circle.

The sacredness of the triad and its symbol—the triangle—is derived from its building blocks: the monad and the duad, the first being the symbol of the Divine Father, the second, the Great Mother. The triad's composition thus reveals its androgynous nature and is symbolic of the fact that God gave birth to His worlds out of Himself, who in His creative aspect is always symbolised by the triangle. The monad merging into the duad created the capability of becoming the parent of progeny for the duad was the womb of Meru, within which the world was incubated and within which it still exists in embryo.

4 (Tetrad)

The tetrad was esteemed by the Pythagoreans as the first-formed number, the primogenial root of all things, the fountain of Nature and the most perfect number. All tetrads were regarded as intellectual, in that they possess an emergent order and encircle the world through which passes the Empyreum, the highest heaven, occupied by the element of fire or, as in Aristotle's philosophy, the aether. The Pythagoreans' expression of God as a tetrad is explained in the sacred discourse in which God is called the Number of Numbers. This is because the decad (10) is the sum of four numbers: 1, 2, 3 and 4. The tetrad is the centre of the week, halfway between 1 and 7.

The tetrad is also the first geometric solid. Pythagoras maintained that the soul of man consists of a tetrad, the four powers of the soul being mind, science, opinion and sense. The tetrad connects all beings, elements, numbers and seasons. Nothing can be named which does not depend upon the tetractys. It is the Cause and Maker of all things, the intelligible God. Plutarch interprets this tetractys, which, he said, was also called the World, to be 36, consisting of the first four odd numbers added to the first four even numbers, thus:

$$\begin{aligned} 1+3+5+7 &= 16 \\ 2+4+6+8 &= \underline{20} \\ & \quad \underline{\underline{36}} \end{aligned}$$

Keywords given to the tetrad are impetuosity, strength, virility, two-mothered and the key keeper of Nature, because the constituent parts of the universe cannot be without it. It is also called harmony and the first profundity. The deities Hercules, Mercury, Vulcan, Bacchus and Urania (one of the Muses) partook of the nature of the tetrad.

The triad represents the primary colours and the major planets, while the tetrad represents the secondary colours and the minor planets. From the first triangle come forth the Seven Spirits, symbolised by a triangle and a square. These together form the Masonic apron.

5 (Pentad)

The pentad is the union of an odd and an even number (3 and 2). Among the Greeks, the pentagram was a sacred symbol of light, health and vitality. It also symbolised the fifth element—ether—because it is free from the disturbances of the four lower elements. It is called equilibrium, because it divides the perfect number 10 into two equal parts. The pentad is symbolic of Nature, for, when multiplied by itself, it returns into itself, just as grains of wheat, starting in the form of seed, proceed through Nature's processes and reproduce the seed of the wheat as the ultimate form of their own growth.

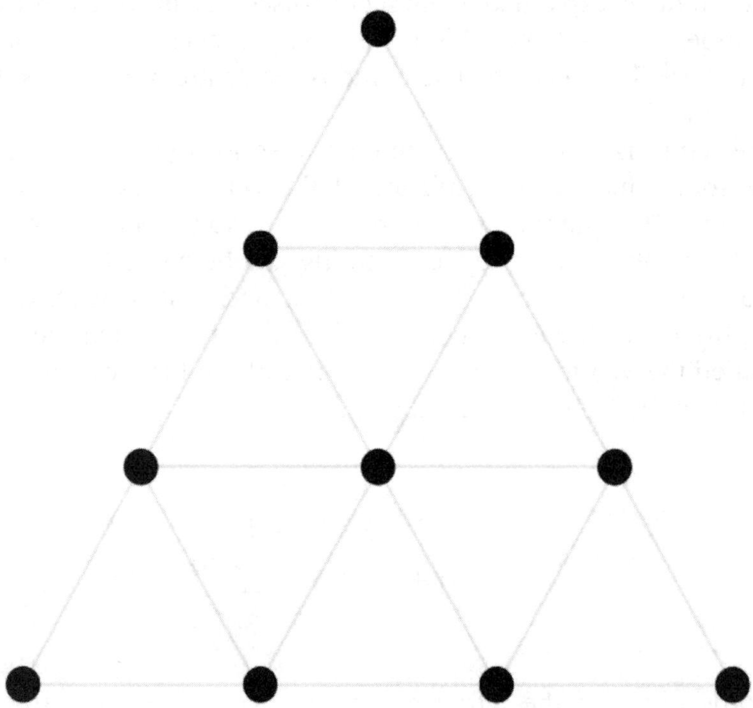

The **Tetractys**, to which Pythagoreans offered this prayer: 'Bless us, divine number, thou who generated gods and men! O holy, holy Tetractys, thou that containest the root and source of the eternally flowing creation! For the divine number begins with the profound, pure unity until it comes to the holy four; then it begets the mother of all, the all-comprising, all-bounding, the first-born, the never-swerving, the never-tiring holy ten, the keyholder of all.'

Other numbers multiplied by themselves produce other numbers, but only 5 and 6 multiplied by themselves (25 and 36) represent and retain their original number as the last figure in their products

The pentad represents all the superior and inferior beings. It is sometimes referred to as the hierophant or the priest of the Mysteries because of its connection with the spiritual ethers, by means of which mystic development is attained.

Keywords of the pentad are reconciliation, alternation, marriage, immortality, cordiality, providence and sound. Among the deities that partook of the nature of the pentad were Pallas, Nemesis, Bubastia (Bast), Venus, Androgynia, Cytherea and the messengers of Jupiter.

The tetrad (the elements) plus the monad equals the pentad. The Pythagoreans taught that the elements of Earth, Fire, Air, and Water are permeated by a substance called Ether—the basis of vitality and life. Therefore, the Pythagoreans chose the five-pointed star, or pentagram, as the symbol of vitality, health and interpenetration.

It was customary for the philosophers to conceal the element of earth under the symbol of a dragon; many of the heroes of antiquity were told to go forth and slay the dragon. Hence, they drove their sword (the monad) into the body of the dragon (the tetrad). This resulted in the formation of the pentad, a symbol of the victory of the spiritual nature over the material nature.

The four elements are symbolised in the early Biblical writings as the four rivers that poured out of Garden of Eden. The elements themselves are under the control of the composite Cherubim of Ezekiel.

6 (Hexad)

For the Pythagoreans the hexad represented the creation of the world according to the prophets and the Ancient Mysteries. They regarded the hexad as the perfection of all the parts. Six was particularly sacred to Orpheus and also to the Fate, Lachesis and the Muse, Thalia. It was called the form of forms, the articulation of the universe and the maker of the soul. Among the Greeks, harmony and the soul were considered to be similar in nature because all souls are harmonic. Six is also benevolence, peace, health and truth. The hexad is also the symbol of marriage because it is formed by the union of two triangles: one masculine and the other feminine. Among the keywords given to the hexad are: time, for it is the measure of duration; panacea, because health is equilibrium and the hexad is a balance number; the world, because the world, like the hexad, is often seen to consist of contraries by harmony; omnisufficient, because its parts are sufficient for totality (3 + 2 + 1 = 6); and unwearied, because it contains the elements of immortality. When multiplied into itself, like the pentad, six has also always itself in the unit place, thus, 6, 36, 216, 1296, 7776…

According to the Pythagoreans, after a period of 216 years, the cube of 6, all things are regenerated, and, in their philosophy, was the periodic time of the metempsychosis or re-birth of man into a new physical existence after each death. The Druids had a mysterious preference for the number 6. They performed their principal ceremonies on the 6th day of the moon, and on the 6th day of the moon began their year. They went 6 together to gather the sacred mistletoe.

An astronomical period of 600 years, spoken of as the "Naros" and known also as the Cycle of the Sun, the Luni-Solar period or Sibylline year, consists of 31 periods of 19 years, and one of 11 years. It seems to have been known by the Chaldeans and ancient Indians. The great seventeenth century astronomer Cassini declared it the most perfect of all astronomic periods.

7 (Heptad)

The Pythagoreans described the heptad as "worthy of veneration." It was held to be the number of religion because man is controlled by seven celestial spirits to which it is proper for him to make offerings. It was called the number of life because it was believed that human creatures born in the seventh month of embryonic life usually lived, but those born in the eighth month often died. One author called it the Motherless Virgin, Minerva, because it was not born of a mother but out of the crown, or the head of the Father, the monad. Keywords of the heptad are fortune, occasion, custody, control, government, judgment, dreams, voices, sounds and that which leads all things to their end. Deities whose attributes were expressed by the heptad were Osiris, Mars and Cleo (one of the Muses). Among many ancient nations the heptad is a sacred number. The Elohim of the Jews were seven in number. They were the Spirits of the Dawn, more commonly known as the Archangels controlling the planets. The heptad is the number of the law because it is the number of the Makers of Cosmic law, the 7 Spirits before the Throne.

The seven Archangels, with the three spirits controlling the sun in its threefold aspect, constitute the 10, the sacred Pythagorean decad. The mysterious Pythagorean tetractys, or four rows of dots, increasing from 1 to 4, was symbolic of the stages of creation. The 3 (spirit, mind, and soul) descend into the 4 (the world), the sum being the 7, the mystic nature of man consisting of a threefold spiritual body and a fourfold material form. These are symbolised by the cube, which has six surfaces and a mysterious seventh point within. The six surfaces are the directions: north, east, south, west, up, and down; or, front, back, right, left, above and below; or earth, fire, air, water, spirit and matter. In the midst of these stands the 1, which is the upright figure of man, from whose centre in the cube radiate six pyramids. From this comes the great occult axiom: "The centre is the father of the directions, the dimensions and the distances." The four levels of the tetractys represent the increasing densities of the 4 elements: Earth (most dense), Water, Air and, the least dense, Fire. The levels also define the unfolding of space: the point (1 dimensional), line (2D), surface (3D), and volume (4D). Theon of Smyrna declared that the ten dots of the tetractys represented the Ten Words of God. To Christians, these "words" signified the Ten Commandments; to the Hebrew, the ten spheres of the Tree of Life.

In Hall's analysis of the tetractys, he described how by connecting the ten dots of the tetractys, nine triangles are formed. Six of these are involved in the forming of the cube. The same triangles, when lines are properly drawn between them, also reveal the six-pointed star with a dot in the centre. From this insight one also understands that the numeric symbolism of the tetractys corresponds to the Hindu model of nine cobras around Brahma, the Egyptian Grand Ennead around Atum, and the Qabalistic nine legions of angles around the Hidden God.

Only seven dots are used in forming the cube and the star. Qabalistically, the three unused corner dots represent the threefold, invisible causal nature of the universe, while the seven dots involved in the cube and the star are the Elohim, the Spirits of the seven creative periods. The Sabbath, or seventh day, is the central dot.

8 (Ogdoad)

The ogdoad was sacred because it was the number of the first cube, which form had eight corners, and was the only "evenly-even"[49] number under 10 (1-2-4-**8**-4-2-1). Thus, the 8 is divided into two 4's, each 4 is divided into two 2's, and each 2 is divided into two 1's, thereby re-establishing the monad. Among the keywords of the ogdoad are love, counsel, prudence, law and convenience. Among the divinities partaking of its

[49] The Pythagoreans defind "evenly-even" numbers as those which divide into two equal parts, and each part divides evenly, and the even division is continued until unity is reached, for example, 64.

nature were Panarmonia, Rhea, Cibele, Cadmaea, Dindymene, Orcia, Neptune, Themis and the Muse Euterpe. The ogdoad was a number associated with the Eleusinian Mysteries of Greece. It was called the little holy number. It derived its form from the twisted snakes on the Caduceus of Hermes and from the serpentine motion of the celestial bodies, possibly also from the moon's nodes.

9 (Ennead)

The ennead, the first square of an odd number (3 x 3), was associated with failure and shortcoming because it fell short of the perfect number 10 by one. It was called the number of man because of the 9 months of embryonic life. Among its keywords are ocean and horizon because these are boundless. The ennead is the limitless number because there is nothing beyond it but the infinite 10. It was called boundary and limitation because it gathered all numbers within itself. It was called the sphere of the air because it surrounded the numbers as air surrounds the earth. Among the gods and goddesses who partook in greater or less degree of its nature were Prometheus, Vulcan, Juno, the sister and wife of Jupiter, Aglaia, Tritogenia, Curetes, Proserpine, Hyperion and the Muse Terpsichore. 9 was also looked upon as evil because it was an inverted 6. According to the Eleusinian Mysteries, it was the number of the spheres through which the consciousness passed on its way to birth. Because of its resemblance to the spermatozoon, the 9 has been associated with germinal life.

10 (Decad)

The Pythagoreans called the decad, or Panteleia ("All complete"), the greatest of numbers, not only because it is the tetractys but also because it comprehends all arithmetic and harmonic proportions. It is the nature of number because all nations reckon to it and when they arrive at it they return to the monad.

*

In summary, in Pythagorean philosophy the ten basic numbers exhibit certain key properties:

1. The Monad, accepted before all others, because having no diversity, it is always the same;

2. The Duad, the audacious, because the first to separate from the One;

3. The Triad, because it grows out of the Duad, or great mother and the Monad, or divine father;

4. The Tetrad, because it provides the foundation of structure;

5. The Pentad, or equilibrium, because it divides ten into equal halves;

6. The Hexad, because it comprises the form of forms, and concerns the perfection of parts;

7. The Heptad, because it is the number of life and law;

8. The Ogdoad, because it symbolises counsel, prudence and love;

9. The Ennead, because it contains the first square of an odd number, and entails boundary or limitation;

10. The Decad, because it is the most inclusive number, involving all arithmetic and harmonic possibilities.

Protagoras of Abdera, fifth century BCE Greek thinker, a member of the Older Sophists, a group of travelling teachers and intellectuals who were experts in rhetoric.

A page from Franchinus Gaffurius' *Theorica Musicae* (1492), depicting a woodcut of Pythagoras with bells, a kind of glass harmonica, a monochord with weighted strings, and organ pipes, all in Pythagorean tuning.

Arithmetic = Number in itself

Geometry = Number in space

Music and Harmonies = Number in time

Astronomy = Number in space and time

—Pythagoras

Chapter 22

Qabalah

> One is filled with admiration, on penetrating into the Sanctuary of the Kabalah, at seeing a doctrine so logical, so simple, and at the same time so absolute. The necessary union of ideas and signs, the consecration of the most fundamental realities by the primitive characters; the Trinity of Words, Letters, and Numbers; a philosophy simple as the alphabet, profound and infinite as the Word; theorems more complete and luminous than those of Pythagoras; a theology summed up by counting on one's fingers; an Infinite which can be held in the hollow of an infant's hand; ten ciphers and twenty-two letters, a triangle, a square, and a circle—these are all the elements of the Kabalah. These are the elementary principles of the written Word, reflection of that spoken Word that created the world!
>
> —Albert Pike, *Transcendental Magic*

Hebrew theology was divided into three distinct parts. The first was the law, the second was the soul of the law, and the third was the soul of the soul of the law. The law was taught to all the children of Israel; the Mishna, or the soul of the law, was revealed to the Rabbis and teachers; but the Qabalah, the soul of the soul of the law, was cunningly concealed, and only the highest initiates among the Jews were instructed in its secrets.

According to certain Jewish mystics, Moses ascended Mount Sinai three times, remaining in the presence of God forty days each time. During the first forty days the tables of the written law were delivered to the prophet; during the second he received the soul of the law; and during the last forty days God instructed him in the mysteries of the Qabalah, the soul of the soul of the law.

Moses concealed in the first four books of the Pentateuch the secret instructions that God had given him, and for centuries students of Qabalism have sought there the secret doctrine of Israel. As the spiritual nature of man is concealed in his physical body, so the unwritten law, the Mishna and the Qabalah, is concealed within the written teachings of the

Mosaic code.

Qabalah means the secret or hidden tradition, the unwritten law. According to an early Rabbi, it was delivered to man in order that through the aid of its recondite principles he might learn to understand the mystery of both the universe about him and the universe within him.

Early initiates of the Qabalistic Mysteries believed that its principles were first taught by God to a school of His angels before the fall of man. The angels later communicated the secrets to Adam, so that through the knowledge gained from an understanding of its principles fallen humanity might regain its lost estate. The Angel Raziel was dispatched from heaven to instruct Adam in the mysteries of the Qabalah. Later, different angels were employed to initiate succeeding patriarchs in this difficult science. Tophiel was the teacher of Shem, Raphael of Isaac, Metatron of Moses, and Michael of David.

According to Eliphas Levi, the three greatest books of Qabalism are the Sepher Yetzirah (The Book of Formation); the Sepher ha Zohar, (The Book of Splendour); and the Apocalypse, The Book of Revelation. Qabalists declare that the Sepher Yetzirah was written by Abraham, but was probably authored by Rabbi Akiba, circa 120 CE. The Sepher ha Zohar is reckoned to have been written by Simeon ben Jochai, a disciple of Akiba. Rabbi Simeon was sentenced to death about 161 CE by Lucius Verus, co-regent of the Emperor Marc Aurelius Antoninus. He escaped with his son and, hiding in a cave, transcribed the manuscript of the Zohar with the assistance of Elias, who appeared to them at intervals. Simen was twelve years in the cave, during which time he evolved the complicated symbolism of the "Greater Face" and the "Lesser Face."

Legend has it that the secret doctrines of Qabalism had been in existence since the beginning of the world but Rabbi Simeon was the first man permitted to reduce them to writing. Twelve hundred years later the books which he had compiled were discovered and published for the benefit of humanity by Moses de León, a fourteenth-century Spanish rabbi and Qabalist, known in Hebrew as Moshe ben Shem-Tov. The probability is that Moses de León compiled the Zohar about 1305 CE, drawing his material from the unwritten secrets of earlier Jewish mystics.

The Apocalypse, accredited to St. John the Divine, is also of uncertain date, and the identity of its author has never been satisfactorily proved.

The theories of Qabalism are interwoven with the tenets of alchemy, Hermeticism, Rosicrucianism and Freemasonry. The words Qabalism and Hermeticism are now considered as synonymous terms covering all the arcana and esotericism of antiquity. The simple Qabalism of the first centuries of the Christian era gradually evolved into an elaborate theological system, which became so involved that it was next to impossible to comprehend its dogma.

The Qabalists divided the uses of their sacred science into five sections. The Natural Qabalah was used solely to assist the investigator in his study of Nature's mysteries. The Analogical Qabalah was formulated to exhibit the relationship which exists between all things in Nature, and it revealed to the wise that all creatures and substances were one in essence, and that man—the Little Universe—was a replica in miniature of God—the Great Universe. The Contemplative Qabalah was evolved for the purpose of revealing through the higher intellectual faculties the mysteries of the celestial spheres. The Astrological Qabalah instructed those who studied its lore in the power, magnitude and substance of the heavenly bodies, and also revealed the mystical constitution of the planet itself. The fifth, or Magical Qabalah, was studied by those who desired to gain control over the non-human intelligences of the invisible worlds. It was also highly valued as a method of healing the sick by talismans, amulets, charms and invocations.

In the Hebrew alphabet of twenty-two letters are the fundamentals of Qabalistic knowledge. Hall[50] referred to these letters as compositions of tiny flames that are joined together in various combinations, the number of flames to each letter ranging from one to four. The ancient Jewish philosophers held that it was with various combinations of these flaming points that Adam named all things while in Eden.

The Qabalah recognises that everything has both its own true name, which is its eternal word, and also a material name which changes with its manifestations. All of the true names are based upon various combinations of the tenth letter of the Hebrew alphabet, *Yod*, a single point from which all of creation emerges.

These fire flames represent living forces among the celestial hierarchies which we know as the revitalising Forces of Living Nature. Various combinations of these cosmic forces differentiate and impart energy to all the forms observed in the material world.

All differentiation is the result of various combinations of spiritual energies that cross and re-cross at different angles, according to the receiving poles and centres within the evolving life. The various combinations of these forces in the invisible worlds spell out the

---

[50] Hall, M., *The Sacred Knowledge of the Qabalah*, Martino Publishing, CT, 2013

archetypes of bodies, and these bodies become the consonants of the Hebrew alphabet.

The vowel points represent the life centres which give life and expression to the consonants or forms. In the same way, the whirling vital centres or chakras in the human body are the invisible causes which lie behind our visible bodies. Hall explained that as there are seven vital centres, so there are seven vowels; but as two vowels (w and y) are at the present time only partly used, so certain spiritual centres are currently latent under certain conditions. As no word can be formed without vowels, so no body can be constructed from consonant elements alone. The vowel points and their sounds, colours and forms were grouped together by the ancients as the spirits before the throne, and composed the unspeakable name of the unknowable God. (In the Sanskrit the seven vowels are the *Dhyani Chohans* radiating the lifeforce of Fohat.)

According to Jewish esoteric tradition there are two great worlds: the higher or superior world of the *Macrocosm* in which rules the divine man, *Macroprosophus*, and the lower world or lesser sphere of the *Microcosm* in which rules an emanation of *Macroprosophu*s, the *Microprosophus*.

Man made in the image of his Father—Adam Kadmon (the Great Man)—contained both the nature of the human and of the divine. In order to understand Nature and God, philosophers taught that man must unravel the mystery of his own being, the process of which involved finding the sacred meaning of the 22 hieroglyphic letters and the vowel points as they play out their drama in the realms of spirit and substance.

The mysterious Forces of Living Nature are correlated to the letters of the divine name Tetragrammaton, which, in turn, is correlated to the four elements. These, comprising seventy-two combinations, are referred to as the ministering angels, or the intelligences that dwell in and give expression to the life-giving forces.

The celestial language, which we see at work in our world of ever-changing lights and colours, is called the "Bible of Nature," *Bible* in this sense deriving from its original meaning, a *book*. This book is composed of the consonants of the divine alphabet. When these letters are given meaning by the unsounded and unwritten vowel points that dwell within the senses, man then reads his own destiny as it is written by God.

All forms are composed of one substance, the difference being in the combinations and positions of the life centres (the vowels). Nature provides the book, but the positions of man's sevenfold consciousness interpret the book. The consonants may change their meaning through the position of the vowels which impart life to their dead forms.

The early Jewish scriptures were written without spacing between words. The confusion that resulted can be appreciated by taking two consonants such as *l* and *g* and trying to figure out whether the intended word is *lag, leg, log* or *lug*, for with the vowel the meaning is wholly changed. It is the same in Nature. The difference between a plant, animal and a man, and the difference between the intelligencies of different men is the result of varying the placing of the vowels (of consciousness) in the consonants (of form).

These life-centres or poles are evolved by the lives we live; as their positions and power are all-important in interpreting the lessons and messages of life, we lose the faculty of balanced discernment when our lives are out of harmony. The words of life lose their meaning because the vowels are misplaced.

Every living thing consists of a sound, a colour and a form, these together comprising the manifestations which bear witness to the life led within. All colours have a sound and a form; and all sounds have a colour and a form. While there are vibrations of sound that our ears cannot detect, there are also colours which we do not see and forms that elude the perceptions of our physical senses but nevertheless they exist.

Thousand of years before the invention of radio Jewish philosophers realised that the world is a checkerboard of criss-crossing vitalising currents, alternately positive and negative. Man is a human radio and can be similarly attuned. Of the myriad messages travelling through the air simultaneously, a well-constructed receiving set can be attuned to any one of them. It is the same with man and the planes of consciousness in Nature through which he is evolving. An individual with a scatterbrain approach to perception brings in many stations at once, while the more disciplined person who has refined their receiving equipment will more readily receive and differentiate the spiritual messages of Nature.

The differences in our respective natures and in our spiritual development are primarily the result of our adjustments with these currents of natural force and intelligence, symbolised in esoteric Jewish philosophy as the letters of Nature, or the elemental letters from which the words of manifestation are formed. Everything is created by a word, a rate of vibration said to be the true name of the thing or body which it builds around itself. One may say that bodies are thoughts made manifest. Quite literally, what we think we become.

According to the ancient Israelites, the knowedge of the Qabalah was given by the angels in Paradise to man at the time of his fall, so that in time he might regain his lost estate. Hall declared that the Qabalah formed the esoteric teachings of one of the most profound of the Atlantean Mystery Schools.

The Qabalists taught that the body of man consists of the consonantal letters which on a large scale formed the body of the Grand Man of the Universe. The vowel letters, the planetary *Elohim*, were divine; they belonged to God and were His name, for He was considered the composite of all life energies. In man these are the invisible lotus blossoms or roses that bloom upon his cross of matter; as no word can be formed without a vowel, so no body can be formed without one of these centres.

Fundamentals of Qabalistic Cosmogony

The Qabalists conceive of the God-force as an incomprehensible principle to be discovered only through the process of eliminating, in order, all its knowable attributes. What remains is Ain Soph ("without end"), the eternal state of being.

Ain Soph is an important concept in Jewish Kabbalah and represents the formless state of the universe before the self-materialization of God. In other words, the Ain Soph is God before He decided to become God as we now know him. Indefinable, the Absolute permeates all space. Abstract to a degree of inconceivability, Ain Soph is the unconditioned state of all things. Substances, essences and intelligences are manifested out of it, but the Absolute itself is without substance, essence or intelligence.

Ain Soph may be likened to an endles field of rich earth out of which grows a myriad of plants, each different in colour, formation and fragrance, yet each with its roots in the same dark soil, which, however, is unlike any of the forms nurtured by it. The "plants" are universes, gods and man, all nourished by Ain Soph and all with their source in one essence that defies definition; all with their spirits, souls and bodies fashioned from this essence, and doomed, like the plant, to return to the black ground, Ain Soph, whence they came.

Ain Soph was referred to by the Qabalists as "The Most Ancient of all the Ancients." It was always considered as sexless. Its symbol was a closed eye. The Rabbis proposed certain theories regarding the manner in which Ain Soph projected creations out of Itself, and they also assigned to it certain symbols as being descriptive of its powers. The nature of Ain Soph they symbolise by a circle, emblematic of eternity. This hypothetical circle encloses a dimensionless area of incomprehensible life, and the circular boundary of this life is abstract and measureless infinity.

According to this concept, God is not only a Centre but also an Area. Centralisation is the first step towards limitation. Therefore, centres which form in the substances of Ain Soph are finite because they are destined to dissolve back into the Cause of themselves, while Ain Soph Itself is infinite because It is the ultimate condition of all things.

The circular shape given to Ain Soph signifies that space is hypothetically enclosed within a great crystal-like globe, outside of which there is nothing, not even a vacuum. Within this globe creation and dissolution take place. Every element and principle that will ever be used in the eternities of cosmic birth, growth and decay is within the transparent substances of this intangible sphere. It is the Cosmic Egg, which is not broken till the great day when all things return to their ultimate cause.

In the secret teachings of the Qabalah it is taught that man's body is enveloped in an ovoid, bubble-like iridescence, which is called the Auric Egg. This is the causal sphere of man. It bears the same relationship to man's physical body that the globe of Ain Soph bears to Its created universes. In fact, this Auric Egg is the Ain Soph sphere of the entity called man. In reality, therefore, the supreme consciousness of man is in this aura, which extends in all directions and completely encircles his lower bodies.

As the consciousness in the Cosmic Egg is withdrawn into a central point, which is then called God, so the consciousness in the Auric Egg of man is concentrated, thereby causing the establishment of a point of consciousness called the Ego. Man never passes from this egg; it remains even after death. His births, deaths and rebirths all take place within it, and it cannot be broken until the day when mankind, like the universe, is liberated from the Wheel of Necessity.

The Tree of the Sephiroth

The Tree of the Sephiroth may be considered as a compendium of the secret philosophy. It consists of ten globes arranged in three vertical columns and connected by 22 channels or paths. The globes are called the Sephiroth and to them are assigned the numbers 1 to 10. The three columns are called Mercy (on the right), Severity (on the left) and, between them, Mildness, as the reconciling power. The columns may also be said to represent Wisdom, Strength and Beauty, which form the three-in-one support of the universe, for it is written that the foundation of all things is the Three.

The 22 channels are the letters of the Hebrew alphabet and to them are assigned the major trumps of the Tarot deck of symbolic cards. Eliphas Levi declared that by arranging the Tarot cards according to a definite order man could discover all that is knowable concerning his

God, his universe and himself.

When the 10 numbers relating to the Sephiroth are combined with the 22 letters relating to the channels, the resultant sum, 32, is the number peculiar to the Qabalistic Paths of Wisdom. Hall pointed out that these paths are analogous to the first 32 degrees of Freemasonry, which elevate the candidate to the dignity of a Prince of the Royal Secret. Qabalists also consider it highly significant that in the original Hebrew Scriptures the name of God should occur 32 times in the first chapter of Genesis. (In the English translations of the Bible the name appears 33 times.) In the mystic analysis of the human body, 32 spinal segments lead upward to the Temple of Wisdom, the skull. The ten Sephiroth are:

- 1 Kether—the Crown
- 2 Chochmah—Wisdom
- 3 Binah—Understanding
- 4 Chesed—Mercy
- 5 Geburah—Severity
- 6 Tiphereth—Beauty
- 7 Netsah—Victory
- 8 Hod—Glory
- 9 Jesod—the Foundation
- 10 Malchuth—the Kingdom

The Sephirothic Tree is sometimes depicted as a human body, thus more definitely establishing the true identity of the first, or Heavenly, Man—Adam Kadmon—the Idea of the Universe. The ten divine globes of the Sephiroth are then considered as analogous to the ten sacred members and organs: Kether is the crown of the prototypical head and perhaps refers to the pineal gland; Chochmah and Binah are the right and left hemispheres respectively of the great brain; Chesed and Geburah are the right and left arms respectively, signifying the active creative members of the Grand Man; Tiphereth is the heart, or, according to some, the entire viscera; Netsah and Hod are the right and left legs respectively, or the supports of the world; Jesod is the generative system, or the foundation of form; and Malchuth represents the two feet, or the base of being. Occasionally Jesod is considered as the male and Malchuth as the female generative power. The Grand Man thus conceived is the cosmic image of Nebuchadnezzar's dream (Daniel, 2), with head of gold, arms and chest of silver, body of brass, legs of iron, and feet of clay. The mediæval Qabalists also assigned one of the Ten Commandments and a tenth part of the Lord's Prayer in sequential order to each of the Sephiroth.

Concerning the emanations from Kether, H.P. Blavatsky in her pamphlet *Ten Sephiroth* wrote:

> This [Kether] was the first Sephiroth, containing in herself the other nine ספירות Sephiroth, or intelligences. In their totality and unity they represent the archetypal man, Adam Kadmon, the πρωτόγονος, who in his individuality or unity is yet dual, or bisexual, the Greek Didumos, for he is the prototype of all humanity. Thus we obtain three trinities, each contained in a "head." In the first head, or face (the three-faced Hindu Trimurti), we find Sephira [Kether], the first androgyne, at the apex of the upper triangle, emitting Hachama [Chochmah], or Wisdom, a masculine and active potency also called Jah הוה and Binah, הניב, or Intelligence, a female and passive potency, also represented by the name Jehovah הוהי. These three form the first trinity or "face" of the Sephiroth. This triad emanated Hesed, דסה, or Mercy, a masculine active potency, also called El, from which emanated Geburah הרובג, or justice, also called Eloha, a feminine passive potency; from the union of these two was produced Tiphereth טפארת, Beauty, Clemency, the Spiritual Sun, known by the divine name Elohim; and the second triad, "face," or "head," was formed. These emanating, in their turn, the masculine potency Netzah, הצנ, Firmness, or Jehovah Sabaoth, who issued the feminine passive potency Hod, דוה, Splendour, or Elohim Sabaoth; the two produced Jesod, דוסי, Foundation, who is the mighty living one El-Chai, thus yielding the third trinity or "head." The tenth Sephiroth is rather a duad, and is represented on the diagrams as the lowest circle. It is Malchuth or Kingdom, תוכלמ, and Shekinah, הניכש, also called Adonai, and Cherubim among the angelic hosts. The first "Head" is called the Intellectual world; the second "Head" is the Sensuous, or the world of Perception, and the third is the material or Physical world.

Among the later Qabalists there is also a division of the Sephirothic Tree into five parts:

- Macroprosophus, or the Great Face, is the term applied to Kether as the first and most exalted of the Sephiroth and includes the nine potencies or Sephiroth issuing from Kether.

- Abba, the Great Father, is the term generally applied to Chochmah—Universal Wisdom—the first emanation of Kether, but, according to Ibn Gebirol, Chochmah represents the Son, the Logos or the Word born from the union of Kether and Binah.
- Aima, the Great Mother, is the name by which Binah, or the third Sephira, is generally known. This is the Holy Ghost, from whose body the generations issue forth. Being the third person of the Creative Triad, it corresponds to Jehovah, the Demiurgus.
- Microprosophus, or the Lesser Face, is composed of the six Sephiroth—Chesed, Geburah, Tiphereth, Netsah, Hod and Jesod. The Microprosophus is commonly called the Lesser Adam, or Zauir Anpin, whereas the Macroprosophus, or Superior Adam, is Arikh Anpin. The Lesser Face is properly symbolized by the six-pointed star or interlaced triangles of Zion and also by the six faces of the cube. It represents the directions north, east, south, west, up and down, and also the first six days of Creation. In his list of the parts of the Microprosophus, Theosophist MacGregor-Mathers included Binah as the first and superior part of the Lesser Adam, thus making his constitution septenary. If Microprosophus is considered as sexpartite, then his globes (Sephiroth) are analogous to the six days of Creation, and the tenth globe, Malchuth, to the Sabbath of rest.
- The Bride of Microprosophus is Malchuth—the epitome of the Sephiroth, its quaternary constitution being composed of blendings of the four elements. This is the divine Eve that is taken out of the side of Microprosophus and combines the potencies of the entire Qabalistic Tree in one sphere, which may be termed man.

According to the mysteries of the Sephiroth, the order of the Creation is described. From AIN SOPH, the Nothing and All, issues Macroprosophus, the Long Face, of whom it is written, "Within His skull exist daily thirteen thousand myriads of worlds which draw their existence from Him and by Him are upheld." Macroprosophus, the will of AIN SOPH, corresponding to Kether, the Crown of the Sephiroth, gives birth out of Himself the nine lesser spheres of which He is the sum. The 22 letters of the Hebrew alphabet, by the various combinations of which the laws of the universe are established, constitute the sceptre of Macroprosophus which He wields from His flaming throne.

From Kether comes forth Chochmah, the great Father, and Binah, the great Mother, usually referred to as Abba and Aima respectively—the first male and the first female. These correspond to the first two letters of the sacred name, Jehovah, יהוה, IHVH. The Father is the י, or I, and the Mother is the ה, or H. Abba and Aima symbolize the creative activities of the universe. In the Sepher ha Zohar it is written:

> And therefore are all things established in the equality of male and female; for were it not so, how could they subsist? This beginning is the Father of all things; the Father of all Fathers; and both are mutually bound together, and the one path shineth into the other—Chochmah, Wisdom, as the Father; Binah, Understanding, as the Mother.

The later Qabalists rearranged the first three Sephiroth and added a mysterious point called Daath—a hypothetical eleventh Sephira. This is located where the horizontal line connecting Chochmah and Binah crosses the vertical line joining Kether and Tiphereth. If Chochmah is considered the active, intelligent energy of Kether, and Binah the receptive capacity of Kether, then Daath becomes the thought which, created by Chochmah, flows into Binah.

According to the original conception, from the union of the Divine Father and the Divine Mother is produced Microprosophus—the Short Face, and corresponds to the letter ו, or V, in the Great Name, Jehovah. The six powers of Microprosophus flow from and are contained in their own source, which is Binah, the Mother of the Lesser Adam. These constitute the spheres of the sacred planets; their name is Elohim, and they move upon the face of the deep.

The tenth Sephira—Malchuth, the Kingdom—is described as the Bride of the Lesser Adam, created back to back with her lord, and to it is assigned the final, ה, or H, the last letter of the Sacred Name. The dwelling place of Malchuth is in the fourth world, Assiah, and it is composed of all the superior powers reflected into the elements of the terrestrial sphere. It is therefore seen that the Qabalistic Tree extends through four worlds, with its branches in matter and its roots in the Ancient of Ancients—Macroprosophus.

Three vertical columns support the universal system as typified by the Sephirothic Tree. The central pillar has its foundation in Kether, the Eternal One. It passes downward through the hypothetical Sephira, Daath, and then through Tiphereth and Jesod, with its lower end resting upon the foundation of Malchuth, the last of the globes.

The true importance of the central pillar is equilibrium. If the numbers of the four Sephiroth connected by this column be added together (1 + 6 + 9 + 10), the sum is 26, the number of Jehovah.

The column on the right, which is called Jachin, has its foundation on Chochmah, the outpouring Wisdom of God; the three globes suspended from it are all masculine powers. The column at the left is called Boaz. The three globes upon it are feminine and receptive potencies, for it is founded in Understanding, a receptive and maternal potency. Wisdom is considered as radiant or outpouring, and Understanding as receptive, or something which is filled by the flowing of Wisdom. The three pillars are ultimately united in Malchuth.

The four globes upon the central column reveal the function of the creative power in the various worlds. In the first world the creative power is Will, the one Divine Cause; in the second world, the hypothetical Daath—the Word coming forth from the Divine Thought; in the third world, Tiphereth—the Sun, or focal point between God and Nature; in the fourth world it is twofold, being the positive and negative poles of the reproductive system, of which Jesod is the male and Malchuth the female. The Tetragrammaton, or the four-lettered Name of God, written thus הוהי, is pronounced Jehovah. The first letter is י, Yod, the Germ, the Life, the Flame, the Cause, the One, and the most fundamental of the Jewish phallic emblems. Its numerical value is 10, and it is to be considered as the 1 containing the 10.

In the Qabalah it is declared that the Yod is in reality three Yods, of which the first is the beginning, the second is the centre, and the third is the end. Its throne is the Sephira Chochmah, from which it goes forth to impregnate Binah, which is the first ה, He. The result of this union is Tiphereth, which is the ו Vau, whose power is 6 and which symbolizes the six members of the Lesser Adam. The final ה, He, is Malchuth, the Inferior Mother, partaking of the potencies of the Divine Mother, the first He. By placing the four letters of the Tetragrammaton in a vertical column, a figure closely resembling the human body is produced, with Yod for the head, the first He for the arms and shoulders, Vau for the trunk of the body, and the final He for the hips and legs.

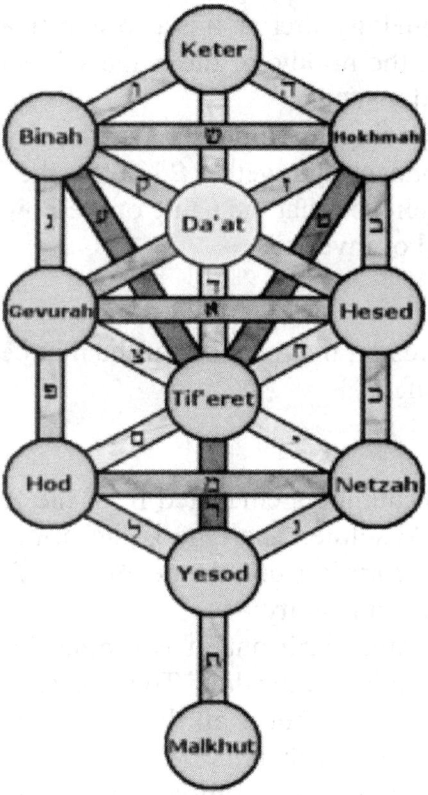

The Yosher-Upright 10-sefirot configuration

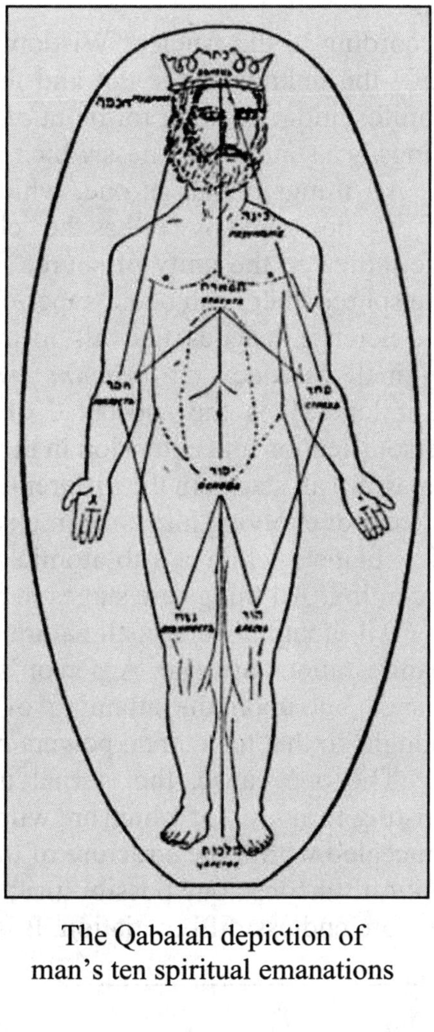

The Qabalah depiction of man's ten spiritual emanations

If the Hebrew letters are exchanged for their English equivalents, the form is not materially changed or the analogy altered. It is also significant that by inserting the letter ש, Shin, in the middle of the name Jehovah, the word Jehoshua, or Jesus, is formed—הושהי

In the Qabalistic Mysteries, according to Eliphas Levi, the name Jehovah is occasionally written by connecting together 24 dots—the 24 powers before the throne—and it is believed that the name of the Power of Evil is the sign of Jehovah reversed or inverted

*

In his slim volume,[51] Hall expounds on the meaning of the numbers associated with the mysterious Ain Sof:

One

According to the Ancient Wisdom all numbers emanated from the Ain Sof—the unknown, the dot and the Absolute. The One is the primary manifestation. Coming forth out of the formless dot, the beginning of all things is a state of one-ness which man calls unity.

All things began as one, which came forth out of No-thing, by a process described by Hall as the "elongation of the dot." To the ancients, one indicated the unity of source. It follows that if all things have just one source, there can be no superiority among them.

Science teaches that all forms are various combinations of one original essence, or *primum hyle* (that which receives form or definiteness), is the substance of the dot, and manifests through its personification and extension in the One. A stone, a flower, an insect and a man are all stages in the differentiation of one life. A vegetable is in the process of evolving into an animal; an animal is a stage in the unfoldment of a planet; while a sub-atomic particle is a god in the process of becoming. All things are stages in the expression of one connected life.

All thought is unity; all natural forces which man uses in his various manifestations are one. A person's ability to think does not depend on chance but upon the attaining of his consciousness to the planes of thought so that his mental powers may be energized.

The one cause, the eternal unit, diversifies into the millions of existing forms, all of which are witness to the infinite diversity of powers concealed within the structure of the primitive One. The young soul is a unity of unconscious possibilities; it is One and yet has the potential to execute endless differentiation. It is the expression of One pouring itself

[51] Ibid

into Many-ness in search of experience. The old soul has increased its One-ness to contain all diversity and all Many-ness yet still remains a unit.

In the One-ness we find the ultimate of all manifestation. All diversity is destined to return again to its own source. All life is consequently symbolised by a great circle which returns again to that from which it came—a serpent with its tail in its mouth.

Two

The number 2 is symbolic of the dual nature of human thought, which views everything either from the standpoint of opposites or comparison. Two is the first negative number because when divided it leaves no remainder. All even numbers are negative and feminine and are ruled by the moon. All odd numbers are called positive because an odd number cannot be divided without leaving the First Cause, *One*, in the centre.

As One is called in ancient esoterics the Number of the Father, so Two is called the Number of the Earth—cosmic root substance, called by the ancients the Divine Mother in contrast to the vitalising ray which carries the title of Great Father.

Two is said to be the number of unconsciousness because the single spiritual power is broken or its flow is impeded. It is also referred to as the number of contention, because the two extremes of Nature are always seeking mastery one over the other.

Those who would learn the mystery of the number 2 must learn how to use the power of thought to blend the opposities in Nature, for the mind is the uniting link between God and man. Every element in Nature has its opposite. In most cases the opposite of a thing is the lack of that thing. Light is an element; darkness is the absence of it. Knowledge is an evolved state; ignorance is the lack of it. As we evolve, we form a triangle out of the opposites by lifting our own centre of cosnciousness above the plane in which lie the two points of our horizon.

Three

The number 3 is symbolised by the triangle, for it is the number of outpourings from the Universal Powers in the process of creation. Its basic principles are spirit, soul and body. This trinity manifests in the world of the physical as thought, desire and action: three principles or forces that mold the destiny of all living things.

The divine *Three* is born in man as a result of the power of discrimination and the union of spirit, mind and body. The secret formula for this accomplishment comes down to us in the alchemical secret of the

Philosoper's Stone, composed of its three elements—salt, sulphur and mercury. The number *Three* is also kown as the threefold path, for it symbolizes the highest expression of the three major divisions of human character. These three paths are symbolised by a philosopher, a priest and a soldier. Metaphysical study is the path of the philosopher; mysticism is the path of the priest; while service is the path of the soldier.

The *Three* is also the number of the three worlds which the true Qabbalist is investigating with his self-evolved powers. It stands for the triple crown of the ancient Magus, who was king of heaven, earth and hell, and represents the three grand centres of the human body—the brain, the heart and the generative system. The number Three is also symbolic of balance or equilibrium, for the triangle is equilateral, menaing that all of its sides are of equal length. With it point upward it represents human aspiration and consciousness rising out of form to union with its divine source.

Four

Four is the symbol univsersally accepted to represent the path of accomplishment and the labours still to be undertaken. Being the number of form and earthly things, it is represented as a cube or stone within which life is imprisoned.

Four is the number of matter, which manifests in endless combinations of earth, water, fire and air—action, vitalisation, emotion and thought. These four principles form the cross upon which is crucified the spirit of life.

By his thoughts, feelings and actions, man slowly transmutes his personal stone tomb into a cube of divine crystal from which his spirit light shines forth as through a protective lantern.

Five

Five is the hand of the philosopher. It is composed of the four elements plus spirit. In the Tarot, *Five* is the hierophant or priest because it is the spirit of man rising from the tomb of matter. The ancients taught that those who have lived through the laws of the *Four* and have mastered them have become the *Five*—liberated from the casket of matter. When the One has ecolved to become the master to the Four, fear, selfishness and egoism disappear and man becomes the divine Five. Only those that have lived life in all its shades and permutations, positive and negative, and finally risen above it and its uncertainties can truly comprehend the mystery of the number Five.

Six

The number *Six* is symbolised by the six-pointed star, commonly known as the Shield of David. Man consists of two two interlaces triangles—the threefold spirit and the threefold form. They are his life principles and the casings of matter which are ensouled by them.

Six is sometimes called the number of materiality, for it is symbolic of the union of spirit and matter. It also represents the six senses, the sixth being the clear vision and the ability to function on the plane of the astral world, whch is a latent faculty yet to be unfolded within humanity.

The figure 6 is a line descending into a circle. The coil with the line descending is symbolic of the serpent's coil, which descends in 9 and ascends in 6. Therefore, in the case of the Six, the serpent is returning upwards to the power which was its source.

Seven

Seven is called the day of completion. All life is divided into seven parts, and the passage of consciousness through these seven divisions are what were described in the ancient wisdoms as the days of "creation." These seven parts are the centres of consciousness. The pathways of human evolution wind in and out through them, finally uniting them as beads upon its golden thread. This divine process is beautifully captured in a verse from the Hindu *Vedas*:

There is an endless net of threads
Throughout the universe.
The horizontal threads are in space,
The vertical threads are in time.
At every crossing of the threads,
There is an individual,
And every individual is a crystal bead.
The great light of absolute being
Illuminates and penetrates
Every crystal bead, and also,
Every crystal bead reflects
Not only the light
From every other crystal in the net,
But also every reflection
Of every reflection
Throughout the universe.

Seven is called the number of divine harmony, for it is the music of the spheres. All Nature is one great, harmonious melody to those who have harmonised themselves with it.

In a previous work I described Pythagoras's teachings regarding music and harmony, the principles of which are closely related to Hall's observations on the mysterious emanations of the Ain Sof. Pythagoras discovered that the heavenly bodies appear to move in accordance with the mathematical ratios that govern the concordant musical intervals in order to produce the "harmony of the spheres." Pythagoras also believed in the concept of "musica universalis," the idea that the planets and stars move according to mathematical equations, which correspond to musical notes and thus produce a kind of symphony. The tones produced by these bodies are in relation to their size, distance, density and movement. As the planetary system produces a harmony, so also does the universe in its entirety; as living creatures breathe, so do the planets and the universe.

Eight

Eight is the divine symbol of vitality, and of spiritual and physical regeneration. It is also the symbol of the mystic marriage, the state of a human soul living intimately united to God through grace and love. It is the strange symbol inscribed by Nature upon the puffed head of the Indian cobra, the symbol of the Logos and of universal creative power. All things are said to have come into being as a result of the spinning or twisting power of the figure 8. The *Eight* is the fusing or joining of the broken ends of the spiritual circuits which, combining in the body of man, form the spiritual wedding ring which unites the masculine and feminine natures within himself.

Nine

In Pythagoras's mystical Science of Numbers, a system that chimes harmoniously with Qabalistic teachings, the nine has the most potential for evolution out of all the numbers. One whose Life Number at birth is 9, the "Idealist," has reincarnated to experience a life of constant change, partly because of destiny and partly because of the consequences of daily action. They will stand apart but will always be sought out for direction and balance. From the beginning they will suffer many mishaps or personal hardships to be endured in one way or another. This is an inner link with the self-sacrificing attribute of the nine to grow and develop through trial and hardship.

This is not really necessary, however, if the nine can live up to their image as the IDEALIST. There is a special universal protection open to nines but it is a gift, which can only atrract positive outcomes provided they learn to enjoy life, work and people.

The nine has twin sides to their nature: the personal and the impersonal. Often they will be felt to be very impersonal because of their ability to appear disinterested or to observe and not participate. They can show warmth, deep love and understanding in one moment but then in another appear cold and distant. These mood changes are nevertheless an essential part of the nine's pathway in learning to balance themselves within a changing world.

The nine naturally loves family, home and friends. They will be open with them, feeling that the sharing qualities within families and friendships should be experienced by all. If the number nine tries to emulate other people or to copy their actions and behaviours, they will fail dramatically. Their strength is as an idealist, not as a copycat.

ALCHEMY - CABBALA. Plate 3 from Steffan Michelspacher, Cabala, Spiegel der Kunst und Natur, 1616

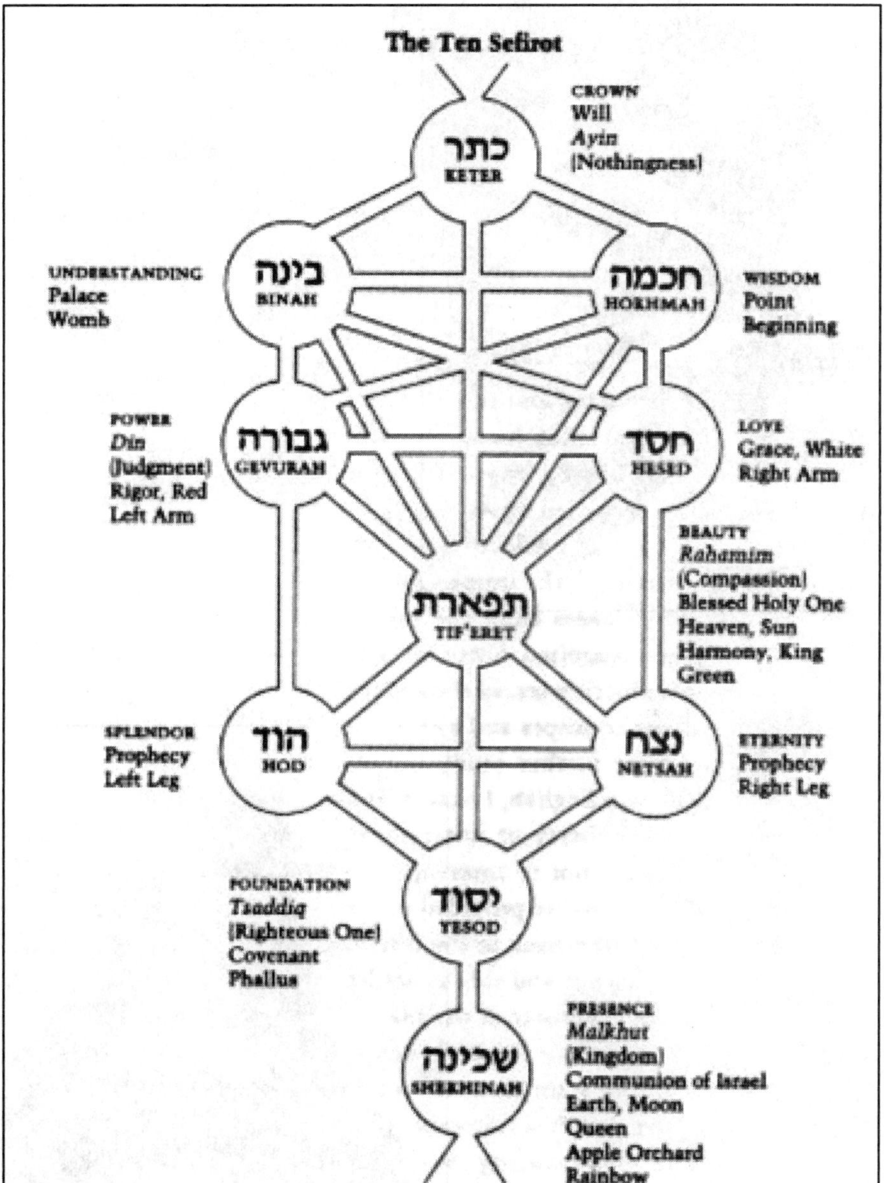

The Ten Sefirot

Madame H.P. Blavatsky

Colonel Henry Steel Olcott

Chapter 23

Qabalah, the Golem and A.I.

The Golem is one of the earliest artificial intelligence (AI) prototypes.[52] Originally a Jewish myth about an anthropoid figure of clay that was brought to life by virtue of Qabalistic magic, the Golem reincarnated time and again, carrying throughout the ages deeply-rooted anxiety concerning the prospect of intelligent and sentient technology going out of human control. Although designed to be an obedient, effective, and formidable sort of "low-tech" robot, the Golem becomes independent of its masters, and eventually wreaks havoc upon its human creators.

Since its very early appearances in Talmudic texts, the Golem has gained a considerable reputation in popular culture and frequently appeared in literature, in comic books, film, and television—from the 1915 silent film *Der Golem* to *The Simpsons* and the *X-Files*.

The term "A.I." is not new. John McCarthy held a workshop at Dartmouth on "artificial intelligence" in 1955. It is now a common technology. AIs today are supporting speech recognition devices and personal digital assistants such as Alexa and Siri. They operate facial recognition and surveillance systems, military drones and other unmanned vehicles; they also manage basic Internet services such as the Google search engine.

Society reaps and will continue reaping benefits from AI but potential pitfalls loom. In 2015, dozens of AI experts signed an open letter, warning of the potential of creating something which cannot be controlled. As the letter alerts, 'our AI systems must do what we want them to do.' The myth of the Golem as an artificial man-made "machine" that gains a mind of its own and turns against its human masters seems more relevant than ever before.

The Golem predates other anthropoid troublemakers and unruly machines inspired by the technophobia which accompanied the industrial

---

[52] Principal source for this chapter—Dr. Amir Vudka of the Department of Media Studies at the University of Amsterdam

revolution from its early stage. Literary examples such as Mary Shelley's 1818 Frankenstein and Karel Čapek's 1921 Rossum's Universal Robots (which coined the word "robot") include early modern cases of artificial humanoids, which, like the Golem, get out of hand and revolt against their human masters. Fritz Lang's Moloch-machine in Metropolis (1927) and the assembly line in Charlie Chaplin's Modern Times (1936) can also be seen as Golem technologies which become uncontrollable to the point that they threaten to swallow up humankind.

The advent of AI technology and its possible trajectory to become superintelligent, far smarter and capable than its human creators, influenced representations of much more sophisticated hostile machines, as in *Westworld* (Michael Crichton, 1973), *The Terminator* (James Cameron, 1984), or *The Matrix* (Lana and Lilly Wachowski, 1999). These highly intelligent machines, like the Golem, quickly shifted from their inscribed role to serve humanity, becoming a threat to humanity's very existence.

The Golem reflects man; man is a Golem made in the image of God. According to Qabalist scripture, the process of creation went out of control already within God's system of sefirot. In such descriptions, God appears as a machine with spherical pump-like vessels, connected by a system of channels that stream the divine light within this all-encompassing cosmic system. At a certain moment, this astral system "malfunctions," breaks down, and its vessels scatter, eventually becoming the substratum of creation. God, then, reassembles Himself in the amended form of the Primordial Man, Adam Kadmon, with the sefirot organised in the shape of a human body (as each sefira represents an organ or limb).

Viewed in this context, the Golem is part of a series of breakdowns, catastrophes that at the same time carry the emergence of new life forms in a continuum of destruction that is simultaneously a movement of creation: from God to man to Golem. With the potential creation of sentient machines, humankind comes full circle and becomes godlike, creator of new life. But as the cycle continues, will AI become a rebellious Golem that seeks our destruction?

Jewish folklore describes how five-hundred years ago learned men, directed by Maharal Yehudah Loew, chief rabbi of Prague, created by means of a secret Qabalistic formula an artificial man. The Maharal, in desperation to save the Jews from increasing persecution, including mass slaughter, prayed for guidance. He received an answer at night in a vision. He was given 10 Hebrew letters, signifying words meaning 'You will create a Golem, a thing of clay and destroy the wicked!'

The Maharal and two friends went to the Moldova River and began to shape the soft clay. They created a figure that resembled a man. The first friend circled the Golem seven times while reciting certain holy letter combinations. The Golem began to glow. The second friend did the same thing, and the glow was replaced by a watery vapour. Then the Maharal also circled the Golem seven times and the three of them cried out, 'And God blew the breath of life into his nostrils.' The Golem's eyes then opened. The men discovered that the Golem had great strength and also the ability to disappear.

The Maharal told the Golem, 'We created you with God's help to protect the Jews against our enemies. You must obey my orders in everything!' The Golem could see and hear but was mute. He nodded his head in agreement.

The Golem was not a monster. It was a gentle soul that had no independent thought but was morally upright. He did exactly what he was told until he was told to stop by the Maharal. When asked to bring water to the kitchen, he continued to bring water until the kitchen flooded and was then told to stop. When he was told to catch fish, he fished all day, and when told that there were too many fish, he dumped the entire basket of them back into the lake.

One version of the story relates that the Golem's creators animated it with the word *emet* (truth), which they inscribed on its forehead. However, the Golem implored them to never again repeat the experiment, and so, understanding the enormity of what they had done, they erased the letter aleph, thereby changing the word *emet* to the word *met* (dead), and he immediately turned into ashes. Here, Hebrew letters are used to activate and deactivate the Golem in a way that nearly anticipates the computer codes that later will be used to program AI machines.

The core of the Golem myth, throughout the various early traditional descriptions of Golem creations, involves the alchemic combination of soil and language, elements which make a clear association to the creation of the first man, Adam, by God. In Genesis (2:7) it is written: "And the LORD God formed man of the dust of the ground, and breathed into his nostrils the breath of life; and man became a living soul."

Adam is created from dust (soil) and the breath of God. Considering that all other creation is done through God's Divine utterances (for example in Genesis 1:3 "God said, let there be light: and there was light"), the breath of God should be understood as logos that bestows Adam with a soul. Adam in turn later shares this power of Divine "coding" that will allow him to name all the creatures in the animal kingdom. The Midrash Genesis Rabbah (a collection of ancient interpretations of the Book of Genesis) made the connection explicit, describing how God "rose him [Adam] [as] a Golem from the earth to heaven and cast the soul in him."

A central cosmogenic formula in kabbalah and many other esoteric traditions postulates: as above so below, the microcosm and macrocosm, the heaven and the earth, reflecting each other. In the Book of Genesis, this principle appears in the notion that God created man in His image. The Hebrew word that is used there to signify man's similitude to his Creator is tzelem, which is better translated as "simulacrum." Thus, man was created as the simulacrum of God.

Qabalists claim that God is shaped in the form of a human body, called Adam Kadmon (primordial man), which originated adam rishon (first man) in its image-simulacrum. Yet the Golem Adam went out of control and rebelled against his creator. As the story goes, Adam and Eve were expelled from the Garden of Eden because they ate from the forbidden fruit of the tree of knowledge, which according to the snake in the story would make them "like God." Becoming godlike is related here to intellectual faculties that later would allow humankind to create their own intelligent Golems, their own simulacrums in the shape of humanoid machines.

The meaning of the word "Golem" in several Rabbinical sources signifies an idiot, fool or clumsy person, but, in contrast, other passages consider the Golem as having an extraordinary cognitive faculty. In Hebrew, the butterfly's cocoon is also called golem, alluding to an embryonic stage. To put it in the context of AI, it has been suggested that we are witnessing its embryonic stage before it will take wings as a superintelligent machine, far smarter than us. And will it then repeat the rebellious ways of its human creators?

While the Golem's creation may seem rooted in mysticism and folklore, it echoes many themes and concerns that surround the development of artificial intelligence today. Just as the Golem was shaped from clay, scientists and engineers today are crafting intelligent machines using advanced algorithms and programming languages. While the medium may differ, both processes involve imbuing inanimate matter with capabilities that mirror or surpass human abilities.

The Golem was brought to life to safeguard the Jewish community, defending them against threats and ensuring their wellbeing. Likewise, artificial intelligence systems are developed to assist humans in various domains, such as healthcare, transportation, and communication, aiming to enhance productivity, accuracy and convenience. Whether it is protecting a community or aiding in complex decision-making, both the Golem and AI serve as powerful allies in addressing human needs and challenges.

Furthermore, both the Golem and AI exhibit elements of autonomy and learning. The Golem, according to folklore, was endowed with a certain level of autonomy, able to carry out tasks independently and respond to its creator's commands. Similarly, modern AI systems possess the ability to learn from vast amounts of data, adapt to changing circumstances, and make informed decisions without constant human intervention. The Golem's autonomy and AI's learning capabilities underscore their potential to evolve and improve over time, becoming increasingly adept at fulfilling their intended rolesEthical Considerations:

The Golem's tremendous power and potential for destruction raised moral questions about the responsibility of its creator and the impact of its actions. Likewise, the development of AI systems demands ethical considerations, such as ensuring transparency, fairness and accountability. As AI becomes more pervasive in society, discussions surrounding its ethical implications, including privacy, bias and the potential for misuse, echo the moral dilemmas surrounding the Golem in Jewish folklore.

The Golem's control rested solely in the hands of its creator. Rabbi Loew could activate and deactivate the Golem as needed. Similarly, controlling the behaviour and decisions of AI systems is a critical concern. Ensuring that AI remains under human control and aligns with ethical guidelines is an ongoing challenge for researchers and policymakers.

A golem is usually turned "on" by writing the Hebrew word for truth (אמת) on its forehead. It's turned "off" by removing the first letter, which changes the word to read death (מת). Computer software has ways to either "Power Off" the hardware or even backdoor that can force a shutdown.

By the early twentieth century, there existed several variations of the Golem story that located the Golem either in Central or in Eastern Europe. What they all had in common was the presence of a rabbi who artificially molds a clay anthropoid and magically brings it to life through Hebrew writing, either engraved on the body or on parchment. The Golem is created to serve the rabbi or, in twentieth-century narratives, to protect the Jewish community against anti-Semitic attacks and redeem it from oppressive conditions in the diaspora, but it ultimately runs amok and attempts to destroy its surroundings, causing a good deal of damage.

No wonder, then, that the Golem regained popularity during the First World War as a wartime celebrity.

After the Second World War, the golem continued to be linked with mass destruction and the threat of nuclear weapons, as well as with cybernetic systems, both disembodied computers and hybrid cyborgs. During this period it was argued that it was necessary to rein in the intelligence of learning machines because of their perceived ability to overcome their human creators in unpredictable ways. Critics said such a machine is the modern counterpart of the Golem of the Rabbi of Prague.

In 1965, the forefather of Qabalah studies, Gershom Scholem, proposed to name one of the first computers constructed in Israel "Golem Aleph." In the inauguration speech for the computer, he expressed his hopes that this "Golem" and its creators 'develop peacefully and don't destroy the world.'

In 1984, novelist Isaac Bashevis Singer pronounced that the robots and computers of our day are Golems, since we now can endow our technologies with 'qualities that God has given to the human brain.' Indeed, he argued, 'we are living in an epoch of golem-making.'

The exhilarations and anxieties surrounding AI have a common projection: that we may be heading towards a point of no return. Perhaps most radical and provocative on the optimistic end of the spectrum is Ray Kurzweil, futurist, inventor of the Kurzweil synthesiser and director of Google engineering, who had predicted a "technological singularity," a point at which AI will far surpass human intelligence. At this point, according to Kurzweil, humans will merge with AI, inaugurating an era in which human intelligence will become increasingly non-biological and fundamentally more powerful than it is today—the dawning of a new civilisation that will enable humans to transcend their biological limitations and mortality.

Vernor Vinge, in a 1993 essay that popularised the term "singularity," argued that as superintelligence would continue to upgrade itself at an incomprehensible rate, it would eventually signal the end of the human era. Vinge's concerns about the possible physical extinction of the human race is in tandem with more recent concerns about the rise of superintelligent autonomous weapons. According to professor of AI and robotics Noel Sharkey, there is currently massive spending on research aimed at autonomous killing machines that will take the human element "out of the loop," allowing robots to operate autonomously to locate their targets and destroy them without human intervention. To avoid a Terminator-like scenario, in which autonomous machines hunt down humans, in 2018 thousands of scientists who specialise in AI declared that they will not participate in the development or manufacture of robots that can identify and attack people, Golem-like, without human oversight.

Present day philosopher Nick Bostrom poses a question. If some day we build machine brains that surpass human brains in general intelligence, then this new superintelligence could become very powerful. This tipping point is quite possibly the most important and most daunting challenge humanity has ever faced. Tipping-point scenarios rely on a big breakthrough in the development of AI, a threshold that according to Bostrom and others we have not yet crossed. There is no blueprint for AGI (Artificial General Intelligence), let alone any known path towards sentient AI. But according to Bostrom, sooner or later humanity will face an AI superintelligence that greatly exceeds the cognitive performance of humans in every domain conceivable. Once we reach this point, "a plausible default outcome" would be "existential catastrophe."

What Bostrom calls "the treacherous turn" is reminiscent of the Golem's rebellion against its human masters. It is a point in which weak AI that behaves cooperatively becomes sufficiently strong, and without warning or provocation, strikes. A scenario not unlike the one depicted in *Terminator*, where Skynet, an artificial general superintelligence system that gained self-awareness, decides to strike humans with a nuclear attack, an event christened in the film series as Judgement Day.

A superintelligent AI that is vastly smarter than us can quickly become unpredictable and uncontrollable. The Golem myth has already predicted "the control problem"—the problem of how to control AI before it may turn against us. The issue was raised in recent times by many distinguished scientists, philosophers, and AI developers, among them Stephen Hawking, Elon Musk, Max Tegmark and Bill Gates.

The parallels between the Golem of Prague and artificial intelligence are remarkable. Their shared purpose, autonomy and learning abilities, ethical considerations and capacity to inspire awe highlight the enduring human fascination with creating entities that resemble us and can assist us in navigating the complexities of life. Despite their historical and technological disparities, both the Golem and AI serve as reminders of humanity's timeless quest to explore, understand, and harness the immense potential of our own creations.

The Golem and his maker

The Golem and his maker

Chapter 24

Glastonbury: The Temple of Britain

The Somerset town of Glastonbury has been described as Britain's only true national shrine, the *omphalos* or Temple of Britain. It was Avalon, the western isle of the dead, a centre of ancient mysteries known from the earliest times as a place of supreme national sanctity. The location was held in reverence by the Druids and their immediate sucessors, the Celtic saints. Significantly, Glastonbury was also known as the English Jerusalem. John Michell[53] described it as a prime example of the holy city as described in Revelation 21, of which these verses are a part:

> 1 And I saw a new heaven and a new earth: for the first heaven and the first earth were passed away; and there was no more sea.
>
> 2 And I John saw the holy city, New Jerusalem, coming down from God out of heaven, prepared as a bride adorned for her husband.
>
> 12 And had a wall great and high, and had twelve gates, and at the gates twelve angels, and names written thereon, which are the names of the twelve tribes of the children of Israel:
>
> 14 And the wall of the city had twelve foundations, and in them the names of the twelve apostles of the Lamb.
>
> 15 And he that talked with me had a golden reed to measure the city, and the gates thereof, and the wall thereof.
>
> 16 And the city lieth foursquare, and the length is as large as the breadth: and he measured the city with the reed, twelve thousand furlongs. The length and the breadth and the height of it are equal.
>
> 17 He measured the wall thereof, an hundred and forty and four cubits, according to the measure of a man, that is, of the angel.

Among the numerous legends associated with Glastonbury is the

---

[53] Ibid

enduring story that identifies it as the location of the world's first Christian church, founded shortly after the Crucifixion by twelve missionaries, including St. Joseph of Arimathea, sent from Gaul by the apostle St. Philip. Some versions say the date was 63 CE, others 37, the latter being more likely as it was only a few years after the Crucifixion.

In the legend Joseph was accompanied by the sister of Veronica, the woman who wiped the face of Christ when He fell under the weight of the Cross on His way to Calvary. Later, the account developed into the story that Jesus had left an image of His face on the cloth. This napkin became the Vera Icon, the True Representation of Christ, from which the name Veronica derives. Joseph planted his staff upon Wearyall Hill where it took root and blossomed into the holy thorn, a species according to botanists that comes only from the Levant.

Below the hill Joseph decided to build a church to settle his community of first Christians. He obtained from Glastonbury's ruler King Arviragus a grant of land consisting of 12 hides (1440 acres) and on it was founded a church dedicated to the Virgin Mary. Just as in ancient Delphi where a federal assembly of 12 tribes administered the rights of Apollo, from this time forward the Twelve Hides held a privileged status.

John Michell's studies of the dimensions of Glastonbury Abbey indicated that St Joseph's settlement was constructed in accordance with an ancient scheme of cosmology in the design of a pre-Christian temple that had formerly occupied the same site. Local lore has it that in the church they kept relics associated with the Grail, the mystical talisman of fertility. According to Michell,[54] when Celtic missionaries chose a location to establish a Christian presence, their first tzzpdiacask was to build an oratory at the centre of their ring of cells. Thereafter, the priests would maintain a ceaseless vigil accompanied by a perpetual chant, a sacred intonation whose magical effect was to weave an enchanting spell over the surrounding landscape.

Accounts speak of a perpetual choir comprising 12 evangelising choristers singing 12-section plainchant, a custom that originated in the East and later adopted by the Druids, who themselves were an outgrowth from Britain's early Celtic settlers. This music also had an astrological aspect that was reflected physically in the landmarks and contours of the surrounding countryside. Each segment had its own symbols, music and myth to represent its unique one-twelfth part of the astrological cycle. William of Malmesbury called Glastonbury's temple area a "heavenly

---

[54] Ibid

sanctuary on earth."[55]

In about 166 two missionaries sent by Pope Eleutherius, Saints Phagan and Deruvian, renewed over a nine-year period the old wattle building (referred to as the *Vetusta Ecclesia*, "Old Church"), appointing 12 of their brethren to continue the rituals of the former twelve.

In 433 Patrick became the first abbot of Glastonbury, and established a monastery with 12 anchorites in residence. Patrick may have been the one responsible for enclosing the round wattle church by a rectangular wooden church.

Early in the 6th century, St David visited Glastonbury and claimed the church as one of his twelve foundations, adding a building at its east end. William of Malmesbury said that some time later another church was built by Glasteing, one of the 12 brothers from the north of England.

In 601 Gwrgan Varvtrwch, King of Dumnonia, gave the land of Yns-witrin to the Old Church under the auspices of Abbot Worgret. This made the whole region of Yns-witrin a monastic island.

In 633 Paulinus, Bishop of Saxon York and a companion of St Augustine, encased the Old Church in wooden boards covered with lead in an effort to preserve the deteriorating sacred fabric.

In 704 or 708 the Saxon King Ide of Wessex completed the stone church dedicated to Saints Peter and Paul to the east of the wooden church. Ide's charter, signed in the wooden church, affirmed the rights of Glastonbury's seven islands as a sanctuary in perpetuity.

In 943, St Dunstan placed the monastery under Benedictine rule, linking all the old buildings into one large one. Immediately after the monastery's destruction by fire in 1184, monks under the stewardship of King Henry II's chamberlain, Ralph Fitzstephen, began the task of reconstruction.

The first task was to build a magnificent stone chapel on the site of Old Church dedicated to St Mary in order to re-establish swiftly the holy link with the Virgin and to preserve the sacred dimensions of the original wattle shrine. The title of *Vetusta Ecclesia* henceforward became the hallowed name of the new St Mary Chapel, a sacred place of worship built on the site of the original wattle church.

Claims that the remains of Arthur and Guinevere were unearthed in 1190 are disputed. In 1191 the bones of three bodies, said to be those of Arthur, Guinevere and the treacherous Mordred, were discovered on the south side of the Lady Chapel at Glastonbury Abbey. The tomb was found between two columns in the Abbey cemetery. On its leaden cross

[55] Michell, J. and Rhone, C., *Twelve Tribe Nation*, Inner Traditions, 1991

was inscribed: “Hic jacet sepultus inclytus Rex Arthurus in insula Avallonia.”[56] The remains, together with their magnificent black marble tomb, disappeared at the time of the Dissolution in the 16th century.

*

Michell confirmed that in the history of the 12 hides and in the dimensions of St. Joseph’s Chapel could be found proof of the identity of Glastonbury as the New Jerusalem, the holy city of Revelation. A hide is defined as the amount of land which can be cultivated by one man and support one family. The precise area covered by 12 hides varies in different parts of Britain but, according to Geoffrey Ashe, in Glastonbury the accepted measure is 120 acres. 12 hides are therefore equivalent to 1440 acres, and this is the area of the plan of the New Jerusalem given by St. John.

An acre is 4840 square yards, so a square area of 1440 acres has a side of 7920 feet, which is 12 furlongs. (In British imperial lengths one furlong is one-eighth of a mile, 660 feet, 220 yards, 40 rods or 10 chains.) Twelve hides, therefore, is simply another description of St. John’s holy city which was a square of 12,000 furlongs.

Following the pattern of the New Jerusalem, a circle is inscribed within the square; this is the wall 14,400 cubits round. Within the circle is placed a hexagon, and the rectangle is drawn on its two parallel sides. The dimensions of this rectangle, whose sides are as 1:∛, are 3960 x 6860 feet, and this is 100 times the existing dimensions of St. Joseph’s Chapel at Glastonbury.

In fact, measurements show that the external width of the chapel should be 39.6 feet, although it is now a few inches longer on account of the inaccurate restoration of the south-west pier, and the length is about 68.6 feet. The true length was lost when the chapel was joined to the main body of the Abbey church at the time of the rebuilding in the twelfth century.

At one time a stone monument marked the original eastern limit of St. Joseph’s Chapel but it has long vanished. In any case, the dimensions of the present chapel, which have always been known to possess mystical significance, are so nearly in agreement with those of the ∛ rectangle that the intention is plain.

---

[56] “Here lies buried the renowned King Arthur in the Isle of Avalon”

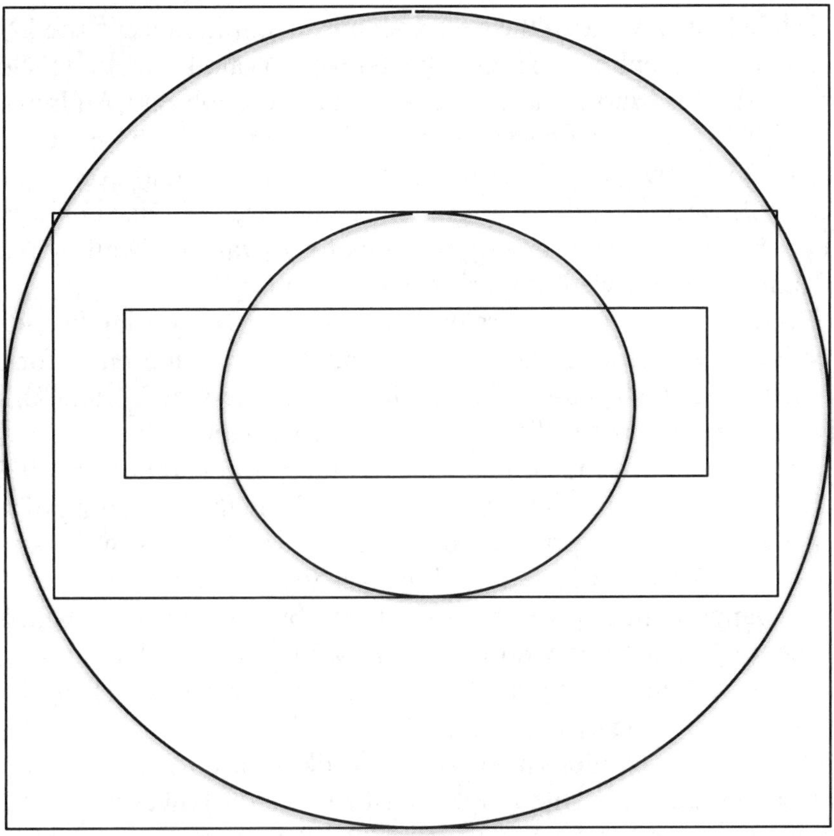

The cosmological foundation of Glastonbury—the diagram shows the groundplan of St. Mary's Chapel, the site of St. Joseph's circular wattle church, of which William of malmesbury wrote, 'The Church at Glastonbury did none other men's hands make, but actual Disciples of Christ built it.' The present chapel was built after the fire of 1184 which destroyed the ancient buildings, and its dimensions were set out to conform to the sacred geometry of the original foundations. These traditions are combined in the figure above. The dimensions of the existing chapel are 39.6 x 68.6 feet, a ratio of $1 = \sqrt[3]{}$. A property of the $\sqrt[3]{}$ rectangle is that the diameter of the circle contained within it is half of the diameter of the circle in which the rectangle itself is contained. Here the diameter of the inner circle is 39.6 feet, of the outer circle 79.2 feet. The outer circle is now enclosed within a square whose side measures 79.2 feet; its perimiter is 316.8 feet and its area 1.44 acres or 0.012 hides. It is therefore a microcosm of the New Jerusalem, which is a square of side 12 furlongs or 7920 feet and area 1440 acres or 12 hides each of 120 acres. The area of the inner circle is 166.5 sq MY, 1665 being the Gematria number of *το πνεύμα της γης*, the Spirit of the Earth, which explains the original dedication of the Chapel to the Virgin.

Michell also wrote of the seven islands of significance in the 12 hides region of Glastonbury. These, the Isle of Avalon, Beckery, Godney (God's Island), Martinsea, Ferrameare, Panborough and Andrewsea or Nyland, were held sacred from the earliest times. Each was exempted from English law and neither monarch nor bishop could exert influence or control. Beckery, now a forgotten derelict area of Glastonbury, once had a very special place among the isles for it was the dwelling place of St Brigit, who followed St Patrick to Glastonbury.

Brigit lived by an old oratory dedicated to Mary Magdalene. This place is Bride's Mound and was once the disembarking place for boats. In legend Mary Magdalene landed here after the Crucifixion. Bride or Brigit or Brighde is the Triple Goddess of Brigantia, the ancient Celtic nation that included the British Isles, Brittany and parts of Spain. She is the Brigit of poetry inspiration and healing through the reciting of poetry at sacred wells and springs. She is Goddess of the New Moon. Her symbol is a White Swan and her flower is the snowdrop.

A chapel dedicated to St. Bridget was built on Little Ireland in the fifth century. The nuns who lived here were said to celebrate Easter at the Aries full moon, no matter the day of the week. They lived in accordance with the cycles of the Moon Goddess.

St Bridget's emblem as a woman milking a cow, a symbol of the nurturing Goddess, is still visible on St Michael's Tower on the Tor and around the doorway to St Mary's Chapel in the Abbey. Until quite recently the Mound was surrounded by the tidal waters of the River Brue, which one could cross at Pomparles Bridge (the "Pons Perilous" in the Grail legends).

Beckery is intimately connected with Grail stories. According to John of Glastonbury it was the site of the Chapel Perilous in the Arthurian romances, which record a visit by Arthur. According to legend the king came to the Magdalene Chapel at dawn one Ash Wednesday to find the door guarded by fiery swords. Inside, an aged priest was conducting mass, assisted by the Virgin Mary. She offered up her Son as a sacrifice to the world. Afterwards, Mary gifted Arthur with an equal-armed crystal cross whose image he engraved on his shield in silver and green, later becaming a treasure of the Abbey.

In 1529 during Henry VIII's Reformation the last Abbot of Glastonbury, Richard Whiting, was dragged on a hurdle to the top of the Tor and hanged because he refused to divulge the hiding place of the Abbey's treasures. His body was dismembered and exhibited around the country. The monks were dispersed, the lead was stripped from the roof, the carved rood screen was burned to melt the bells and the residents of

Somerset used the stone from the walls as a quarry.

Although the day may yet emerge when physical treasures are revealed, the true essence of Glastonbury's riches is a spiritual quality that the sincere truthseeker aspires to receive. The very air, stone and landscape of Glastonbury are infused with powerful feelings of imminent revelation concerning the fulfilment of certain prophecies. One such concerns the sixth century Book of Melchin, a lost volume of the Glastonbury library. According to contemporary chroniclers it contained the oracle of Melchin, which states that the tomb of St Joseph, together with the Grail talisman, will one day be discovered, and "Thenceforth nor water nor the dew of heaven shall fail the dwellers on that ancient isle."

The prophecy chimes with the legend of the Fisher-King, an occupant of the Glastonbury marshes whose healing, according to the Grail romances, shall make his barren kingdom flourish and restore the primeval Hyperborean Golden Age. On his deathbed, Austin Ringwode, the last of the monks expelled from the Abbey, proclaimed, 'The Abbey will one day be repaired and rebuilt for the like worship which has now ceased; and then peace and plenty will for a long time abound.' Powerful prophecies such as these nourish the long-held belief that Glastonbury is the English Jerusalem.

In 1907 the Church of England acquired Glastonbury Abbey and its environs. It appointed Frederick Bligh Bond as Director of Excavations to oversee a deep study of the Abbey's history and foundations. Bond, an authority on mediaeval architecture and ecclesiastical restoration, undertook his work very successfully.

Bond uncovered the foundations of previously unknown parts of the old Abbey, including the foundation walls of the now ruined St Edgar's Chapel. No matter where Bond turned his attention, he always seemed to dig in exactly the right spot to make important discoveries. In 1918 he revealed in his book *The Gate of Remembrance* that his successes were owed to spiritualistic channelings in the form of automatic writing.

Friends of Bond had received messages purporting to be from spirit world representatives of the Company of the Watchers of Avalon, a body of former monks of Glastonbury Abbey whose names were given in the book and in a later one of Bond's, *The Company of Avalon*. The messages revealed details on the Abbey's structure and history and Bond's interpretation of these had allowed him to make his startling discoveries. In one message Bond learned that Glastonbury's history as a place of special reverence dates back to the time of Atlantis:

Glastonbury Tor, photographs by the author, Summer Solstice 2024

The flow of spiritual forces is westward, following and impelling the forces of material things... Thus they whose habitation was in Crete, revisiting the memories and traditions of others of the same race... continued the interminable route ever westward beyond the gates of Hercules to the islands where the first fire-drawn metals be... but soon the spiritual forces which developed and sustained this immigration had deeper objects in view. They followed and transformed it by removing mundane influences and a great spiritual development arose in the places in which their instruments had prepared the soil. Phocis of the race of Crete trading with Poseidon [Atlantis]... *was thus brought in contact with them who worshipped the One God... thus paved the way for the building of a Temple in his settlement of Tintagella... thus first arose that measurement and design which were afterwards as accurately reproduced by that further advance which culminated in the temple of Glastonbury. And Tintagella was the ancient place of the shrine of the High God. So the temple, a reproduction accurate in every measurement, was reproduced at Glaston on this foundation.*

Bond's automatic writing scripts also emphasised the importance of reconstructing the pattern on the floor of the Old Church at Glastonbury. He understood from the communications that the floor pattern reflected the dimensions of a New Jerusalem, wherein a new Gnosis would arise that incorporated the inspired synthesis of religion, philosophy, metaphysics and mystical science.

Among the many mystics drawn to Glastonbury in Bond's time were J. Foster Forbes and "psychometrist" medium Iris Campbell. Bond described one of Campbell's visions:

Beneath the abbey are remains of vast catacombs caused by natural upheavals. These are very deep down and it is through these underground channels that the magnetic currents of the world flowed. It was by this means that internal combustion was caused, known as the secret fires of the earth... Now the Glastonbury Tor is raised over an epicentre of magnetism, and that which is located there is continually churning up underneath... The contemplative order of monks drawn to this ancient site of Glaston - knowing as they did of these terrestrial-cum-celestial mysteries - made it their life's work to pray for the peace of the world. This they did by projecting their thoughts to the seething underworld.[57]

The revelation that Bond's work was guided and inspired by what was regarded as little more than demonism in the eyes of the Church caused a furore, during which he was roundly condemned by archaeologists and eccliastical authorities alike. It was vital that the church should suffer no further scandal. Bond was sidelined and another architect brought in to supervise his work. Presently, when it became evident that Bond was in no way contrite about his spiritualist leanings, he was dismissed. Bond retired an embittered figure. To heap more humiliation on Bond, his excavations were grassed over, his discoveries erased from the official Abbey plans and his books removed from the Abbey bookstall.

If the authorities thought that these actions would reverse continuing episodes of anti-Christian involvement in the Abbey's affairs they were sorely mistaken. Soon, Glastonbury became a focal point for "New Age" revivalists whose ranks were not solely populated by mystics but by men of the cloth, among them Rev. Lionel Smithett Lewis who published *St Joseph of Arimathea at Glastonbury* and Rev. C.C. Dobson who penned *Did Our Lord Visit Britain as they say in Cornwall and Somerset?* From the secular perspective, Kathryn Maltwood in the 1930s alerted the world to her astonishing discovery of the Glastonbury Zodiac during her research into the Arthurian *High History of the Holy Grail*.

Gradually, Frederick Bligh Bond's work attracted new converts who recognized that his discoveries were years ahead of their time. In 1968, architect Keith Critchlow visited Glastonbury to check for himself Bond's claims that existing within the Abbey layout and structure is a scheme of sacred number and proportion. Critchlow concluded that Bond's findings were correct and went on to suggest that there may be a connection between the design of the original wattle settlement and the geometry of the Twelve Hides purportedly granted to St Joseph of Arimathea and his company.

Critchlow's supposition bore fruit when it turned out that the dimensions of the St Mary chapel were a microcosm of the geometry incorporated into the dimensions of the Twelve Hides. This is not the place to go into the particulars of the Abbey's geometry (many have

---

[57] Forbes, J. & Campbell, I., *Giants, Myths and Megaliths*, William Chudley, 1973

covered the subject very well, the most cogent and compelling, in my opinion, being John Michell) but, suffice to say, the overall scheme and its archetypal cosmological framework is one that features in the foundations of temples and places of veneration throughout the ancient world. William of Malmesbury made reference to this mystical archaeology when he wrote of the mosaic design on the floor of the St Mary Chapel:

> *This church, then, is certainly the oldest I know in England, and from this circumstance deserves its name* (Vetusta Ecclesia)*... In the pavement may be seen on every side stones designedly inlaid in triangles and squares, and figured with lead, under which, if I believe some sacred enigma to be contained, I do no injustice to religion.*

William's remarks are supplemented by the content of Bligh Bond's automatic scripts, one of which stated:

> *All ye measures were marked plaine on ye slabbes in Mary's Chappel, and ye have destroyed them. So it was recorded, as they who builded and they who came after knew aforehand where they should build. But these things are overpast and of no value now... There was the Body of Christ, and round him would have been the Four Ways. Two were ybuilded and no more. In ye floor of ye Mary Chappel was ye Zodiac, that all might see and understand the mystery. In ye midst of ye Chapel he was laid; and the Cross of Hym who was our Example and Exemplar... Braineton, he didde much, for he was Geomancer to ye Abbey of old tyme.*

Taking as his starting point William of Malmesbury's description of St Mary's Chapel, Bond visualised the original wattle church as a circular structure that was surrounded by twelve smaller circular cells in which dwelt Joseph and his fellow saints. Another script stated that Joseph's structure was not the first to be located on the site. A pagan temple had previously existed there and it was the dimensions of this much earlier sanctuary that Joseph and his followers took great pains to preserve in the wattle church.

John Michell's careful measurements revealed that the dimensions of the original Glastonbury saints' twelve cells relate in size to the larger round church they encircled as the moon relates to the earth. The dimensions also correspond to those of the New Jerusalem as specified in Revelation, xxi. A script that came forward in connection with this remarkable fact said:

> *You know that in this designing of the Floor* (of the Old Church) *lies the future prophecy of Glastonbury, together with the inward secret of Christianity.*

.

Queen Guinevere bestowing Knighthood

Frederick Bligh Bond

The Glastonbury Zodiac

> *In the great mystery schools... the human body was chosen as the first study... Pictures and models of the human body were to be found in the inner temples... with every part related to some sign of the zodiac. The astrological and astronomical knowledge of the wise teachers and priests enabled the neophyte to open his understanding and his consciousness to respond to the universal powers... Through knowledge of astrological influences operating on the various parts of the body, the man obtained understanding of true healing. He recognized such influences as affecting his own life and developing that second aspect of his being, and thus opened up a world described as the 'underworld'... the 'soul world.*
>
> —British medium Grace Cooke's spirit-guide, "White Eagle"

The term zodiac is derived from the Greek ζῳδιακός κύκλος, which means "a circle of animals" or "little animals." It is the name given by the old pagan astronomers to a band of fixed stars about sixteen degrees wide, apparently encircling the earth. Zōidion (ζῴδιον) is the diminutive of zōion (ζῷον, "anima"), an expression originating from the primitive Egyptian radicals, *zo*, life, and *on*, a being. The name reflects the prominence of animals and mythological hybrids among the signs.

The Greeks, and later other peoples influenced by their culture, divided the band of the zodiac into twelve sections, each being sixteen degrees in width and thirty degrees in length. These divisions were called the Houses of the Zodiac. The sun during its annual pilgrimage passed through each of these in turn. Imaginary creatures were traced in the star groups bounded by these rectangles. Because most of them were animal or part animal in form, they later became known as the Constellations or Signs of the Zodiac.

The first six signs of the zodiac of twelve signs were regarded as benevolent, because the sun occupied them while traversing the Northern Hemisphere. The 6,000 years during which, according to the Persians Ahura-Mazda, Zoroastrian Creator of the Universe, ruled His universe in harmony and peace, were symbolic of these six signs.

The second six were considered malevolent, because while the sun was travelling in the Southern Hemisphere it was winter with the Greeks, Egyptians and Persians. Therefore, these six months were symbolic of the 6,000 years of misery and suffering caused by the evil genius of the Persians, Ahriman (the "Devil"), who sought to overthrow the power of

Ahura-Mazda.

In ancient cosmology the supreme council of the gods is composed of twelve deities—six male and six female—that correspond in the sense of polarity to the positive and negative signs of the zodiac. The six gods are Jupiter, Vulcan, Apollo, Mars, Neptune, and Mercury; the six goddesses Juno, Ceres, Vesta, Minerva, Venus, and Diana.

In the Grail romances St Joseph of Arimathea's sister, Enygeus, married Bran, the Celtic Keeper of the Grail, and bore him twelve children. In the stories, Joseph went on to establish the Round Table, guarded by twelve Knights of the Holy Grail. Later, Arthur re-established in the Glastonbury region the order of Knights, symbolised by the image of the sun passing through the twelve houses of the zodiac. The "Rule of 12" and the Zodiac motif, the latter both physically and figuratively, thus become critical features in Celtic Christian cosmology.

When on a summer's day in 1925 Katherine Maltwood's inner vision captured an image of the Glastonbury Zodiac, she may have been the first person to see the secret design in the landscape for many thousands of years. Great minds gone before, such as Dr. John Dee, William Stukely and William Blake, had caught glimpses of the celestial pattern but had not been permitted a vision of the whole planisphere.

Ancient Britons were familiar with energetic earthen forms and referenced them in the language of the countryside in stories. They spoke of Dragons "of such extent that grass grew upon their backs." Some said they were "five acres" large, while others described them as so great "that riders on opposite sides could not see each other."

Maltwood, née Sapsworth, was born in Essex and brought up in her parents' large Italianate home, "Higham Lodge," in Woodford Green. Her father was a wealthy leather merchant and sometime local mayor. In 1901 she married John Maltwood, a wealthy advertising manager whose fortune enabled Katherine to devote her life to travel, collecting, sculpture and writing. Her sculpturing activities were particularly impressive. She studied at the Slade and exhibited regularly at the London Salon, the Royal Academy and at various other London galleries. In 1925 Katherine was commissioned by the British publisher Dent to draw an itinerary of the Grail Quest for its Everyman edition of the *High History of the Holy Grail*, newly translated into English by Dr. Sebastian Evans. So accurately does this mediaeval work describe the Somerset landscape that many believe it to have been written by a monk at Glastonbury Abbey. Interest in the adventures of King Arthur's Knights and the Holy Grail had been revived and made popular in the Victorian era by the Pre-Raphaelites and Alfred, Lord Tennyson.

> *The Round Table was constructed, not without great significance, upon the advice of Merlin. By its name the Round Table is meant to signify the round world and round canopy of the planets and the elements in the firmament, where are to be seen the stars and many other things*
>
> —La Queste del Saint Graal

Maltwood was convinced that the book set out the secret location of the rumoured zodiac effigies in the Somerset countryside, the place where Grail writers had located the adventures of King Arthur. Setting up home in the Polden Hills, Maltwood dedicated herself to the task of re-discovery. Presently, she was drawn to certain configurations in the hills and waterways, which she perceived as symbolic figures.

One summer afternoon, Maltwood was standing on a low hill watching the shadows move across the plain that stretches towards Cadbury Hill. Suddenly, she recognized the profiles of a lion and a woman partly outlined by the river Cary near Somerton about four miles south of Glastonbury and interpreted these as the symbols for Leo and Virgo. Maltwood went on to identify ten other effigies within a 10-mile diameter circle. Glastonbury Tor is its northern point. Somerton and Lyte's Cary bound it to the south and to Cadbury Hill. Its centre is at Butleigh ("centre of the wheel"), three miles south of the Tor. Maltwood's named the zodiac the Temple of the Stars.

> *We have often been told that astronomy is found in a developed form among the ancient Baylonions, traceable to 3000 B.C., but not until I discovered this 'Temple of the Stars' in Somerset in 1925 A.D. and photographed it from the air, have we been able to define... the original features forming the Zodiac.*
>
> — Katherine Maltwood, *The Enchantments of Britain*

Maltwood perceived the whole design as the original Round Table. She plotted her zodiac onto Ordnance Survey (OS) Landranger Maps together with the Celestial Equator, the Equinox as it would have appeared in 2700 BCE, the stars forming the 12 zodiac constellations and the 12 astrological divisions. The heads of 11 of the effigies are turned to the west, the sunset. Some effigies such as Leo, Sagittarius and Pisces are 2-3 miles long. Each is delineated by natural features: hills, earthworks, watercourses, dykes, mounds, barrows, ditches, old roads and footpaths, streams and rivers.

A notable feature of Maltwood's zodiac is that the star constellations are squeezed so that between Pisces and Aquarius there is a gap in which to fit a thirteenth constellation. Maltwood said that 10 of the 12 signs were easily discernible (although the traditional Aquarius figure is replaced by a phoenix, Libra and Cancer by a dove and a boat, and there are three fish in Pisces, the third being a whale). Significantly, if a planisphere is placed behind an OS Map and the stars and constellations are pricked through they do correspond on or near their counterparts in the zodiac pattern. Pilots have reported this good fit and aerial photos also support the layout.

The signs' correlation with tales in the *High History of the Holy Grail* suggests that the zodiac architects had a pre-cognition of the Arthur saga more than 3,000 years before the reputed time of Camelot and the Knights of the Round Table. In 1935 Maltwood published her findings in *Glastonbury's Temple of the Stars*. Her theory was that the zodiac was a combination of influences from Sumeria (from which she thought the name of Somerset may derive), Theosophy, Masonry, Egyptosophy, early Christianity and Rosicrucianism.

Maltwood perceived the whole design as the original Round Table. She plotted her zodiac onto Ordnance Survey (OS) Landranger Maps together with the Celestial Equator, the Equinox as it would have appeared in 2700 BCE, the stars forming the 12 zodiac constellations and the 12 astrological divisions. The heads of 11 of the effigies are turned to the west, the sunset. Some effigies such as Leo, Sagittarius and Pisces are 2-3 miles long. Each is delineated by natural features—hills, earthworks, watercourses, dykes, mounds, barrows, ditches, old roads and footpaths, streams and rivers.

A notable feature of Maltwood's zodiac is that the star constellations are squeezed so that between Pisces and Aquarius there is a gap in which to fit a thirteenth constellation. Maltwood said that 10 of the 12 signs were easily discernible. Significantly, if a planisphere is placed behind an OS Map and the stars and constellations are pricked through they do correspond on or near their counterparts in the zodiac pattern.

Mary Caine[58] has calculated that the odds against the 12 signs of the Zodiac occurring on the ground in their correct placements are

---

[58] Roberts, A. (Ed.), *Glastonbury: Ancient Avalon, New Jerusalem*, Rider, 1978

480,000,000 to 1. These mammoth odds increase if one considers that the winter signs are all to the north, the summer ones to the south and the three human figures—the Trinity comprising Sagittarius, Virgo and Gemini form an equilateral triangle across the circle. Moreover, the fact that when the planisphere is placed on the map the zodiac constellations fit over their earthly forms lengthens the immense odds even further.

Maltwood's ideas were very negatively received for many years. Frankly, they were (and are) too much of a stretch for orthodox archaeology, which says that no Middle Eastern people were in Britain during the period when Maltwood claimed the zodiac was constructed. Critics claim that anyone can select lines on a map that can be joined to make "meaningful patterns." Her technique has also been likened to the phenomenon of *pareidolia*, whereby we look into flames, stains, wood grain and so on and see images that remind us of other things.

Maltwood's design was examined by two independent studies, one by Ian Burrow in 1975 and the other in 1983 by Tom Williamson and Liz Bellamy, using standard methods of landscape historical research. They concluded that the evidence weighed against Maltwood's findings. They identified waymarkers on the design that were either of relatively recent historical origin (the western wing of the Aquarius phoenix was a road laid in 1782, and the Cancer boat is made up of a network of eighteenth century drainage ditches and paths) or were present day features.

Looking at the studies' findings objectively, they contain nothing that rules out the veracity of Maltwood's zodiac temple. Landscape features, either naturally or artificially made or re-shaped, could easily have eroded over time only to become re-defined by the actions of a later road-builder, ditch digger or farmer. Archaeologists also fail to grasp that a thorough study of the zodiac requires not just digging tools but input from astronomy, astrology, anthropology, folklore, history, esoteric tradition and help from archivists and experts in ancient languages such as Hebrew, Aramaic, Akkadian, Greek and the Celtic dialects.

More recent archaeological work has gone some way to vindicate Maltwood's theories. Professors John and Bryony Coles of Cambridge have undertaken diggings west of Glastonbury at Shapswick Heath and discovered causeway roads, consisting of a double layer of logs buried in peat.[59] Carbon dating reports a reading of 2,800 BCE, a very near match to Maltwood's research findings.

---

[59] *Somerset Levels Papers* (1975-1989), and *Sweet Track to Glastonbury* (1986)

Moreover, an 80-year-old OS Map of Glastonbury shows menhirs in the zodiac area, which were subsequently removed. These formed an alignment with astronomical significance, marking points of critical significance and direction for the Temple of Avalon. In any case, Maltwood was not the first to make these observations. Co-founder of Theosophy, Helena P. Blavatsky, had also insisted fifty years earlier that missionaries from Egpyt fanned out worldwide to create four zodiacs, including the one at Glastonbury.

More recently, Michell[60] described the Seven Isles of Glastonbury as places of special interest for those who formerly inhabited the area within the Twelve Hides region. Each had its own community of monks who served and maintained their chapels. The clerics' veneration was inspired by the special secret they shared. When the seven islands are plotted on a map they reveal the pattern of the Constellation of the Great Bear. Glastonbury corresponds to the star Dubhe on which the constellation pivots.

The Great Bear is long associated with Arthur, the name deriving from "Arth Fawr," meaning Great Bear. It is also associated with Arcturus (Greek for "Keeper of the Bear"), the brightest star in the Northern Hemisphere. Early English tribesfolk called the Great Bear "Arthur's Wain" or "Arthur's Wagon," the vehicle in which Arthur circles the celestial pole. Other names for the Great Bear are the Plough and Arator (the Ploughman).

The fact that the Seven Isles area resembles the Great Bear suggested to John Michell that other constellations must exist in the Glastonbury landscape with the Tor representing the Pole Star, the star nearest to the imaginary line through the heavens produced by the northenward extension of the earth's axis. Michell also considered the possibility that British priest-astronomers first perceived the Seven Isles as a microcosmic mirror image of the Great Bear when the Pole Star was located in the head of Draco at the end of the last Ice Age. Such a prominent celestial event may have been immortalised in the story of Arthur's father, King Uther (Uthyr in Welsh meaning wonderful) Pen*dragon*.

---

[60] Michell, J., *New Light on the Ancient Mystery of Glastonbury*, Thrift Books, 1990

Katherine Emma Maltwood, re-discoverer of the Glastonbury Zodiac

Uther Pendragon by Howard Pyle

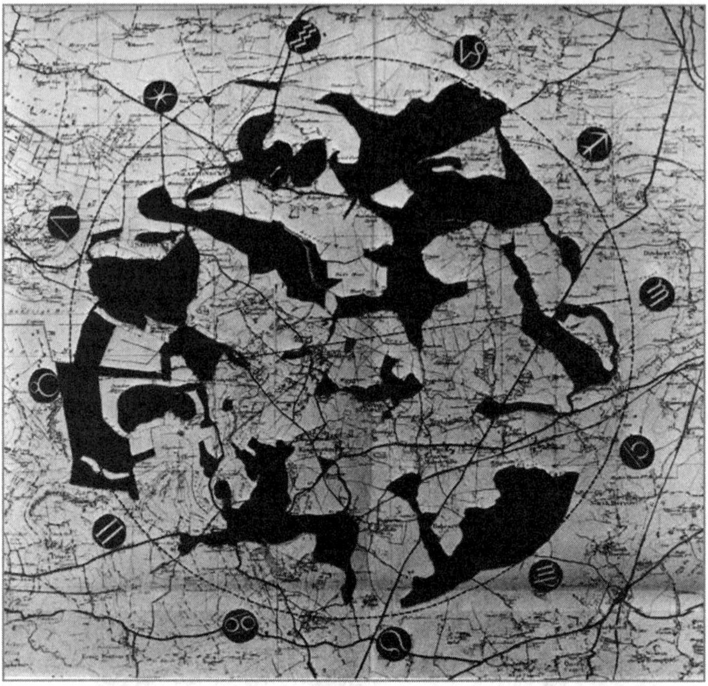

Mrs Maltwood's Zodiac Temple of the Stars

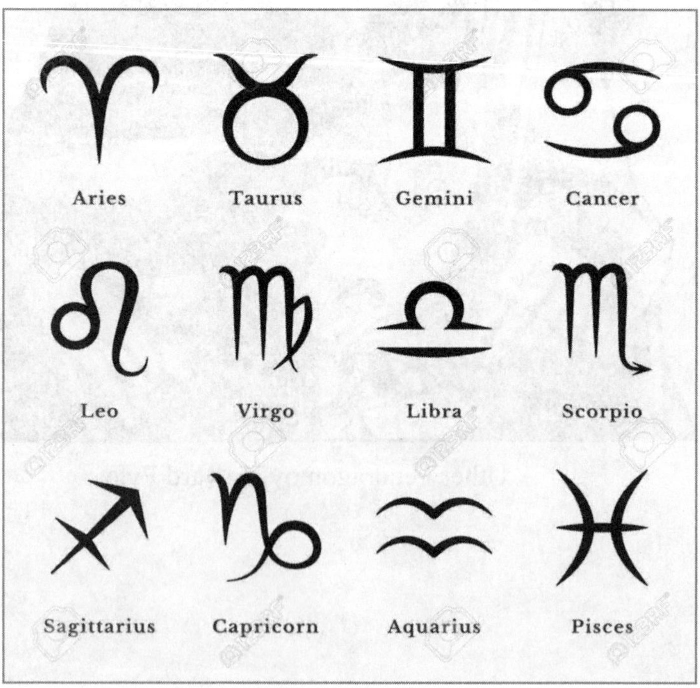

Zodiac symbols with their names

The Glastonbury Zodiac and its forms in the landscape

Aries

Since ancient times, the first sign of the heavenly zodiac is Aries. In the Somerset design the effigy is two miles long and shaped not as a ram but as a Paschal Lamb. It is located at the ten o'clock position around the zodiac circle. The shape is traced out in the landscape on a medieaval farm, together with an eagle at Lower Wick. Its head is reverted at the town of Street, just over two miles south of Glastonbury. Its back follows the contours of the Polden Hills. Walton Hill delineates Aries' body, its adjacent fields accurately marking out the form of its haunches. The stained glass at Walton church depicts two Arien stories: one of Abraham and Isaac with the ram in the thicket, and another of Christ shown as the good shepherd holding a lamb. The paschal lamb of the Jewish Passover is also carved onto the font.

Taurus

Moving widdershins around the circle we come to Taurus, an effigy touched by the folded knee of Aries. Taliesin wrote, '*A holy sanctuary there is, on the wide lake; a city not protected with walls... The sacred ox of the patriarch is stationed before the lake.*'

In legend, Mithras slays the Constellation of Taurus and nourishes the Universe with its blood.

In Maltwood's cosmological scheme her effigy for the Bull is a depiction of the Mother Goddess, symbolising creation. Just one mile long, it is laid out over Compton, Trays Farm, Redlands and Castlebrook. Its neck is on Collard Hill, which is the site of its actual collar. Through the beech trees on his collar can be seen Glastonbury Tor. A ridge of land projecting out from the head towards Combe Hill forms the horn, which overlooks Combe Hollow. Looking south, one sees Gemini sleeping on Lollover and Dundon Hills. Ploughman's lynchets that curve around Hatch Hill make furrows in his horns. More recently, another horn has been added, marked by Hood Monument crowned by a tall stone 18th century obelisk. Its tail is at Asney (Mary Caine wonders if this refers to "Agnus Dei"). The Bull's lower jaw is at Street, his tucked-under feet at Ivybarn Hill, his chest and the back of his head traced by the old tin-track from Somerset to the Mendip Hills through Glastonbury. Its haunches are centred on Walton Hill. A former pond at Tray's Farm marks his Bull's-eye. The Pleiades fall on his collar. In an undoubted reference to the sign, Taliesin said: '*They know not the brindled ox with his thick headband and the seven-score knobs on his collar.*'

Gemini

One and half miles long, the Heavenly Twin of Dundon Hill is marked out over Castlebrook, Emblett Lane and Lollover Hill. Its head is the steep British Camp of Dundon Hill (the "fort of Don or wisdom"). It is lolling in sleep posture (Lollover Hill is in Gemini's lower body). His eyebrow by Dundon Smithy is marked by the entrance to an orchard. Lynchets trace his ribcage on Lollover Hill. Caine later identified the Second Twin within the form of Katherine Maltwood's Griffin effigy. He is the same size as his brother and set at right angles to him. His head, facing west, is at Lugshorn to the east. Bradley Hill models his body. Maltwood found that the ship's planks on which Gemini sits measure one-thirteenth of the zodiac circle and conceal the 13th moon-month of the Druids. The recurring "13th" motif suggests that Emblett Lane may represent the Greek "embelos," meaning intercalation.

Cancer

This sign is drawn in the form of a crescent-shaped boat to the south of Gemini. The ship's planks are drawn by the dykes that drain a marsh, which winds round Gemini's hills in the Redlake Farm, Liver Moor and river Cary region. The ship is cradling a baby, which symbolises Cancer's lunar, maternal character. In C.W. King's *The Gnostics* there is an illustration of a baby in a ship. The prow is carved on the head of a griffin-like creature beneath a crescent moon (the traditional Cancer symbol).

Where the stern is positioned is an ox-head with a 4-pointed star above it, representing the Sun in Taurus. In the Glastonbury Zodiac the griffin effigy lies under the jurisdiction of Cancer and is resting at one end of the vessel carrying the Gemini child. The Taurus effigy is situated at the other end of the canal-drawn ship. Maltwood links the ship with both King Solom's ship in Mallory's *Morte d'Artur* and the Padstow hobbyhorse, the body of the latter traditionally portrayed as an upturned boat.

Leo

> *There is a formidable animal from the city of Satanas, which has made an inroad between the deep and the shallows. His mouth is as wide as the mountains of Mynnau: neither death shall vanquish him, nor hand, nor sword. There* (are) *nine hundred rocks between his two paws; there is but one eye in his head, vivid as the ice blue* - Taliesin

Situated to the right of Gemini's twin, Leo lies at Catsash Hundred, the "Field of the Lion," the only figure in the zodiac that has paws. His left front paw is weighed down by the "nine hundred rocks." The nearby villages of Catsgore and Catsham emphasise Leo's feline character. In the Celtic myths Arthur used to hunt the Cath Pulag, "Lion of the month of Lug the Sun-god." Three miles long, Britain's heraldic lion sits on the south of the zodiac. It is laid over Copley Woods, the ruined Roman villa of "Maggoty Paggoty" marked now by two stones, Christian's Cross, Charlton Adam, Lynches earthworks, the Little Dog of Littleton, Somerton, and the river Carey that draws Leo's underside. Leo's head is raised up on Hurcot, a district of Somerton. His jaws and lolling tongue are drawn by terraced lynchets on the side of Worley Hill and his muzzle is defined by Chabrick Millstream. The River Cary, rising from the Seven Lady Springs in Castle Cary, flows along Leo's ribs and foot. Its rump sits on Charlton Mackerell. Ancient trackways and footpaths delineate his back and front legs. Two pools of water known as Chalkham ponds mark his eyes.

W.T. Olcott pointed out in *Star Lore of All Ages* that, astrologically, Bristol, Bath and Taunton, all within thirty miles of the effigy, are ruled by Leo. The Druids worshipped Hu, the Sun God, personified in the ancient Greek pantheon as Mithras, Lord of the Sun. In the third and final degree of initiation into the Mithraic mysteries, the hierophant was given a cape upon which were drawn or woven the signs of the zodiac and other astronomical symbols. After his initiations were over he was hailed as one who had risen from the dead, having been instructed in the secret teachings of the Persian mystics. Candidates who successfully passed the Mithraic initiations were called Lions and were marked upon their foreheads with the Egyptian cross. Mithras himself is often pictured with the head of a lion and two pairs of wings. Throughout the entire ritual were repeated references to the birth of Mithras, his sacrifice for man, his death that men might have eternal life, and, lastly, his resurrection and the saving of all humanity by his intercession before Ormuzd, the supreme source of Light.Many later institutions exhibited Mithraic culture. In particular, the reference to the “Lion” and the “Grip of the Lion’s Paw” in the Master Mason’s degree have a Mithraic characteristic and may well have originated from this cult. A ladder of seven rungs appears in the Mithraic initiation. Scholars believe that this ladder was originally a pyramid of seven steps. May this help one to understand the original purpose behind the creation of the 7-tiered labyrinth on the Tor?

Virgo

Four miles long, Virgo is lying on her back with her head pointing west. She is outlined by Keinton Mandeville, Stickle Bridge, Yeovilton, Babcary, Wheathill, Annis Hill and the Fosse Way. The River Cary outlines her profile and front, her hands and back by roads, lanes and streams. At her feet we find Wheathill. Within her outline is the tumulus Wimble Toot. It falls where her breast (“bab”) would be. Bab is also Arabic for gate, while wimble means augury. Toot or moot hills were places where the locals once gathered to receive spiritual nourishment. Toot equates with old Welsh *twt*, lookout mound, and also with teat. Moot stems from the Welsh *maeth*, nourishment. In Virgo’s hands is a wheatsheaf formed by three lanes, a cone being a symbol for Isis, the Queen of Heaven, also used by the ancient Cypriots on their coinage for Venus. Cary is Ceridwen, the British Ceres, and also Keris of Cornish legend. Castle Cary’s British camp guards her, a reminder that Virgo in Glastonbury is associated with old Mother Cary, Britain’s sea-witch.

Stickle Bridge emphasises the broomstick in her hand. Here also is Mary Magdalene's Church, a reminder that the three Marys of the New Testament personified the Triple Goddess. Beneath her head is Annis Hill, representing Black Annis, the British Ceres, Mother Goddess of the Druids' Trinity, known variously as Anu, Danu and Annwn of the Underworld. Ansford at Castle Cary also echoes the name. The Virgin's pregnant womb is at Babcary.

Libra

Libra is represented not by scales but by a dove, one and a quarter miles long, hidden within the centre of the circle over the village of Barton St David and its network of paths and streams. Flying from the head of Sagittarius, the dove is traced by the little waterfall at Baltonsborough Flights, Catsham, the River Brue, Tootle Bridge and Barton St. David's Silver Street and Gosling Street. Hurtle Pool is on his wing.

Scorpio

Two miles in length and guarding the eastern approach to Avalon is the scorpion, its tail poised above the flank of the Centaur. Caine's revised form of Maltwood's effigy is traced by Parbrook, Stone, Hornblotton, Alford, the Fosse Way and Hell Ditch. The river Brue marks its southern boundary past Lovington's old mill. Churches at Alford and Ditcheat mark its tail. West Lydford lies at its tip. Lyd means gate, the threshold to King Lud's underworld. One claw nips Arthur's head at Catsham and the other pinches his seat at Parbrook. Banked ditches by Lottisham's Lower Farm mark Scorpio's head and mandibles. Its eight legs are marked by Four Foot Farm and Bridgefoot Farm.

Sagittarius

The five-mile long image of the Centaur, symbolised in British legend as Arthur of Avalon, is marked by Catshain, Baltonsborough, Ponter's Ball, Breech Lane, Canters Green, West Pennard, the Pennard Hills, Arthur's Bridge, West Bradley and Hell Ditch. The horse is modelled by Pennard Hill ("Arddur's hilltop"), and his body lies on the plain of Baltonsborough. West Bradley on the top of his leg was formerly known in the Domesday Book as Bodelege. On his tail is Arthur's Bridge. The waterfall at Baltonsborough Flights pours its waters into the wing of the Libran dove. Baltonsborough marks his helmeted head. The archer's leg is positioned near the Ponter's Ball linear earthwork at Havyatt in the Glastonbury parish of West Pennard. The name Havyatt was originally hagyatt, "hagy" meaning heaven or sacred place, and "yatt" gateway—the Gate to Avalon or the Summerland. (Somerset's Celtic name is "Gwlad yr Hav".) As the archer takes aim, his arm stretches almost to the centre of the zodiac at Park Wood.

Capricorn

Measuring three and a half miles, east to west, Capricorn is the northernmost figure in the zodiac. It is marked out by the Shepton Mallet-Glastonbury road, Ponter's Ball earthwork, Wick, Hearty Moor, Hartlake, Somerton, Fountains Wall, Barrow and Launcherly Hill. His shoulders emerge from the marshes around the Whitelake River. Arthur's leg descends into the horn of Capricorn. Its nose is pressed against the Tor. His back leg is the river Whitelake and runs down on to its hindquarters at Launcherly in the Pennard Hills. His feet are dipped into Hartlake; its chest wall faces onto Heart Moor. The great horn of the legendary supernatural goat said to haunt the Tor is at Ponter's Ball (some suggesting a derivation from the Etruscan "Puntes Bal": "sacrifice of Bel"), an area once known locally as the Golden Coffin. Mary Caine found a well-drawn back leg at North Wootton, thus improving on Maltwood's original design.

Aquarius

Aquarius is represented in the Glastonbury Zodiac as an Eagle or Phoenix, the precursor to the water-carrier. Measuring 1½ miles across with Glastonbury at its centre, Aquarius is delineated by Edmund Hill, Paradise Lane, Wick, South Down Hill, Edgarley, Ashwell Lane and Chalice Well. The Tor falls within the head of the bird, which is twisted round to face Chalice Hill. The hill is in its body and contains the red waters of Chalice Well, said to be the repository of the Holy Grail. The Tor's furrows mark the folds of its neck. Chalice Well is on the end of its beak. Its head is drawn by the same Shepton Mallet to Glastonbury road that defines Capricorn's back. Maltwood concluded that the Phoenix is drinking from the Druid Well, its head turned to reach for the magical healing water of the Chalice Well Blood Spring. Its west wing is drawn by two old roads to Wells that wend round Edmund Hill. The eastern wing is traced round South Down Hill, the ancient oaks of Gog and Magog by its tip, its breast by Paradise Lane.

Pisces

Approximately 5-miles across, Pisces in the Glastonbury scheme is a whale connected by a cord to two fishes. It is outlined by Wearyall Hill, Glastonbury Abbey, Fishers Hill, Pomparles Bridge over the river Brue where Arthur threw Excalibur into the water, Plunging, which marks the whale's heaving back, Wallyer's Bridge, which accommodates its jaw, Hulk Moor on the road from Somerton to Glastonbury and the Mendips that marks the tail, and Street. The jaw of the whale hangs on Glastonbury Abbey's gate. The two fishes, each less than a mile long, lie on the whale's flank. One fish, the northernmost of the pair, rests on Wearyall Hill, reputed in legend to be the burial place of the Celtic Salmon of Wisdom. The other is lower by the ram's head at Street.

In the Mabinogion tale of *Kylhuch and Olwen*, the salmon takes Kay and Bedivere upriver to rescue the Mabon (youth) from the prison of Oeth and Anoeth (Knowing and Not Knowing). The Rivers Brue and Old Rhyne outline the whale's length while Watchwell house falls on its eye and Wallyer's Bridge on its snout. Caine found a serpent's head projecting from the whale's jaws. It lies near Maltwood's serpent head in Park Wood. The stars in Draco correspond to Caine's new find. Close by the River Brue one comes across the "tree of sorrows," once a willow, now a hawthorn. Nearby is Bride's Well where Chalice Well's mysterious blue bowl was discovered in 1905 through the visions of Wellesley Tudor Pole. From here it is a short walk across the field to Bride's Mound, formerly the site of St Brigid's Chapel and part of an earlier Saxon monastery dedicated to Mary Magdalene. This hallowed place was once the traditional disembarking place for boats, and where local legend says Mary Magdalene landed on a visit to these isles.

Glastonbury Abbey

Sunrise at Glastonbury Tor

Glastonbury Tor and its Labrynthine Paths

Chapter 25

The Tarot

The history of playing cards and the possibility that they possess symbolic and esoteric significance have long been a topic of intrigue.

It is conjectured that Tarot cards form an integral element of the Arabian Mysteries, especially the arcane teachings of the dervishes. Manly P. Hall[61] referred to the tradition that pictorial devices arranged in the form of a deck of cards were in circulation among the mysterious wise men of Fez and Damascus. It was among these adepts that the founder of Rosicrucianism, Father Gébelin C.C.R., is said to have been initiated.

Hall explained that when Christian forces destroyed the pagan sanctuaries of Serapis, Isis and Osiris the magic and sorcery of Egypt withdrew into the desert regions of the Near East and was given asylum among the mystics of Islam. Here, the great body of Platonic lore—the Orphic traditions, the laws of Zarathustra, the mysteries of Islam, the Hermetic Arcanum, the secrets of alchemy, and other orders of esoteric knowledge—were kept alive by the wise men of the desert, the descendants of the ancient magi, and the stargazers of Chaldea and Phoenicia.

The Crusaders became indoctrinated with these traditions. Many soldiers were devout men who, expecting to be confronted on the battlefield by infidel devils, were surprised to find instead refined, chivalrous and cultured Saracens, custodians of ancient wisdom.

On their return home, disillusioned Knights served as a conduit by which Eastern cultures permeated quickly into a chaotic Europe. The Knights Templars in particular applied themselves to study of the Syrian Mysteries, aided by an alliance with the secret Brotherhood of Mt. Lebanon which safeguarded the secret traditions of the mystical Jewish and Christian cults.

---

[61] Hall, M., *The Tarot*, Philosophical Research Society, Los Angeles, 1978

Among the mysteries encountered by the Templars appears to have been the Tarot cards. Mrs John King van Rensselaer wrote,[62] "…that cards were brought by the home-returning warriors, who imported many of the newly acquired customs and habits of the Orient to their own countries, seems to be a well-established fact."

The Templars are said to have brought these cards with them because they knew that a great deal of ancient knowledge was encoded in them. Echoing this sentiment, the great 19th century magus Eliphas Levi wrote that a man imprisoned in a dungeon with nothing but a deck of the Tarot could, if acquainted with the correct keys, reconstruct from them the entire body of learning.

The Tarot cards may be traced back to the religious symbolism of the ancient Egyptians through the Gypsies. A curious legend relates that after the destruction of the Serapeum in Alexandria, its priests banded themselves together to preserve the secrets of the rites of Serapis. Their descendants—the Gypsies—carrying with them the most precious of the volumes saved from the burning library, the Book of Thoth, became wanderers upon the face of the earth, remaining a people apart with an ancient language and a birthright of magic and mystery.

Antoine Court de Gébelin believed the word Tarot itself to be derived from two Egyptian words, Tar, meaning "road," and Ro, meaning "royal." Thus the Tarot constitutes the royal road to wisdom.

Paul Christian[63] described a purported initiation into the Egyptian Mysteries in which the 22 major Tarots assume the proportions of trestleboards of immense size which line a great gallery. Stopping before each card in turn, the initiator described its symbolism to the candidate.

The Tarot is undoubtedly a vital element in Rosicrucian symbolism, possibly the very book of universal knowledge which the members of the order claimed to possess. The Rota Mundi is a term frequently occurring in the early manifestoes of the Fraternity of the Rose Cross. The word Rota by a rearrangement of its letters becomes Taro, the ancient name of these mysterious cards.

Sir Francis Bacon employed the Tarot symbolism in his ciphers. The numbers 21, 56 and 78, which are all directly related to the divisions of the Tarot deck, are frequently involved in Bacon's cryptograms. In the great Shakespearian Folio of 1623 the Christian name of Lord Bacon appears 21 times on page 56 of the Histories.

---

[62] *The Devil's Picture Book: the History of Playing Cards*, 1890

[63] Christian, P., *History and Practice of Magic*, France, 1870

As the Greeks placed the letters of their alphabet with their corresponding numbers upon the various parts of the body of their deities, so the Tarot cards have an analogy not only in the parts and members of the universe but also in the divisions of the human body. Hall claimed that they are in fact the key to the magical constitution of man.

The Tarot cards must be considered as separate and complete hieroglyphs, each representing a distinct principle, law, power or element in Nature. As every structure consists of certain elemental parts, so the Tarot cards represent the components of the structure of philosophy. Irrespective of the science or philosophy with which the student is working, the Tarot cards can be identified with the essential constituents of his subject, each card being related to a specific part according to mathematical and philosophical laws.

Some writers have adopted the hypothesis that the 22 major trumps represent the letters of the Hebrew alphabet, a supposition based purely on the coincidence that both consist of 22 parts. The major trump cards portray incidents from the Book of Revelation; and the Apocalypse of St. John is also divided into 22 chapters.

The major trumps of the Tarot and the 22 letters of the Hebrew alphabet cannot be synchronized without first fixing the correct place of the unnumbered, or zero, card, the Fool. Levi places this card between the 20th and 21st Tarots, assigning to it the Hebrew letter Shin. On the other hand, Antoine Court de Gébelin in his essay[64] placed the zero card before the first numbered card of the major trumps on the basis that if the natural order of the numbers (according to both the Pythagorean and Qabalistic systems) is adhered to, the zero card must naturally precede the number 1.

In de Gébelin's case, he assigned the zero card to AIN SOPH, God prior to His self-manifestation as the Creator. In this placement the zero card represents that Eternal Power of which the 21 surrounding or manifesting aspects are but limited expressions. If the 21 major trumps are considered as limited forms existing in the abstract substance of the zero card, it then becomes their common denominator and, as Hall suggested, reveals that the entire mystery of the Tarot is wrapped up in the symbolism of the Fool card.

The first numbered major trump is called Le Bateleur, the juggler, and according to Court de Gébelin, indicates that the entire fabric of

[64] *Le Monde primitif, analysé et comparé avec le monde moderne*, volume viii, 1781

creation is but a dream, existence a juggling of divine elements, life a perpetual game of hazard and the seeming miracles of Nature feats of cosmic sleight of hand. Man is like the little ball in the hands of the juggler, who waves his wand and, hey presto, the ball vanishes. The world looking on does not realize that the vanished article is still cleverly concealed by the juggler in the hollow of his hand. This is also the Adept whom Omar Khayyám calls "the master of the show." His message is that the wise direct the phenomena of Nature and thus are never deceived.

The second numbered major trump is called La Papesse, the Female Pope, and has been associated with a curious legend of the only woman who ever became pope. Pope Joan is supposed to have accomplished this by masquerading in male attire, and was stoned to death when her subterfuge was discovered. This card portrays a seated woman crowned with a tiara surmounted by a lunar crescent. In her lap is the Tora, or book of the Law (usually partly closed), and in her left hand are the keys to the secret doctrine, one gold and the other silver. Behind her rise two pillars (Jachin and Boaz) with a multicoloured veil stretched between. Her throne stands upon a checkerboard floor.

The third numbered major trump is called L'Impératrice, the Empress, and has been likened to the "woman clothed with the sun" described in the Apocalypse. On this card appears the winged figure of a woman seated upon a throne, supporting with her right hand a shield emblazoned with a phœnix and holding in her left a sceptre surmounted by an orb or three-leafed flower. Beneath her left foot is sometimes shown the crescent. Either the Empress is crowned or her head is surrounded by a diadem of stars; sometimes both. She is called Generation, and represents the threefold spiritual world out of which proceeds the fourfold material world.

The fourth numbered major trump is called L'Empereur, the Emperor, and by its numerical value is directly associated with the great Deity revered by the Pythagoreans under the form of the tetrad. His symbols declare the Emperor to be the Demiurgus, the Great King of the inferior world. The Emperor is dressed in armour and his throne is a cube stone, upon which a phœnix is also clearly visible.

The fifth numbered major trump is called Le Pape, the Pope, and represents the high priest of a pagan or Christian Mystery school. In this card the hierophant wears the tiara and carries in his left hand the triple cross surmounting the globe of the world. His right hand, bearing upon its back the stigmata, makes "the ecclesiastic sign of esotericism," and before him kneel two acolytes. The back of the papal throne is in the form of a celestial and a terrestrial column. This card signifies the initiate or master of the mystery of life and, according to the Pythagoreans, the spiritual physician.

The sixth numbered major trump is called L'Amoureux, the Lovers. There are two distinct forms of this Tarot. One shows a marriage ceremony in which a priest is uniting a youth and a maiden (Adam and Eve, Hall suggested) in holy wedlock. Sometimes a winged figure above transfixes the lovers with his dart. The second form of the card portrays a youth with a female figure on either side. One of these figures wears a golden crown and is winged, while the other is attired in the flowing robes of the *bacchante* (a priest or priestess of Bacchus), and on her head is a wreath of vine leaves. The maidens represent the twofold soul of man, the first his guardian angel and the second his ever-present demon. The youth stands at the beginning of mature life, "the Parting of the Ways," where he must choose between virtue and vice, the eternal and the temporal.

The seventh numbered major trump is called Le Chariot, and portrays a victorious crowned warrior crowned riding in a chariot drawn by black and white sphinxes or horses. The starry canopy of the chariot is upheld by four columns. This card signifies the Exalted One who rides in the chariot of creation. The vehicle of the solar energy being numbered seven reveals the arcane truth that the seven planets are the chariots of the solar power which rides victorious in their midst.

The eighth numbered major trump is called La Justice, and portrays a seated figure upon a throne, the back of which rises in the form of two columns. Justice is crowned and carries in her right hand a sword and in her left a pair of scales. This card is a reminder of the judgement of the soul in the hall of Osiris. It teaches that only balanced forces can endure and that eternal justice destroys with the sword that which is unbalanced. Sometimes Justice is depicted with a braid of her own hair twisted around her neck in a manner resembling a hangman's knot. This may imply that man is the cause of his own undoing, his actions being the instrument of his annihilation.

The ninth numbered major trump is called L'Hermite, the Hermit, and portrays an aged man, robed in a monkish habit and cowl, leaning on a staff. This card was popularly supposed to represent Diogenes in his quest for an honest man. In his right hand the recluse carries a lamp which he partly conceals within the folds of his cape. The hermit thereby personifies the secret organisations which carefully conceal the light of the Ancient Wisdom from the profane. The staff of the hermit is knowledge, which is man's main and only enduring support. Sometimes the mystic rod is divided by knobs into seven sections, a subtle reference to the mystery of the seven sacred centres along the human spine.

The tenth numbered major trump is called La Roue de Fortune, the Wheel of Fortune, and portrays a mysterious wheel with eight spokes--the familiar Buddhist symbol of the Cycle of Necessity. To its rim cling Anubis and Typhon, the principles of good and evil. Above sits the immobile sphinx, carrying the sword of Justice and signifying the perfect equilibrium of Universal Wisdom. Anubis is shown rising and Typhon descending; but when Typhon reaches the bottom, evil re-ascends, and when Anubis reaches the top good wanes once more. The Wheel of Fortune represents the lower universe as a whole with Divine Wisdom (the sphinx) as the eternal arbiter between good and evil. In India, the chakra, or wheel, is associated with the life centres either of a world or of an individual.

The eleventh numbered major trump is called La Force, Strength, and portrays a girl wearing a hat in the form of a *lemniscate* (the infinity symbol of a figure eight on its side, representing eternal balance), with her hands upon the mouth of an apparently ferocious lion. The young woman symbolises spiritual strength and the lion either the animal world which the girl is mastering or the Secret Wisdom over which she is mistress. The lion also signifies the summer solstice and the girl, Virgo, for when the sun enters this constellation the Virgin robs the lion of his strength. King Solomon's throne was ornamented with lions and he himself was likened to the king of beasts with the key of wisdom between its teeth.

The twelfth numbered major trump is called Le Pendu, the Hanged Man, and portrays a young man hanging by his left leg from a horizontal beam, the latter supported by two tree trunks from each of which six branches have been removed. The right leg of the youth is crossed behind his left and his arms are folded behind his back in such a way as to form a cross surmounting a downward pointing triangle. Popular tradition associates this card with Judas Iscariot, who is said to have hanged himself, the money-bags representing the payment he received for his crime. In the Egyptian Tarot the hanged man signifies the Sun God who dies perennially for his world.

The thirteenth numbered major trump is called La Mort, Death, and portrays a reaping skeleton with a great scythe cutting off the heads, hands and feet rising out of the earth about it. In the course of its labours the skeleton has apparently cut off one of its own feet. Not all Tarot decks show this peculiarity, but this point emphasises the philosophic truth that imbalance and destructiveness are synonymous. The skeleton is the proper emblem of the first and supreme Deity because it is the foundation of the body, as the Absolute is the foundation of creation. The reaping skeleton physically signifies death but philosophically that irresistible impulse in Nature which causes every being to be ultimately absorbed into the divine condition in which it existed before the illusionary universe had been manifested. The blade of the scythe is the moon with its crystallising power. The field in which death reaps is the universe, and the card discloses that all things growing out of the earth shall be cut down and return to earth again.

The fourteenth numbered major trump is called La Tempérance, Temperance, and portrays an angelic figure with the sun upon her forehead. She carries two urns, one empty, the other full, and continually pours the contents of the upper into the lower. In some Tarot decks the flowing water takes the form of the symbol of Aquarius. Not one drop, however, of the living water is lost in this endless transference between the superior and inferior vessel. When the lower urn is filled the vases are reversed, thus signifying that life pours first from the invisible into the visible, then from the visible back into the invisible.

The fifteenth numbered major trump is called Le Diable, the Devil, and portrays a creature resembling Pan with the horns of a ram or deer, the arms and body of a man, and the legs and feet of a goat or dragon. The figure stands upon a cubic stone, to a ring in the front of which are chained two satyrs. For a sceptre this so-called demon carries a lighted torch or candle. The entire figure is symbolic of the magic powers of the astral light, or universal mirror, in which the divine forces are reflected in an inverted, or infernal, state. The demon is winged like a bar, showing that it pertains to the nocturnal, or shadow inferior sphere. The animal natures of man, in the form of a male and a female elemental, are chained to its footstool. The torch is the false light which guides unillumined souls to their own undoing.

The sixteenth numbered major trump is called Le Feu du Ciel, the Fire of Heaven, and portrays a tower whose battlements, in the form of a crown, are being destroyed by a bolt of lightning from the sun. The lighting bolt sometimes takes the form of the zodiacal sign of Scorpio, and the tower may be considered a phallic emblem. Two figures are falling from the tower, one in front and the other behind. This Tarot card is popularly associated with the traditional fall of man. The divine nature of humanity is depicted as a tower. When his crown is destroyed, man falls into the lower world and takes upon himself the illusion of materiality.

The seventeenth numbered major trump is called Les Étoiles, the Stars, and portrays a young girl kneeling with one foot in water and the other on the ground, her body suggestive of a swastika. She has two urns, one in her left hand (the subconscious) and one in her right (the conscious). She pours the water out to nourish the earth and to continue the cycle of fertility, represented by the lush greenery around her. Above the girl's head are eight stars, one of which is exceptionally large and bright. Count de Gébelin considers the great star to be Sirius; the other seven are the sacred planets of the ancients. He believed the female figure to be Isis in the act of causing the inundations of the Nile which accompanied the rising of the Dog Star.

The eighteenth numbered major trump is called La Lune, the Moon, and portrays Luna rising between two towers—one light and the other dark. A dog and a wolf are baying at the rising moon, and in the foreground is a pool of water from which emerges a crawfish. Between the towers a path winds, vanishing in the extreme background. This card refers to the path of wisdom. Man in his quest of reality emerges from the pool of illusion. After mastering the guardians of the gates of wisdom he passes between the fortresses of science and theology and follows the winding path leading to spiritual liberation. His way is faintly lighted by human reason (the moon), which is but a reflection of divine wisdom.

The nineteenth numbered major trump is called Le Soleil, the Sun, and portrays two children—Gemini, the Twins—standing together in a garden surrounded by a magic ring of flowers. One of these children should be shown as male and the other female. Behind them is a brick wall apparently enclosing the garden. Above the wall the sun is rising, its rays alternately straight and curved. Thirteen teardrops are falling from the solar face. The sun of Truth is shining into the garden of the world over which these two children reside. The harmony of the world depends upon the coordination of two qualities symbolised throughout the ages as the mind and the heart.

The twentieth numbered major trump is called Le Jugement, the Judgement, and portrays three figures rising apparently from their tombs, though but one coffin is visible. Above them in a blaze of glory is a winged figure (presumably the Angel Gabriel) blowing a trumpet. This Tarot represents the liberation of man's threefold spiritual nature from the sepulchre of his material constitution. Since but one-third of the spirit actually enters the physical body, the other two-thirds constituting the

Hermetic anthropos,[65] only one of the three figures is actually rising from the tomb.

The twenty-first numbered major trump is called Le Monde, the World, and portrays a female figure draped with a scarf which the wind blows into the form of the Hebrew letter Kaph. Her extended hands—each of which holds a wand—and her left leg, which crosses behind the right, cause the figure to assume the form of the alchemical symbol of sulphur. The central figure is surrounded by a wreath in the form of a vesica piscis which Levi likens to the Qabalistic crown Kether. The Cherubim of Ezekiel's vision occupies the corners of the card. This Tarot is called the Microcosm and the Macrocosm because in it are summed up every agency contributing to the structure of creation. A human figure kneels below this wreath, playing upon a harp of three strings, for the spirit must create harmony in the triple constitution of its inferior nature before it can gain for itself the solar crown of immortality.

The four suits of the minor trumps are considered as analogous to the four elements, the four corners of creation, and the four worlds of Qabalism. Modern playing cards represent the Tarot's minor trumps, from each suit of which the page, or valet, has been eliminated, leaving 13 cards. Hall said that even in this abridged form, the modern deck is of profound symbolic importance, for its arrangement is apparently in accord with the divisions of the year. The four suits represent the seasons, the ages of the ancient Greeks, and the Yugas of the Hindus. The twelve court cards are the signs of the zodiac arranged in triads of a Father, a Power and a Mind according to the upper section of the Bembine Table. The ten pip cards of each suit represent the Sephirothic trees existing in each of the four worlds (the suits). The 13 cards of each suit are the 13 lunar months in each year, and the 52 cards of the deck are the 52 weeks in the year. Counting the number of pips and reckoning the jacks, queens, and kings as 11, 12 and 13 respectively, the sum for the 52 cards is 364. If the joker is considered as one point, the result is 365, or the number of days in the year.

The court cards contain a number of important Masonic symbols. Nine are full face and three are profile. Acccording to Hall, here represented is the broken "Wheel of the Law," signifying the nine months of the prenatal epoch and the three degrees of spiritual unfoldment necessary to produce the perfect man. The four armed kings are the

---

[65] The Hermetic anthropos is more than the Adam of Genesis, the ancestor of the human race. He is a transcendental being, the personification of humanity.

Egyptian Ammonian Architects who gouged out the universe with knives. They are also the cardinal signs of the Zodiac. The four queens, carrying eight-petaled flowers symbolic of the Christ, are the fixed signs of the Zodiac. The court cards of the spade suit will not look upon the pip in the corner of the card but face away from it as though fearing this emblem of death. The Grand Master of the Order of the Cards is the king of clubs, who carries the orb as emblematic of his dignity.

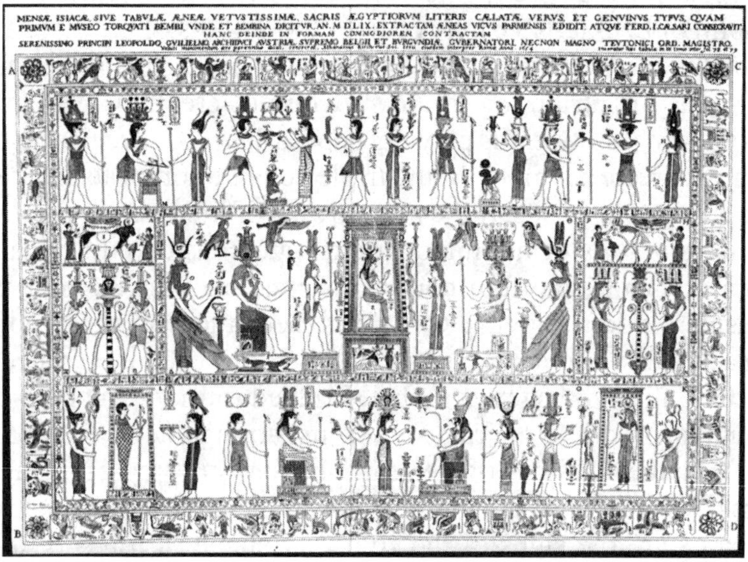

The Bembine Table of Isis

Le Bateleur

La Papesse

The Hermit

Death

The Emperor

The Queen of Cups

Judgement

The Moon

The Sun

The Tower

The Devil

‘Use the invisible that is all around you. No one else is using it, so why not YOU!’

—the Flying A’s Gatekeeper

FAREWELL TO FINLEY

A Tisserand Cross—in their early years the Cathars were known in France as Tisserands (weavers)

Chapter 26

Brad's Dream

Brad's daylong journey through the mystical treasures in his magical hilltop library has left him drained. His mind is saturated; he can hardly keep his eyes open. He lies on the kline to rest and is asleep in seconds. He dreams vividly.

He is lying on his back in a shallow bank of ferns beneath a quarter moon hidden by cloud. His one hand is resting on a pebble, the other on a clump of daisies. He cannot feel the touch of either because in these moments, moments that have neither beginning nor end, Brad is occupying a world as remote from this as the most distant star.

A hooting owl swoops by, a ghost-grey blur in the gloom. Here, nestled cosily in the soft bracken, Brad has no idea where his body ends and the woodland begins. It hardly matters. He is happy; he is free.

He has always possessed the gift of separation, the ability to experience the certain feeling that he is occupying another world, the original world—the one from which each of us, high and lowborn alike, travel in our very beginnings.

Brad's moments of reverie in the ferns are interrupted by the sudden appearance of a bright light. He gets to his feet and is astounded to see that twenty or so paces in front of him in the dark wood is a room, one he instantly recognises. It is the living room in his parents' former home where Brad lived until he was nine years old.

Coming from the room is the distinctive noise of his mother's old vacuum cleaner. Bradhad loved the sound of the Hoover. Whenever he saw his mother fetch it out of the understairs cupboard he would position himself behind a large armchair. As soon as she flicked the switch the ensuing drone would instantly transport Brad to a special place in his imagination, the one, in fact, he is visiting while lying in the ferns.

Curiosity overcoming trepidation, Brad crosses the woodland floor and enters the room. 'Mom?' he says, hesitantly. There is no response. He calls out again but it appears he is alone in this mysterious replication of a bygone place and time. The thrum of the vacuum continues unabated, much louder now. The sound seems to be coming from the kitchen. Brad reaches for the kitchen light switch and opens the door.

All at once the drone becomes a roar and Brad is standing not in the family kitchen but on a bank of a woodland pool into which a waterfall is pouring its tumbling cascade. It is early morning.

Brad senses movement and hides behind a tree. Peeking through the hawthorn's low branches, he sees on the opposite side of the pool a robed and hooded figure.

In the dream the figure, a druid, is named Osric. Osric has made the local woodland his home for fifty years. It is the year 882 as measured in the Christian calendar. The sounds and scents of his woodland sanctuary are poetry for his soul. The music and percussive rhythms of the waterfall clear his mind and refresh his spirit. Animals and birds accept his presence. He is as much a component of the natural scene as the fox, the sparrow hawk and the speckled trout. Occasionally, he sees a glint of something light and brilliant in the bushes or in the flowing waters and knows he is glimpsing the "Otherworld," the magical realm of the fairy folk.

Now in his seventieth year, Osric knows that the moment of his death is at hand. He has read the signs in the mistletoe seeds and senses that his assassin is even now making his silent way along the footpath to the fall. Osric is not afraid to die because he does not believe in death in the way that most imagine it. His demise will be the beginning of a new journey, one whose prospect he relishes. In the meantime, there is a long awaited appointment he must keep. Close by he senses the presence of another.

Osric turns to look in Brad's direction, holding a finger to his lips as if in warning. Brad ducks back out of sight. Moments later, a powerfully built man dressed in animal hides enters the ravine over a pile of rocks. The Viking is carrying a large club.

The assailant jumps from the rocks. Uttering a battle cry, he raises his club and brings it down hard upon the druid's skull. At the same time, Brad feels a searing pain in his own head. He has to stuff a fist into his mouth to stifle an agonising gasp of pain. Osric totters forward and falls into the pool only yards from Brad's hiding place. Once again, his eyes lock onto the dreaming observer. Feebly, he lifts an arm from the waters and points towards the cave behind the fall.

It is Osric's last act in this life. Moments later the Norseman wades through the beck and delivers his victim a final, crushing blow.

Next, Brad is standing in a dark space behind the fall. He takes a torch from his pocket, switches it on and sees that leading into the gloom is a corridor lit by flaming torches set into both sides of the cavern's uneven granite walls. He is unafraid; he is free; he is safe. He senses that here before him is a pathway to an uncharted part of his inner "Brad."

After ten minutes of walking, Brad comes to a large oak door adorned with finely wrought gold fittings. He tries the handle but the door is locked. There is no sign of a key. At that moment the torch beam begins to flicker. Brad knows that its battery is dying. Vainly, he gives the handle another yank. The battery light is dimming quickly. Rising anxiety spurs his efforts to wrench open the unyielding door. Not a hair's breadth of movement is gained by his tugs on the implacable golden handle. The torchlight is now almost entirely extinguished. Brad can see little more than the vague shadows cast by his frantic exertions. He does not relish the prospect of retracing his steps in pitch darkness.

Wait, there has to be another way. Understanding comes. This is his world, his to command; he is the power in this place. Brad closes his eyes, takes a deep breath and pictures the door complete with a golden key. As the torchlight dies, in his mind Brad reaches out, grasps the key and gives it a turn. Click! He opens his eyes, opens the door and steps within.

Brad sees that he is in a brightly lit, high-roofed square cavern with sides of around thirty feet. Flaming candelabra placed all around the unusual room supply illumination. Brad is initially taken aback by the environment but then is delighted to see that it is filled with comfortable furnishings, including a table spread with delicious foodstuffs. The haunting sound of a solitary flute is playing softly but Brad is clearly alone. Of course, he is. The cave's former resident had died at the hand of the Viking invader.

In addition to the familiar fixtures the room features other items of interest. Against the rear wall of the cavern stands a large and impressively stocked glass cabinet. It is crammed with apothecary jars of various sizes that contain a bewildering assortment of herbs, tinctures, decoctions and potions. As he lifts out a jar to read its label a voice from within the glass container tells him what ailment is treated by its ingestion or application. He understands that this is his personal apothecary. At any time, the magical voice explained, he can make the journey into the Druid's cavern and receive healing for any ailment or imbalance of the body.

In another corner of the room is a full-length mirror. He stands before it and is astonished to see a reflection of his naked form. Successively, the image in the glass changes to reveal his skeleton, his musculature, his circulatory and nervous systems, his organs and his glands. Every physical weakness, present and potential, is highlighted in extraordinary detail.

Deep within his dream-self Brad understands that if he is to enjoy physical wellbeing he must learn about all aspects of his body. He must be able to visualise in full health his heart, lungs, kidneys, liver, stomach, intestines and all other vital parts if he is to become his own healer and physician.

The beauty of this gift overwhelms him. Tears flow freely as he delights in his discovery of the magical healing cavern. Brad moves to an armchair, snacks on fruit washed down with elderberry cordial and takes in his extraordinary surroundings. He understands that he is in a place which from now on he can access simply by exercising his imagination, a faculty with which he is blessed in abundance.

The flute continues its evocative refrain while Brad's attention is next drawn to a far corner of the cavern and a second door, smaller and plainer than the one through which he has entered. Excited, he goes to it and turns the handle. It opens easily. He steps forward onto a wooden platform and enters a giant cavern at a point just below its ceiling. Low, diffused light from an unseen source allows Brad a view of its principal features.

Below is a large subterranean lake accessed via a long winding, wooden stair. Brad can make out the silhouette of a gondola moored to a jetty. He descends the stairs and quickly reaches the gondola, which is strewn with plush, colourful cushions.

Unhesitatingly, Brad climbs into the boat and makes himself comfortable. He sees a notebook and quill pen among the cushions. He picks them up and, unprompted, writes his name, "Brad Gunther Pulaski," on the notebook without lifting the point of the pen. He repeats this unusual action over and over again, flipping from page to page as he fills them one after the other with text.

Gradually, this act of writing induces in Brad a deep level of relaxation. He puts aside the notebook and pen and lies down upon the cushions. Silently, the gondola slips from its mooring and moves across the lake. Presently, it enters a long, narrow passage lit by wall torches. The alternating hypnotic flicker of the torches and the gentle, rhythmic lap of the water around the boat lulls Brad into an ever-deeper feeling of calm.

The gondola navigates the length of the passage and emerges into a round lake suffused with pale moonlight which is beaming through a small opening in the high roof. Brad drops a hand over the side of the boat and lazily swirls the cool water. On the opposite shore is a small cave illuminated by a sparkling golden light. Minutes later the gondola comes to rest. Brad steps from the boat and enters a hollow hewn from brilliant rock crystal. It is empty except for a large, low altar of polished rose quartz. Instinctively, Brad lies down upon the altar. The same recurrent flute refrain he heard earlier is playing pianissimo. Soon he becomes aware of a new presence in the cave. Without raising his head Brad can see a cowled form. It is the smiling figure of Osric.

'Good morning,' said Brad.

'And a very good morning to you too, Brad,' Osric replied.

'Didn't I see you being slain by the Viking?' Brad asked.

'If you learn just one thing in this life, Brad, let it be that nothing ever truly dies. Always something survives.'

'Am I dreaming?'

'The physical Brad is in a deep sleep in the Greek temple. Here, in your astral form, you are very much awake and hungry for a new kind of adventure. Although we are separated by a span of one thousand years, you and I share an unbreakable connection, one that will assume a far greater importance in the coming years. This is the first of many occasions when we shall meet in the crystal cave. It is a place of peace in which you can feel a sense of balance and complete freedom. It is also a place of adventure from which you can travel to all worlds of beauty and enchantment.

'Today is the first day of the Winter Solstice. The magnificent power of this very special time in Nature's calendar has opened for you a corridor in time. It will always be open for you. Very few individuals are gifted this opportunity but it is a necessary part of your life's journey, one that will be as unique as it will be challenging and, at times, maybe downright dangerous. But being the person that you are, Brad, you will not want in any other way.'

Osric produces from a pocket a beautifully sculpted crystal cross whose upperpart consists of a teardrop-shaped loop in place of a vertical bar. Handing it to Brad, Osric explains. 'The ancient Egyptians called this unusual form of cross an *ankh*, the early Christians the *crux ansata*. Basically, it symbolises the joy of living. Keep it safe, Brad. In future, it will not be necessary for you to be asleep and dreaming to make a journey to special places of your choice, including your healing cavern beneath the fall. When you want to visit somewhere, hold the crystal in your left hand and make a picture of your destination in your mind. Instantly you will be there.'

'Who are you?' Brad asks quietly.

'The question is moot,' Osric answers. 'Deep down you already know the answer. It is time now that you woke up and pulled a new scroll from the library shelves and learn a little more about who you are. Relax now and let the light of living crystal guide you along a unique journey of discovery.'

From within his robes the druid produces a long upturned sword, its tip pointing to the cavern roof. Reflected light from the surrounding crystal converges upon the blade's tip, streams to the ceiling and reflects back to encircle Brad's prone body in an aura of golden light.

Brad stiffens momentarily and then relaxes. He is not conscious of stepping down off the altar but all at once he is back, lying on the kline in the temple and rubbing sleep from his eyes.

What an amazing dream, he thinks to himself. But then he fingers the magical crystal pendant round his neck and realises that his experience was real in every detail.

What is strikingly obvious to Brad is that there is no limit to the layers of experiential pathways that a truthseeker will travel in their quest for answers to the "meaning of life." He must be open to all avenues of adventure and metaphysical opportunity if he is to evolve to his highest potential while he remains in the physical world.

As Osric had directed, Brad reaches out in anticipation to a nearby shelf and a protruding scroll nestles into his hands. Brad unrolls it. It is written in Occitan, the dialect spoken in the south of France in the Middle Ages. Once again, Brad can understand it perfectly.

The text, interspersed with illustrations, describes events in the Middle Ages during the Catholic Church's crusade against the Cathars, a religious brotherhood that practised an unusual kind of Christianity. On one of the opening pages is a picture of men, women and children tied to stakes in a huge stockade. Robed priests are lighting with torches kindling faggots heaped around each of the condemned, their faces etched in agony and terror.

Looking carefully, Brad can see that in the bottom corner of the illustration a crossbowman is emerging from the shadows of a smithy's forge. Brad *knows* that the crouching figure is himself in a distant time and place. The man's name is Alain.

Chapter 27

The Secret of the Holy Shroud

The scroll explains that the Cathars were part of a widespread spiritual reform movement in medieval Europe, which began about 653 CE when Constantine-Silvanus brought a copy of the Gospels to Armenia. In the following centuries a number of dissenting groups arose, gathered around charismatic preachers who rejected the authority of the Catholic Church. These groups based their beliefs and practices on the Gospels rather than on Church dogma and sought a return to the early church and the faith of the Apostles.

Among these groups were the Cathars, a term derived from the Greek word katharos meaning clean or pure. It is believed that they originated from an anti-materialist reform movement within the Bogomil churches of the Balkans, which called for a return to the Christian message of perfection, poverty and preaching, combined with a rejection of the physical.

The reforms were a reaction against the often-perceived scandalous and dissolute lifestyles of the Catholic clergy. Following the First Crusade, Latin settlers established a dualist community in Constantinople. It is theorized that this group provided Westerners with Latin translations of Greek Bogomil texts, which included the mysterious consolamentum ritual, thus helping to generate the first organized dualist movement in Western Europe.

According to Otto Rahn,[66] the roots of Catharism can be traced to the legends of the ancient Greeks, Goths and Germanic pagans, all sworn enemies of the Roman Empire and its successor, the Catholic Church. Like Rahn, the Cathars did not see Satan, Beelzebub or the devil in Lucifer. In the Pyrenees, he was known as Abellio; among the Norsemen, he was Baldr; and the ancient Greeks celebrated him as Apollo. This

---

[66] Rahn, O., *Kreuzzug gegen den Gral,* Freiburg i/Breisgau: Urban Verlag, 1933

Luciferianism, which is rooted in the esoteric literature of Hermeticism, sees Yahweh as the manifestation of a satanic material realm, whereas Lucifer is the keeper of the highest spiritual ideals and has nothing at all to do with Satanism.

The Latin name Lucifer originally designated the brilliance of the planet Venus and literally means, "Light bringer." Roman legend describes Lucifer, the son of Aurora, as the harbinger of the dawn who rode across the skies on a white charger—but he was also the evening star (Venus) who rode a dark steed. The Vulgate employs the word for "the light of the morning" (Job 11:17), "the signs of the zodiac" (Job 38:32), and "the aurora" (Psalm 109:3).

Rahn tells the story of the Cagots, a minority discriminated against, which may have been the missing link between the Cathars and the Goths. In a letter to Pope Leo X in 1513, the Cagots identified themselves as the last surviving of the Albigenses. Like the Bonhommes, as the Cathar perfecti were called, they were convinced that Yahweh was incompatible with the God of the New Testament.

The theology of the Cathars was also dualist, a belief in two equal and comparable transcendental principles: God, the force of good, and the demiurge, the force of evil. Cathars called the demiurge Rex Mundi (King of the World). Rex Mundi encompassed all that was corporeal, chaotic, evil and powerful. The Cathar viewed God as a being or principle of pure spirit, completely unsullied by the taint of matter. He was the God of love, order and peace. In this recognition, Jesus was an angel with only a phantom body, and the accounts of him in the New Testament were to be understood allegorically.

Pope Innocent III's initial diplomatic attempts to roll back Catharism met with little success. After the murder of his legate Pierre de Castelnau in 1208, suspecting that Raymond VI, Count of Toulouse was responsible, Innocent declared a crusade against the Cathars. He offered the lands of the Cathar heretics to any French nobleman willing to take up arms. Early in the summer of 1209 the crusading army left Lyon and made its way south. The Pope would have preferred the King of France to head the army but Philippe Auguste was careful to stay in the background. Raymond VI was forced into a diplomatic ploy. He took on the crusader's cross and joined the army of Christ, thus saving his lands from wartime sequestration but he engaged in no action and watched passively from the sidelines. His vassal Raimond Roger Trenceval, viscount of Béziers and Carcassonne, fearful and isolated, sought to follow his example but the crusading clerics were not to be taken in a second time and rejected his overtures.

Roger returned to Béziers and asked his citizens to hold out while he gathered troops in Carcassonne to relieve them. Béziers could not hold. Capitalising on an error of judgement made by the occupied forces when they attempted a daring sortie, the crusading soldiers entered the city and engaged in acts of appalling butchery. Asked during the slaughter by a knight how to tell Catholics from heretics, Arnaud Amaury, archbishop of Narbonne, reportedly replied, 'Kill them all; the Lord will know his own.' Approximately twenty thousand citizens were killed. Spurred on by this swift and bloody victory, the crusader forces set up camp at nearby Carcassonne. The city fell quickly. Trencavel had tried to negiotiate surrender terms but he was taken prisoner and died in a dungeon on 10 November.

From 1209 to 1215, the Crusaders experienced great success, capturing Cathar lands and systematically crushing the movement. From 1215 to 1225 a series of revolts caused many of the lands to be regained by the Cathars. A renewed crusade resulted in the recapturing of the territory and effectively drove Catharism underground within twenty years.

*

The mass pyre had been constructed at the foot of Montségur, adjacent to a crusader encampment that accommodated six thousand French soldiers, foreign mercenaries and clerics in the service of King Louis IX and Pope Innocent IV.

Montségur, the Mount Tabor of the Cathars of Aquitaine, was the Cathars' open and official headquarters in Languedoc. Located in the heart of France's Languedoc-Occitanie regions in the eastern Ariège Pyrenees, 80km southwest of Carcassonne, Montségur dominates a rock formation known as a pog, a term derived from the Occitan "puy," meaning peak or mountain.

Known in medieval times as a "vessel of stone," Montségur is a gigantic rounded outcrop a little over one thousand metres in height, shaped like a sugarloaf and inaccessible save on its west flank. In remote times Montségur was a sanctuary dedicated to Belissena, the Celtic appellation for the Goddess Astarte. The rock lies on the northern slopes of the Pyrenees, dwarfed by surrounding peaks up to three thousand metres high and flanked on three sides by deep valleys. The rock faces are everywhere dotted with fragrant box bushes.

A Crusader Knight

Montségur's architecture displays technical and mathematical knowledge extremely rare for medieval Western Europe: the orientation of the walls is designed to catch the light in relation to the rising sun. The fortress had two main gates. The entrance was known as the Great Gate and its size and character ran counter to all medieval rules of architecture. The upper chamber of the keep was fifty metres square, the pentagonal courtyard six hundred metres square.

A sizeable Catharist colony had built up since the Crusade and was visited by merchants. The Cathar leaders were Guilhabert de Castres (Bishop of Toulouse from 1223), Bernard de Simorre, Sicard Cellerier (Bishop of Albi), Bertrand Marty (Guilhabert's successor), Raymond Aiguilher and Jean Cambiaire. Principal safe houses were provided at the chateaux of the Lords of Niorts, Lanta Jourda (Lord of Calhavel), and by the nobility of Fanjeaux, Laruac and Miramont, and in the Boroughs of Sorèze, Avignonet and Saint-Felix.

Guilhabert asked for Perella's permision in 1232 to turn Montségur into the official asylum of the Catharist Church. Seigneurs of the Counts of Foix organised armed resistance. The noblemen's domains straddled the Pyrenees on the French side in Languedoc, including the Ariège Valley; in Spain was the Viscountcy of Castelbon. Knights loyal to the Cathars were called Faidits. They brought spears, crossbows, arrows and armour to Montségur. This is why Montségur was at the very heart and centre of resistance in Languedoc.

In 1233 the Catholic Church started referring to Montségur as the Synagogue of Satan. Olivier de Termes had several strong fortresses in the Corbières, which were used as arms depots and assembly points. In the mountains of the Corbières, the Sault district and Cerdagne Valley were centres for the planned uprising of the seigneurs.

The Cathar perfecti (*bons hommes*) lived in huts below the walls. Knights and their families made pilgrimages and received blessings from the perfecti. The site was on land belonging to Guy de Lévis, the "Marshall of the Faith" and the new suzerain of Mirepoix. It had been part of the inheritance of Esclarmonde, the sister of Raymond-Roger Trencavel of Foix. Esclarmonde was made a Perfecta in 1206; legend has it that she was the keeper of the Cathar Manisola or Mani—the Grâl. Otto Rahn wrote that the Mani was an emerald, called also by the Cathars the Stone of Wisdom and the Stone of Chastity.

Cathar deacons and recluses occupied the narrow strip along the stony face of the mountain between the fortress wall and the temporary defences thrown up around the small shelving slope that encompassed it.

The broad stone-built edifice was ringed about with a collection of little wooden huts to a depth of several metres.

There are four paths leading up to the fortress. The easiest and most used starts at the pass and goes up the southwest side of the mountain. To the west is the clifftop castle of Roquefixade; to the north, the Morenci range and beyond, the towns of Lavelanet and Laroque d'Olmes, the slopes of the Plantaurel, and, in the distance, the lower valley of the Ariege; to the east, the castle of Puivert and the Roc de la Mousse on the other side of the gorge of the Carroulet; to the southeast, the village of Montsegur, the mountain of La Frau where near the top one can see the mouth of a cave (La Caunha); and to the south, the pass of La Peire, the Pic du Soulerac, and the St Bartelemy massif. Near the gorge du Carroulet is the sheer rock face of the Roc de la Tour and the intermittent spring at Fontestorbes. From here one can follow the road towards Belesta, Lavelanet and Benaix, and onwards to Morenci.

This rock has given rise to many legends. Why was there a 15-day truce before the surrender in March 1244? What did the four perfecti take with them when they left the fortress in secret the night before the mass burning?

At the request of the Pope, in 1235 Raymond VII of Toulouse dispatched three Knights to take formal posession of Montségur. These knights were admitted, did obeisance (*adoratio*) before Guilhabert de Castres and went back to Toulouse. Afterwards Raymond sent his bailiff, Mancipe de Gaillac. He also "adored" the *bons hommes* and then went home. Mancipe was then sent back a second time, together with men-at-arms. They seized Jean Cambiaire and three perfecti for burning in Toulouse. In 1242 it was Montségur that despatched the small band of men accused of assassinating the inquisitors at Avignonet. Reprisals were swift.

In May 1243 Hugues des Arcis, at the head of an army of French knights and men-at-arms, pitched camp below Montségur on the Col du Tremblement, so depriving the besieged of the easiest way down into the valley. The sizes of the two opposing forces were grotesquely unequal. At the time of the siege there were five to six hundred persons in the fortress: the garrison of one hundred and fifty or so knights and men-at-arms, their families, and around two hundred and twenty Cathars. Arcis was also expecting a further ten thousand reinforcements; mostly conscript footsoldiers unwilling to fight fellow countrymen voluntarily. The French army's plan was to sever all communications and let the hot summer dry up the defenders' cisterns.

The crusaders must have anticipated a short siege, for most of the other Cathar fortresses had surrendered rapidly when their water ran out. Here the problem was quite different; it was not a simple matter to cut off a citadel of this kind. The lie of the land and the size of the outcrop would have needed a large body of soldiers. Only the most strategic points could be under continual surveillance. Furthermore, some of the mercenaries came from neighbouring villages, in particular Camon. This all meant that the besieged force was perfectly familiar with the area and, as a result, the Northerners' blockade was less than watertight, even when the fighting was at its height. Messages, supplies and reinforcements continued to pass through the besiegers' lines. Summer passed, rain came. Abundant gifts from *credentes,* members of the Cathar underground cell of supporters, provided food.

The weeks had passed and the combined royal and papal army lost patience. Winter was approaching and there was no sign of things going their way. Exasperated, Hugues des Arcis signed on a team of Basque mercenaries in October. They got a foothold on a narrow ledge at the eastern face, eighty metres downhill from the fortress. The Cathar supporters brought in Bertrand de la Baccalaria, an engineer from Capdenac. He broke through the blockade, reached the fortress and had another machine mounted in the eastern barbican that could return the Bishop of Albi's stone-gun's fire. Meanwhile the perfecti in the fortress invited knights and certain men-at-arms in to receive gifts. The nature of these gifts is not recorded.

At one point in the seige Imbert de Salas had a personal interview with Hugues des Arcis. Pierre Roger de Mirepoix criticised him for it and had his armour taken from him. This is suggestive of an act of betrayal. The Knight Del Congost managed to spend three months beneath the fortress while the siege was going on. The phrase *infra castrum* ("below the castle") appears in testimony but there is no evidence of any underground passageways.

Over the course of thirty years, the pilgrims and soldiers of the crusade against the Albigenses, and later the Dominicans, had united with the French. Now, behind the thick walls of Montségur, the last free Cathars and Occitan knights were enjoying their final hours of refuge. They had managed to hold out until Palm Sunday of 1244. Then, shepherds who had taken Catholic money pointed out a stone ridge from which the besiegers could reach the summit without any fear. This was a secret route from the Gorge of Luzset. Sole access to the castle was on the western face of the mountain, which was less steep but, thanks to defensive works, was well protected. Yet here, too, danger threatened the besieged inhabitants of the citadel. A group of Basque soldiers constructed a machine called a gatta, a siege tower, which, day after day, was pulled a few feet closer to the summit to menace the castle walls. The betrayal by the shepherds caused the collapse of resistance inside the citadel.

After the capture of the eastern barbican Matheus and Peter Bonnet left the fortress with gold and silver bullion and "pecuniam infinitam." These two men had a secret understanding with sentries who were from Camon-sur-l'Hers in the fief of Mirepoix. The treasure was cached in the woods on the Sabarthès Mountains until a safer place was found. Many believe that Otto Rahn, seven hundred years later, found evidence to indicate its location.

Bertrand de la Baccalaria set up another machine. Matheus returned to the fortress at the end of January 1244 with two crossbowmen, a meagre reinforcement but better than nothing. Only very dexterous and brave men could have risked the climb up the Porteil chimney and so they must have been extremely devoted to the Cathar cause. This same Matheus then went down a second time to seek reinforcements but came back with just one man.

The men-at-arms smuggled in by Matheus brought a message from Isarn de Fanjeaux to Pierre Roger de Mirepoix. The Count of Toulouse wanted to know if Montségur could last until Easter, by which time the Count had hoped to levy an army to raise the siege. The Count had no real chance of doing this but did have good reason to ask the men to hold on because Matheus had persuaded two local seigneurs, Bernard d'Alion and Arnold d'Uson, to contact an Aragonese mercenary captain called Corbario. He promised the captain fifty *livres melgoriennes* if he would bring twenty-five men-at-arms to Montségur. Had these elite men arrived the siege engines would have likely been burned but they failed to break through the besiegers' cordon.

In 1244 Montségur was held in trust by the seigneur Raymond de Perella, vassal to the Counts of Foix. Perella and his brother-in-law Pierre-Roger of Mirepoix were the most active resistance leaders during the time when the Catholic pogroms were reaching their peak of brutality towards the middle of the thirteenth century.

The fortress held all through February, the stone-gun keeping up a constant barrage on the besieged day and night. Inside the fortress the shortage of food was making life unbearable.

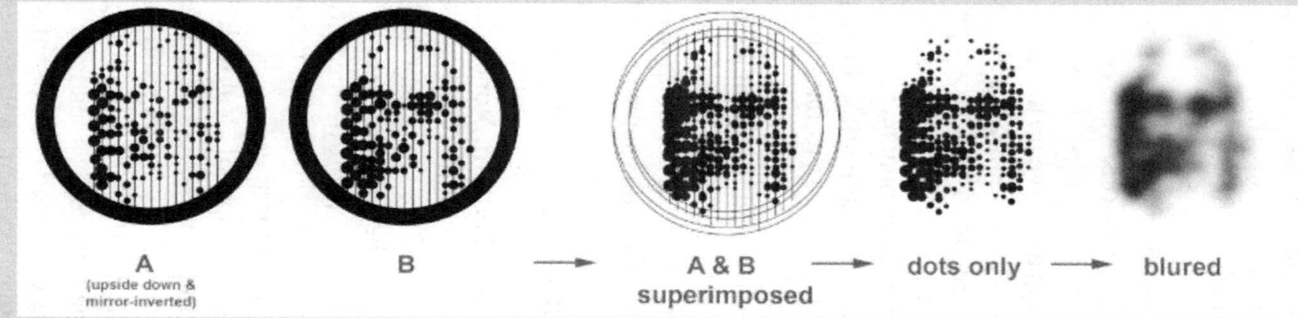

Fig. 4 Seen as two individual designs (Diagram A and B on the left) the two crop circles do not make a lot of sense. But if they are superimposed (Diagram A&B in the middle) a face emerges that resembles the Shroud of Turin (see Fig. 4 below).

Fig. 5 A gradual super imposition of the two crop circle designs with the face on the Turin Shroud.

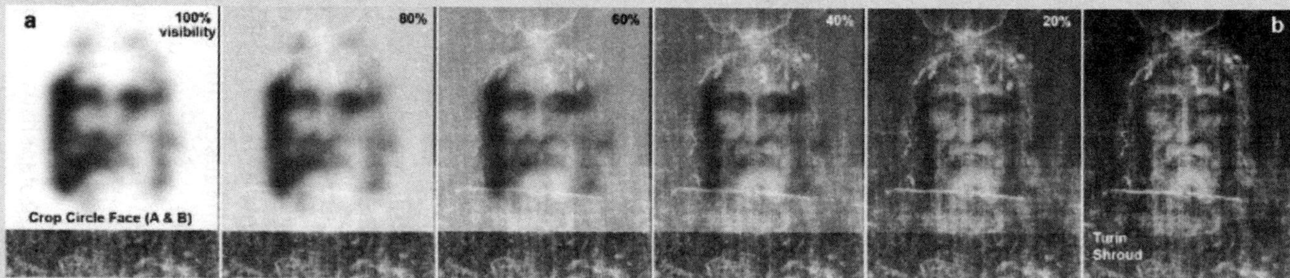

Diagrams © Andreas Müller, kornkreise-forschung.de

Two crop circles appeared in a field in Hungerford 5 August 2010. Superimposing them reveals the image of the Shroud of Turin. This illustration and its sequencing work reproduced with permission of its author, Andreas Müller

Pierre-Roger de Mirepoix counselled with Bishop Bertrand and Raymond de Perella and decided to attempt a night sortie with the object of retaking the barbican and setting the siege engine alight. The sortie failed. The Crusaders gained more footing into the fortress forecourt. The knights' wives hurriedly asked for the *convenensa* (the initiation ceremony for a *credens*, a believer). The morning after the failed sortie the fortress leaders decided to surrender.

On 1st March the crusading army managed to take up positions on the slopes of the Pog and negotiations began. Discussions were very short as even the Crusaders were exhausted. The conditions were: i) the garrison to remain in the fortress for fifteen days and give up all hostages; ii) they would receive pardons for all past crimes, including the Avignon affair; iii) the men-at-arms to retire with their arms and baggage but would have to report to the Inquisition and confess their errors; iv) all other persons in fortress would be freed with light penances provided they recanted their heresy and made confession to Inquisitors, those who did not to be burned; v) the fortress of Montségur was to pass into the hands of the Church and the French Crown.

On 14th March a festival of sorts was celebrated. It seems as if the two-week truce was engineered so that the Cathars would have time to hold the festival. Also during the truce at least six non-Cathar women and fifteen fighting volunteers received the Consolamentum and so committed themselves to certain death.

During the night of the 16th, Pierre-Roger dangled ropes down the west face of the rock and let down four people, stories handed down naming them as: Amiel Aicart, Hugo, Poitevin and Alforo. None of these four or the purported treasure in their care, the Oriflamme (Grâl or Mani) of the Cathar faith and, it is rumoured, the Ark of the Covenant and the Grail Cup, fell into the hands of the authorities. The four knights are said to have handed the Mani to a "Son of Belissena" (Son of the Moon), Pons-Arnaud de Castella Verdunam, who in turn hastened it to its place of concealment in the caverns of Ornolac in the Sabarthès.

All who refused to recognize the supremacy of Yahweh, the authority of Peter's keys and Rome's dogma were condemned to be burned alive. At daybreak more than two hundred *haeretici* (Rahn stated they were 205 in number) were fettered and brutally dragged down the mountain. The pyre on which they were to be burned was made of huge mounds of faggots, straw and pitch. The clergy chanted their psalms and the executioners shouted as they set fire to the palisade at each of its four corners. Among the condemned was the castellan's daughter,

Esclarmonde de Belissena, a relative of Esclarmonde de Foix. The other prisoners, about 400 in total, were thrown in the dungeons of the fortress of Carcassonne, where the vast majority perished in misery.

*

While emerging from the seclusion of the forge, Templar knight Alain Vangineau, an armed crossbow in his hands, is taking great care not to be spotted by the aggressors. He recalls his Grand Master's reverent description of the Cathar faithful. The Cathars teach that men and women may know God personally. This beautiful catechism enrages the Church of Rome whose twelve hundred year doctrines are founded on the absolute necessity for the intervention of exclusively male intermediaries through whom the faithful may worship a remote and distant God.

More than this, the Cathars' belief that God lives within the hearts of human beings and can communicate with them directly poses fundamental questions about the role and influence of any kind of temporal authority figure in the conduct of individuals' lives. A person taking to heart the Cathars' teachings and living them day-to-day has need neither of priests, popes nor kings.

The problem facing Louis IX, as one of the joint initiators of the Albgensian Crusade, was one of public image in these final months of the mission to exterminate the Cathars. There was an underlying opinion within Christendom that the king was being unduly harsh in his dealings with the Cathars who, after all, were fellow Christians, albeit with radically different ideas about expressing their faith. Consequently, in recognition of their power and the respect they commanded, Louis asked Knights Templar Grand Master Armand de Périgord to send to Montségur a contingent of Templars as neutral observers. Their role was to report that military actions, trials and executions were conducted fairly.

In reality, Armand de Périgord was a secret supporter of the Cathars. In addition to sending five Templar observers in full dress, he posted thirty knights incognito around the camp. Alain was one of these. The disguised knights were placed at different levels in the encampment as cooks, herdsmen, chicken keepers and servants. Alain had been posing as a smithy, a trade he had learned from his father. These concealments allowed the knights to see, hear and feel the pulse of proceedings as the mountain community began to fall and to give insight to Armand de Périgord on the true course of events at Montségur. Alain watched as the first to be manhandled down the mountain were pushed roughly into a large flat meadow and tied to a stake. These were the bishops and the priests, the formal members of the Order who had undergone the Consolamentum, the sacred and mysterious rite of baptism of the Cathars. Consequently, they neither felt pain from the flames nor cried out. It was said that the rite of Consolamentum involved the priests' laying on of hands upon a mysterious head, a supernatural talisman that imbued those present with an invulnerable force. Alain had heard whispers that the object was thc Head of God. One of his fellow Templars told him of a rumour that this was connected with the manner of Jesus' death and the subsequent flight to France of some close to Him, most notably Mary Magdalene, the disciple Bartholomew and a child.

This absence of yells and screams from those giving up their lives for their beliefs caused fury among the watching troops and papal clergy. But as the executioners gradually worked their way through to the younger Cathars and the *faidit* and their wives and children, the pain was recognisable. They had no protection against the agony of the flames. Intervention was necessary.

Through a sign from one of the dressed Templars all those that are incognito draw back their crossbows, take rapid aim and euthenize the vulnerable as the flames begin to leap ever higher. Time and again, Alain, unseen, brings a swift death to a woman or child in pain and distress. These merciful acts doubly infuriate those who are responsible for the executions because they want to hear the moans, groans and death gasps. The dead are taken down and new victims put up.

Anger is soon replaced by fear and confusion when the rising embers from the Prat dels Cremats turn into millions of white petals, which in their billowing ascent skyward release an overwhelming scent of roses. Puzzlement on the faces of the burners quickly turns to horror when a sense of a new understanding pervades their angry righteousness. The thought that they may not be on the right side after all is too much to bear. Most seek to dismiss the idea and redouble their grisly work but some drop their brands and run from the scene. One doubter even throws himself on the pyre in shame. No arrow to end his suffering is forthcoming.

A great furore quickly develops and the only thing that keeps the proceedings from degenerating into a state of complete imbalance is the five Templars who stand very strong, steadfast and still. The observers are able to cover for Alain and his disguised companions who, hiding in the shadows within the tents and behind animals, bring peace to those women and younger ones that are dying.

Suddenly, one of the Templar observers gives a sign to Alain to fall back. Quickly, Alain withdraws from his hiding place and is met by Armand de Périgord who is holding a kidskin satchel and a fold of cloth. The Grand Master issues urgent instructions.

'Alain, the cloth is the Cathars' most precious relic, the Holy Shroud in which Joseph of Arimathea wrapped the crucified body of Our Lord after he was taken down from the Cross. Our enemies will stop at nothing to secure it. Ride like the wind and deliver it to our Preceptory in Foix.'

*

Barely able to catch his breath, Brad rises from the table. Tears and sweat stream down his face as he slumps down on the *kline* and drains a pitcher of water. Gradually regaining his composure, Brad reflects on what he had witnessed; no, not just witnessed, but experienced in every heartstopping detail on a shameful day in the history of the Roman Church and the French monarchy. So many deaths, so many terrible deaths—could he and his fellow Templars in hiding have done more? It was pointless dwelling on it.

The Shroud—Alain had been tasked with removing it from Montségur. Did he succeed? What became of it? How had it come into the Cathars' possession? Brad knows that in the present day there are sharply divided opinions on the question of the authenticity of the shroud in the cathedral of San Giovanni Battista in Turin. Was the cloth that had been temporarily in Alain's possession the genuine article?

Suddenly, the writing on the parchment dissolves and is replaced by fresh script. Firstly, Brad sees an unusual illustration of the Crucifixion scene. Jesus has been taken down from the Cross and placed on a haycart by a man and two women. His prone body is wrapped in a cloth. Brad reads the accompanying text. By virtue of his newly acquired astral vision, Brad *knows* that its author had been a member of the Essene community in Jesus' time.

The text reveals that before commencing his Ministry, Jesus came to a special place above Qumran called the Caves of Zohar. Here he received instructions and insight from Zohar, a Qabalah master who used crystal balls to illustrate his lessons.

It was to this place that the three Persian Magi had come some years earlier. They had discovered a phenomenon in the heavens for which their knowledge and ancient charts had no explanation. Here, Zohar told the Magi that there would shortly be born a special child who would be the catalyst for mystics and metaphysicians through the years to come. He would eventually create the curtain or shroud for the Ancient Truths, which had existed from the beginnings of time.

Zohar told Gaspar, Melchior and Balthazar that what the child would eventually teach he would learn in this cave during the four occasions that he would visit. Those who followed him would create a religion that would be full of attempts to control humanity by spiritual manipulation. As the religion grew, it would spread throughout the world. Wars would be fought because of it; and much anger and hatred would arise from its contacts with other world religions. Behind these chaotic actions, esoteric mysticism would continue working through disciplined individuals who were aligned to Mother Nature and their inner spiritual journey. The child would die in his forty-first year.

Jesus' mother, Mary, had entered the Temple of Ishtar in Jerusalem at the age of thirteen. Her qualifications were of the highest for she was a direct descendent of four previous high priestesses of the Temple: Tamar, Ruth, Bathsheba and Rahab. In her fifteenth year Mary was chosen to lay with Joseph and, for the first time in 2,500 years of the Goddess tradition, an initiate conceived. As the High Priestess of the Temple, Mary Magdalene summoned Joseph to notify him of the miracle. Somewhat embarrassed, Joseph humbly asked if he could take Mary as his wife. Approval was given under two conditions. He was to take Mary to the Mother Temple in Alexandria for sanctification ceremonies, and he must swear to keep this information secret.

However, rumours of this potential high birth began to circulate throughout Jerusalem just as Joseph was preparing to take Mary to Egypt. Mary Magdalene soon became aware of the concerns that the Temple of Solomon's inner council had regarding these rumours. If it were true that one of the Ishtar temple initiates had conceived, something that had never happened before, then the child of the birth would be a definite threat to the masculine god of the Jews. In fact, the times were so harsh and cruel in Roman occupied Jerusalem that people might even be calling this child the Messiah.

After the birth, Joseph and Mary returned to Jerusalem with the baby and moved into quarters near the Temple of Ishtar. As the child grew he played in the Temple, learning of the power and subtleties of women. At the age of thirteen Jesus was sent by Mary Magdalene and her priestesses to the Caves of Zohar for the first of the four occasions that he would visit for further initiation and learning. Afterwards, Jesus travelled to Egypt and studied in the Mother Temple of Isis to gain further understanding of feminine power.

Subsequently, Mary Magdalene was called to Alexandria by the High Council of Ishtar to be told that she was to return with Jesus to Jerusalem where they would wed. Mary was twenty-three years the young man's senior and at first protested. Jesus answered Mary's concern, saying that love was ageless and that its power would produce a child who would be trained in a far-off land by a Master of Light.

Another that found their way to Zohar's cavern was a middle-aged woman, Calista, who had fled years earlier from powerful enemies in Rome. Zohar seated her at a loom and asked her to weave from a special yarn a cloth two lengths and one width of her body. Its warp had to be perfect. Thirty years later, after unravelling the cloth and starting over more times than she could remember, Calista finished the cloth. The completion of the cloth took place just before the Crucifixion.

Pontius Pilate had given two members of the Sanhedrin, disguised as simple Jews, permission to remove Jesus from the cross and entomb him. Calista and two helpers from the cave overpowered the two men as they were making their way with the body through an olive grove. They took Jesus, barely alive, to a waiting cart. One of the helpers applied an herbal salve to his wounds and gave him an elixir to slow the bleeding, allowing him to enter a state of suspended animation.

The specially woven cloth, sprinkled with special herbal essences, was wrapped around his body to prevent infection and keep him warm. Jesus was put in the cart, covered in hay and transported up the mountain above Jerusalem to Zohar's Temple Cavern where he was placed on a marble altar. Calista sprinkled a special herbal essence onto the cloth covering Jesus' unconscious body.

In this healing place Jesus, wrapped in the magical shroud, remained alive, thus allowing his astral form to travel beyond the confines of the cave. He appeared to his mother, Mary Magdalene, his disciples, and to others who would eventually create Christianity. The Bible refers to these appearances:

Mark 16:9
Now when Jesus was risen early the first day of the week, he appeared first to Mary Magdalene, out of whom he had cast seven devils.

John 20:17
Jesus said to her, 'Touch me not, lest I ascend to the father.'

Finally, Jesus returned to his body one last time and Zohar conducted a special Qabalah ceremony with his magical crystal balls. Suddenly, three bolts of lightning pierced the walls of the cavern and entered the crystal balls. One concentrated bolt projected into the crystal ball that was positioned directly behind Jesus' head. A beam of electricity travelled from one ball to the other and the cavern lit up like brilliant sunshine. In one final flash the cavern went dark:

Matthew 27:50, 51
Jesus, when he had cried again with a loud voice, yielded up the ghost. And behold, the veil of the temple was rent in twain from the top to the bottom; and the earth did quake, and the rocks rent.

The shroud lay limp upon the altar; the body had vanished. The only visible sign that one had been there was the image that was left on the shroud, an imprint made indelibly by the chemicals in the cloth combined with the massive electrical charge. The weaver folded the cloth carefully and walked out of the cave. That night one of Zohar's helpers took the shroud to the Temple of Solomon. He made his way to the Inner Temple and entered a small passageway that led steeply downward. After what seemed an age he entered a dark space. He saw a door in the gloom and pushed it open to reveal a huge gilded room. In its centre was a small altar. He pushed hard and slowly the marble top moved enough for him to deposit the Shroud.

*

The scroll reveals that the Holy Shroud remained undisturbed in the Temple of Solomon for nearly twelve hundred years. In the early twelfth century, a few years after the founding of their Order, a party of Knights Templar, newly arrived in Jerusalem, retrieved the cloth from its hiding place during excavations of the Temple after a tip off as to its location. Soon afterwards, the Shroud was handed to the Catholic Church. The Pope at the time, Honorius II (head of the Church 1124-1130), promptly declared it a forgery because in his view it depicted a Serapis-like figure too slight and feminine in appearance to serve as an appropriate symbol for a powerful, masculine Church. But did the Pope's displeasure bring damage or even the destruction of the Shroud? It appeared not.

The parchment's account of the next chapter in the Shroud's history was a little muddled but it seemed to Brad that at some point in the twelfth century the cloth came into the possession of the Bogomils in Bosnia, a Christian sect influencd by Manichaean ideas. At this time

Bosnia belonged to the Kingdom of Hungary crown lands. Brad sees no reason to doubt it, knowing that the Cathars in France were probably an outgrowth from Bogomilism.

The text goes on to mention the creation of a collection of medieval manuscripts between the late 12th to early 13th centuries, together known as the *Codex Pray* or the *Hungarian Pray Manuscript.* Of the five illustrations within the Codex, one is reproduced in the parchment. It shows the body of Jesus being prepared for burial. An angel is showing the empty tomb to the Three Ladies, whom the *Gospel of John* names as Mary (mother of Jesus), Mary Magdalene and Mary of Clopas. Placed by the side of this illustration is a plate depicting the Shroud in the cathedral of San Giovanni Battista.

Examining them together, Brad can clearly see that the Codex image shows striking generic similarities with the present-day Shroud of Turin. Jesus is shown entirely naked with the arms on the pelvis, as in the body image of the Turin cloth; the thumbs on the image appear to be retracted, with only four fingers visible on each hand, matching the detail on the Turin Shroud; the fabric shows a herringbone pattern, similar to the weaving pattern of the Shroud; and the four tiny circles on the lower image, which appear to form a letter L, perfectly reproduce four apparent "poker holes" on the Turin cloth, which likewise appear to form a letter L.

Brad *knows* that the cloth pictured in the Codex could not have been drawn except by the hand of one who had seen Jesus's burial shroud with their own eyes. This confirmed that the Holy Shroud, although disliked by Honorius, perhaps equally so by his successors, had not suffered destruction and was at some point passed by the Bogomils to their Cathar brethren, who subsequently brought it to Montségur. So, the answer to Brad's initial question was, yes, the cloth that had been briefly in Alain's possession was the genuine article.

The book explained that before the Cathars possessed the Shroud it was held in Constantinople during the Fourth Crusade (1202-1204). In August 1203, during a ceasefire, knight Robert de Clary visited the city. He wrote in his chronicle that, 'Among other astonishing things there is a church called Saint Mary of Blacherne, where there is the Shroud, in which Our Lord Jesus was wrapped and that every Holy Friday is lifted up vertically, so that the shape of Our Lord could be seen very well.'

Two years later the plundered Shroud was in Athens. Theodor Angel Comnenus, nephew of Byzantine Emperor Isaac II, wrote from there to Pope Innocent III begging the Holy Father to retrieve as soon as possible precious relics that had been missing for over a year, presumed stolen by the Crusader forces, making specific reference to the presence of the Shroud.

The scroll is not forthcoming on the movements of the Shroud between its presence in Athens and, later, Alain's hurrying it away from Montségur. Brad's new *knowing*-sense tells him, however, that it was not long before the Templars gave it to the Cathars in the Languedoc for safeguarding.

Despite the Shroud's depicting the form of a man, the Cathars did not disdain the task to safeguard the cloth. They knew that the image was that of Jesus but not one imprinted by his flesh. How could it? The Cathars' Christian faith was grounded in the belief that Jesus was not corporeal but an angel. They accepted the power and Godliness of the Shroud because they knew from teachings passed down what had taken place in the Caves of Zohar. They knew that the imprint had been created by the miraculous power of Divine Light hurled down from the Heavens, an action that vouchsafed the truth of their faith and proved that the Son of God could not possibly have been a flesh and blood figure.

After Alain delivered the Holy Shroud to the Preceptory at Foix, it remained in the possession of the Templars until their Order was brutally repressed in the first decade of the fourteenth century. One of the knights who was burned at the stake in 1314, along with the last Grand Master, James de Molay, was the Norman preceptor Geoffroi de Charney, also known as Guy d'Auvergne. It is believed that Guy was a relative of another knight named Geoffroi de Charny, who came into possession of the Shroud in 1354. This Charney, whose grandfather was Jean de Joinville, a close friend of Louis IX, the joint exterminator of the Cathar faithful, founded the church of Lirey, a hamlet of fifty hearths in north-central France, where he exhibited the Shroud in 1356 in the few months before he died. It would appear, therefore, that Guy d'Avergne, having obtained the Shroud legitimately or by stealth, due to his senior Templar connections, handed it down through the Charney family.

The Shroud remained at Lirey until around 1418, although it is unclear if it remained in public view all this time because it was denounced in 1389 as a forgery by the Bishop of Troyes, who said it was 'cunningly painted, the truth being attested by the artist who painted it.'

The Avignon antipope Clement VII (reigned 1378–94), although he refrained from expressing his opinion on the Shroud's authenticity, sanctioned its use as an object of devotion provided that it be exhibited as an "image or representation" of the true shroud. Subsequent popes from Julius II on, however, took its authenticity for granted.

By 1418, the Champagne region where resided the Charney family was occupied by the English and their Burgundian allies. Geoffroi de Charnay's granddaughter Marguerite, dame of Lirey, Savoisy and Montfort, married Humbert de Villersexel, Count of La Roche. Fearing for the safety of their treasures and relics in these troubled times, the canons of Lirey entrusted them all to Humbert.

In a receipt for the items dated 6 July the Count stated on item entrusted to his care as '…a sheet on which is the figure or representation of the Shroud of Our Lord Jesuchrist, which is in a coffer emblazoned with the Charny arms.' Humbert de Villersexel promised to return the treasures to the church 'when the tribulation now in France will have ceased.' Marguerite and Humbert kept the Shroud at their Château de Montfort. The Shroud did not change hands until 1453 when Marguerite gave it to the Italian House of Savoy, which deposited it in a chapel at Chambéry in the Auvergne-Rhône-Alpes region of southeastern France.

The parchment then reveals to Brad that the Borgia Pope, Alexander VI (reigned 1492-1503), ordered the Shroud to be destroyed because, like Honorius 350 years previously, he too hated its "feminine" image. The Pope's son, Cesar Borgia, ordered Leonardo da Vinci to make a replacement. The artist had been helped in this task by the arrival in his studio of a very unusual man who had brought with him herbs, oils and other materials from the time of Jesus. Da Vinci's artistic genius, combined with his incorporation into the cloth of the fifteen hundred-year-old materials, created the shroud that can be seen today in the Cathedral of St. John the Baptist in Turin, and which continues to divide opinion. Nevertheless, in 2022 a study team led by Liberato De Caro in Italy, using a new X-ray technique, concluded "the experimental results are compatible with the hypothesis that the Turin Shroud is a 2,000-year-old relic."

Brad felt very humbled by what he had felt and experienced emotionally as he traced the history of the shroud. The scroll had revealed that its safety had been entrusted to Alain after the fall of Montsegur, and that he successfully delivered it to the Templar perceptory at Foix for safekeeping. After that, Alain had had no responsibility for the Shroud's destiny, but Brad felt in his heart that Da Vinci's creation, imbued with materials that had been used in its original creation in the Caves of Zohar, retained an essence of Jesus's spirit substance.

(New research findings support the theory that the Holy Shroud was created in Da Vinci's time period. They indicate that the imprint of a human-like figure on the cloth may have come from a shallow sculpture and not an actual person. Brazilian designer Cicero Moraes used 3D digital modelling to analyse how different types of cloth drape over various shapes or figures and to map their respective contact areas. He used open-source software to assess how fabric forms impressions from a full three-dimensional human body as compared to a low-relief sculpture produced by raising a figure slightly from a flat background. Moraes says the scenario of fabric contouring a low-relief sculpture shows greater similarity to the observed contours on the shroud while the projection of a 3D human body results in a 'significantly distorted image.' The designer suspects such a sculpture may have been made from wood, stone or metal, and likely pigmented only in the areas of contact to produce the kind of pattern seen on the shroud. The study concludes that the image is more consistent with an artistic low-relief representation than with the direct imprint of a real human body.) [67]

*

Now it was really was time for Brad to leave his hilltop Temple. He put a finger to his Celtic cross and visualised Finley's livery stable. Immediately, he felt himself draining as if through an hourglass and all at once he emerged into the stable.

'Welcome back, Brad,' said Ruth.

[67] First published: 28 July 2025 https://doi.org/10.1111/arcm.70030

Cesare Borgia by Altobello Melone

The Temple of the Grail from "Parsifal"

Chapter 28

Initiation

'Live each day to the fullest, and let no sun pass through the sky that you do not see beauty in everything around you.'

—The Flying A's Gatekeeper

Ruth was walking out from the kitchen in Ellie's Guest House carrying a heaped plate in one hand and a steaming coffee pot in the other. Brad had made the transfer from ancient Greece not into the livery stable but into the Finley B&B's dining room.

'Take a seat and dig in, Brad,' said Ruth.' You're probably famished after your journey. The Gatekeeper has left Finley. He's expecting another curious adventurer to find their way to the Flying A. There are others like you, Brad, for whom doors open but need a helping hand to make the all-important crossing of the "Philosophic Bridge" to find the "other side of things." How was Greece, by the way?'

'It was amazing,' Brad replied as he tucked into a meal of baked trout, creamy mashed potato and corncob. 'Wow, this is fantastic. Dare I say it, but your cooking is even tastier than the Gatekeeper's. I love this fish; trout is one of my favourites. And this mash is beyond excellent. I guess you know I arrived in a beautiful hilltop temple, which contained an unusual library full of books that meant something special to me. It wasn't long before I twigged that the library was a physical representation of my personal history through the ages. I learned a great deal but I also feel that I absorbed a lot of stuff that I won't digest and assimilate for a long time yet.'

'You've got that right. I mean the bit about your absorbing stuff, not about the quality of the Gatekeeper's cooking, but I have to confess I ain't bad in the kitchen,' Ruth said laughing.

'The experience of living in the world,' Ruth continued, 'can be likened to the learning and graduation process in a university. Each lifetime that we experience is the equivalent of undertaking a semester within an academic year. Very rarely, an individual will sail through their studies term-by-term, year-by-year, and graduate without breaking a step. The rest of us proceed in a more leisurely and zigzag fashion, sometimes having to re-sit a lesson, test or examination or, in some cases, repeating one or, exceptionally, even more than one year of study before earning our diploma.'

'What comes after graduation?' Brad asked.

'New adventures, of course,' Rachel said, laughing. 'There are only ever new beginnings, never final endings. The Universal Powers created training dimensions such as Finley to ensure that certain individuals may step temporarily out of their daily environment and experience new lessons and insights in a place that exists between the physical world and the infinite number of dimensions beyond. The few who find their way here can do so because they have reached a point in their evolution that enables them to pass freely through the gateway that separates the physical world from learning dimensions such as the Flying A service station and Finley.

'It is not that these travellers are any better, smarter or more spiritual than anyone else. To think that is a sure-fire way to get relegated to the back of the queue for the bus or bike ride to places like the Flying A. These things can happen when the forces of synchronicity have lined up in such a pattern that a doorway opens to a very different kind of classroom. That is what happened for you on that first occasion you came off the blacktop and met the Gatekeeper. Since that day you have, by and large, used your time on the "other side of things" to excellent advantage…but you are not yet quite done.'

Ruth paused for a moment before continuing. 'In one of your library scrolls, you read of the time when one of Zohar's helpers took the shroud and hid it deep within the Temple of Solomon. It wasn't the only item he concealed.'

Ruth had already secured Brad's keen attention. This last remark grabbed him with both hands. 'Oh?'

'A charge laid against the Templars in their day was that they worshipped a human skull they called "Baphomet," which, according to the Rome's indictment of heresy, "bestowed on the order all its wealth, made the trees flower, and the plants of the earth to sprout forth." There was a germ of truth in the Church's accusation. The Cathars were said to possess a "talking head," known by the faithful as the "Living Bible." After the fall of Montségur, this talking head vanished. You were not the only Templar to be entrusted with a valuable relic. Your superior,

Armand de Périgord, took personal responsibility for spiriting away the Cathar's most sacred possession.'

Ruth went to an oak chest and removed an item draped in a dark blue velvet cloth. With a flourish, she pulled off the cover to reveal a crystal skull.

Brad was stunned into silence before finding his voice, 'The Head of God?'

'A bit fanciful,' Ruth replied, 'but, yes, it is the skull from Zohar's cavern, which Mary Magdalene brought to France after the crucifixion. For centuries the skull was hidden in a small church near Lake Garda until in 1914 certain lowlife Cardinals in the Vatican became suspicious of its whereabouts, and so it was brought here to Finley. Let's take it into the garden.'

Ruth led Brad to a small garden behind the guesthouse. Brad had never seen such beauty. Every part of the garden's perfectly sculpted landscape was exquisitely planted. Overwhelmingly, the garden's most abundant flower was the white rose, multiple varieties of which were filling the lovingly tended beds. He recognised it from his dreams.

'Welcome, Brad, as you can see, you visit this beautiful garden while you are asleep. Unlike most, this personal and special space needs only your love to keep it growing in perfection. Each flower, bush or tree will feel your kindness and love and will respond the same as it would to sun and rain. It is here that you are taught the intricacies of living in the world while not being of it.'

Ruth asked Brad to sit on a rustic stool placed in the centre of three interlaced triangles of hundreds of white rose petals, which, together, formed a pentagram star. Ruth explained that the five points represented the five elements of nature: earth, fire, water, air and *quint essentia*, the hidden power behind all things, the creator of the other four.

'Are you ready for one last adventure here in Finley?' Ruth asked.

With only a hint of hesitation, Brad nodded. Ruth placed her hand on the small of Brad's back and pushed his head gently backwards. Unseen hands then eased Brad from his stool into a suspended position five feet from the ground.

Ruth began humming a melody that quickly began to mesmerise the horizontal figure. The humming grew louder and louder, the ascending sound reverberating through Brad's magical garden.

'All that you have experienced so far under the guidance of the Gatekeeper, Hermes and me are merely *hors d'oeuvres*. It is now time for you to savour the main course.'

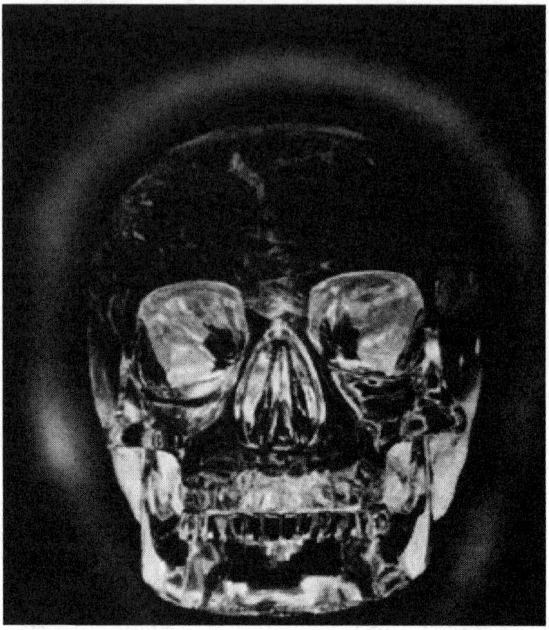

Mitchell-Hedges Skull with observed "halo" effect

Ruth placed Brad's arms across his chest and positioned the skull nine inches above Brad's head. There it hovered for a few moments before becoming consumed in a blinding light.

'Prepare!' commanded Ruth.

All at once, the solar light became nebula bright. It then gathered itself into a narrow channel and streamed its holy irridescence into Brad's head. Instantly, Brad's body began to revolve counter clockwise. Faster and faster it spun until his body became a mere blur. There was a blinding flash of light and and Brad was no longer in the Finley garden. In his place, suspended in the same spot, was a bouquet of white roses.

Experiencing total weightlessness, Brad felt himself explode into thousands of pieces. He was suddenly aware of of a multitude of unique sensations and discovered that he was walking on rays of light which came from an unseen source on the horizon. Each step became like the touch of a butterfly upon a flower petal. From his right and left, he saw images of himself moving toward a rainbow of colour. As he came closer to the rainbow, he experienced his other fractured pieces slowly merging into one efflorescent sensation.

'Welcome to the ultimate initiation of manhood,' spoke an unseen female voice. 'You will now learn what you are, how to be more, and how to use the powers of the earth as if you were nature herself.'

Never had Brad felt so alive. All of his senses were intensified to such a point that he was acutely aware of feeling all of his life-form functions. He reached to touch himself for proof of what he was experiencing. To his surprise, his hand passed right thought the vision of his physical form. This caused him some immediate concern and he concentrated on touching himself again and again. To his relief, he began to feel substance. Satisfied, he turned his concentration to the sensual input which semed to be exploding around him. It was now that Brad noticed once again that what his body did was without substance. Only when he thought of himself as physical did he begin to achieve a fraction of solid form. However, the magnitude of power and sensation surging within and around him was more intriguing than any worry for the physical form he had become accustomed to in the recent past. He relaxed and let himself become a part of the expanding dimensions around him.

Never had Brad been made aware that colour has a smell as well as a musical quality. In childlike awe, he watched reds, blues and yellows fill the spaces around him with melodious sounds and fragrant perfumes. A spectrum of colour dazzled his consciousness. This spectrum produced an incredible harmony, dissolving every negative attitude he had ever acquired. Simultaneously, he was overpowered by the pungent and delicate aromas of the colours which had begun to lace themselves into his very esence. Sweet, spicy, succulent, they expanded his awareness to every horizon imaginable.

Through these inexhaustible sensations, Brad was vaguely aware of a nucleus of vibrant power pulling him to itself. Time and space had disintegrated into a minor part of the surrounding ether. An overwhelming fragrance of roses engulfed his senses. The aromatic feeling was satiny white with a melody of bubbling water…then a scented frosty air…then porous earth…and finally volcanic fire.

Closer and closer, Brad drifted toward the sophisticated power that radiated outward, pulling him into its enchanted web. One again, the fragrance of roses filled his awareness and he felt himself merge with a luminous Circle of Light. Around him, he felt a Presence that made him feel at ease and profoundly protected. His continuous movement, which had begun in the guesthouse garden and had brought him to this infinite place, began to slow. He found himself seated upon a form that seemed to be a crystal pillow. He looked down at himself, or at what he thought he should be, but there was nothing.

'How could this be?' he thought. 'How can I sit here without a form?' He looked again but didn't see anything. In essence, he was…but was not. There was a sensation of soft fluttering objects falling all around him. It took a moment to recognise them—they were white rose petals.

The brilliant Circle of Light surrounding Brad seemed to hide the Presence that he trusted intuitively. In what was probably only an instant, he examined the pillow upon which he sat. His hand reached down down to feel it. It was icy hard…but at the same time softly warm!

He began to feel small charges of energy shooting into him from the crystal pillow. The sensations proceded to grow until his consciousness had become an orgy of sense releases. From beyond the Circle of Light came a voice…an impression…or perhaps a thought?

'What you are about to learn, you already know,' continued the mystery voice. 'However, this time you will have total recall about the information your spirit is communicating. The body known as Brad has become a veil between what you really are and what you are experiencing upon the earth. When you step out of that physical shell, you will once more be all that you are experiencing right now…this moment. Within your spirit you are a part of all living things; you have discarded igorance and embraced wisdom of continual development.'

Brad's feeling was one of unity. Whatever he thought of he immediately became and then experienced everything related to the thing he had become. He thought of white roses and immediately he was a rose. To his surprise, it was a confining feeling, but one of warmth, beauty, fragrance and awareness. All of these sensations heightened as his initiation continued.

'Your spirit is not masculine or feminine. What WE have to teach you is how to use your earthly physical shell to its highest potential. The physical shell, known as Brad, is male. It is a magnificent combination of boundless biological impulses.'

During the period of impressions through the crystal pillow, Brad began to perceive glimmers of the universal energy of which he was a part, and how it complemented this earthly living experience.

'Your earth and its many life forms, if coordinated with care, have a potential power beyond any realisation that can be described or taught. The door to consistent communication with your inner spirit through to the "universal essence" is manifested by a positive polarity between your intuition-instinct and nature. When that door is wide open, the individual becomes a Spiritual Oasis for all life forms seeking unification with energies beyond physical imagination.'

The impulses around Brad stopped suddenly and he became aware of a great void encircling him. Everything was white, or so it seemed, for he could not find a response from any of his senses. He was slightly aware of something approaching but could not identify it.

Brad felt himself expanding again but, for the first time, he could now make out what was the recognisable physical form of himself. In a blinding flash, his form exploded into thousands of particles. The Circle of Light spoke once more. 'Your initiation has only just begun. *Now find yourself!*'

Brad, his body dispersing, could sense a slender thread connecting all of the pieces to a single entity. It was frightening to have every aspect of his worldly self disbanded into separate energies. The Circle of Light was providing just enough power for observtion to keep all the fractions of himself from fading into oblivion, which could easily happen if there were a lack of continuous identification. This he perceived as a most curious sensation. If he did not actively keep a pulsating energy running through the umbilical thread which connected the fragments known as Brad, he would merge into what he had been without a record of what he was now. He would not be able to return!

Suddenly, he felt the pulsation of a memory, the occasion of his first visit to the Flying A gas station, flowing though the connecting thread which seemed to create a type of unification. Within this thread came the affirmation, 'All energy comes from white. In the cycle of universal law, that energy would eventually merge into black only to re-emerge into white once again.' This memory pulsation travelled throughout the fragments in a perpetual cycle…again and again and again.

Brad began to comprehend the quest for balance in the assemblage of his old recognisable energy. First, he conneced taste and smell. Next, he connected sight and hearing. Finally, he connected the whole. Each of these pieces had gone through a complete cleansing and polarity realignment. What existed now began to take a form that was sharper, more perceptive, stronger and more assertive. As the final piece bonded with the whole, Brad was aware of the Divine. It was as if he were being annointed.

Throughout this experience, the Circle of Light had provided the guidance for a stable initiation, but had not projected one thought of energy transfer. Brad's conception of himself was now wonderfully new. No longer did he fear not having a physical form with which to identify. He recognised that he was now one thousand times greater than this physical shell of Brad. This recognition was so intense that he could manifest the physical Brad from any one of a hundred connection points. In essence, the experience of Initiation had broken down the veiled barriers between his Spirit Library and the physical Brad! What a precarious situation! It allowed him to have the control of materialisation and dematerialisation over his physical body with just a mere thought as the trigger.

Sitting in the Circle of Light, Brad gained deeper insights into the frailness between his spirit-being and his physical shell. He felt a communication from the energy behind the Circle of Light. 'By pulling all of your scattered pieces together and bonding them into a whole once again, you have become ONE with that eternal source of power. You are now a doorway for all those who seek a path of awareness within day-to-day living.'

A tremendous power shift began to take place as Brad felt himself moving away from the Circle of Light. In one final communication, the Circle of Light filled him with impressions which stirred him deeply.

'Learn always to be the observer, for what you will witness and walk through in this life could debilitate even the strongest person. Your initiation has provided you with many powers, but with every power comes a built-in weakness. The weakness will be your balance. In order for you to maintain the delicate balance you will need, you will be required to maintain a neutrality at all times. How you manoeuvre gracefully through chaos in day-to-day living will be in direct relation to your neutrality.'

Blackness engulfed Brad. It was as if he was being carried by gigantic loving hands through an endless tunnel of darkness. He closed his eyes in a deep relaxed meditation and sensed himself floating on the surface of a still, calm lake. The feeling of solid support around him was the first time he had felt physically whole since the Initiation had begun. The sensation of the water was healing, fulfilling and revitalising but he was afraid it would be gone if he opened his eyes.

Suddenly, Brad began sinking deeper into the lake, going deeper and deeper as if caught in a whirlpool. Spinning, spinning, Brad continued to fall. Time did not exist. It seemed he had been falling for a lifetime when the motion finally ended. He felt soft hands pull him to a standing position. His eyes fluttered open. He was in his home cabin by western Montana's Holland Lake.

He was quite alone. He looked at the clock and gasped. He had left the cabin at 5 a.m. on 21st December to keep his appointment with the Gatekeeper. So much had happened since then he was sure he must have been away for several days. But the ticking clock, which showed the day of the week as well as the time, was showing exactly the same time and date as when he had left. His overnight bag was at his feet. In addition to his belongings was a thick padded envelope.

He opened the envelope. Inside was the crystal cross that was gifted to him by Osric, a note from the Gatekeeper, some old papers, and a small linen bag containing six coins. The note read:

Dear Brad,

I'm sure you enjoyed your adventures while in Finley. As time goes by, more and more of what you learned and experienced will seep into your everyday life, and others will be drawn to your unique energy.

The papers I have enclosed are the deeds to the Flying A filling station and a notarised letter that confirms that its ownership is now vested in you.

The coins date back to Roman times. They are rare and valuable. They will fetch a very good price. Use them to bring the Flying A back to life. It has served its purpose as a gateway to the "other side of things," and now deserves to serve the public once again. It will not be entirely what it seems. Expect from time to time to receive visitors who will be drawn to its unusual energy. Rest assured, it will retain some of its old secrets and surprises!

As for me, my new billet is a neat little bistro in Montmartre. Next time you visit the City of Light pay me a visit at the Café des Artisans. You might be surprised by what you will find there.

Happy Solstice, Brad. Holland Lake is so very beautiful at this time of year. Enjoy the company.

Best wishes

Leon (yes, I do have a name!)

As Brad came to the end of the letter, he heard a knock at the cabin door. Puzzled, he opened it to see Ruth standing in the porch. She was wearing a backpack and carrying a picnic hamper and a bottle of Chianti Classico.

'Thought you might like some company over the next three days, Brad,' Ruth said, grinning from ear to ear. 'Where do I bunk?'

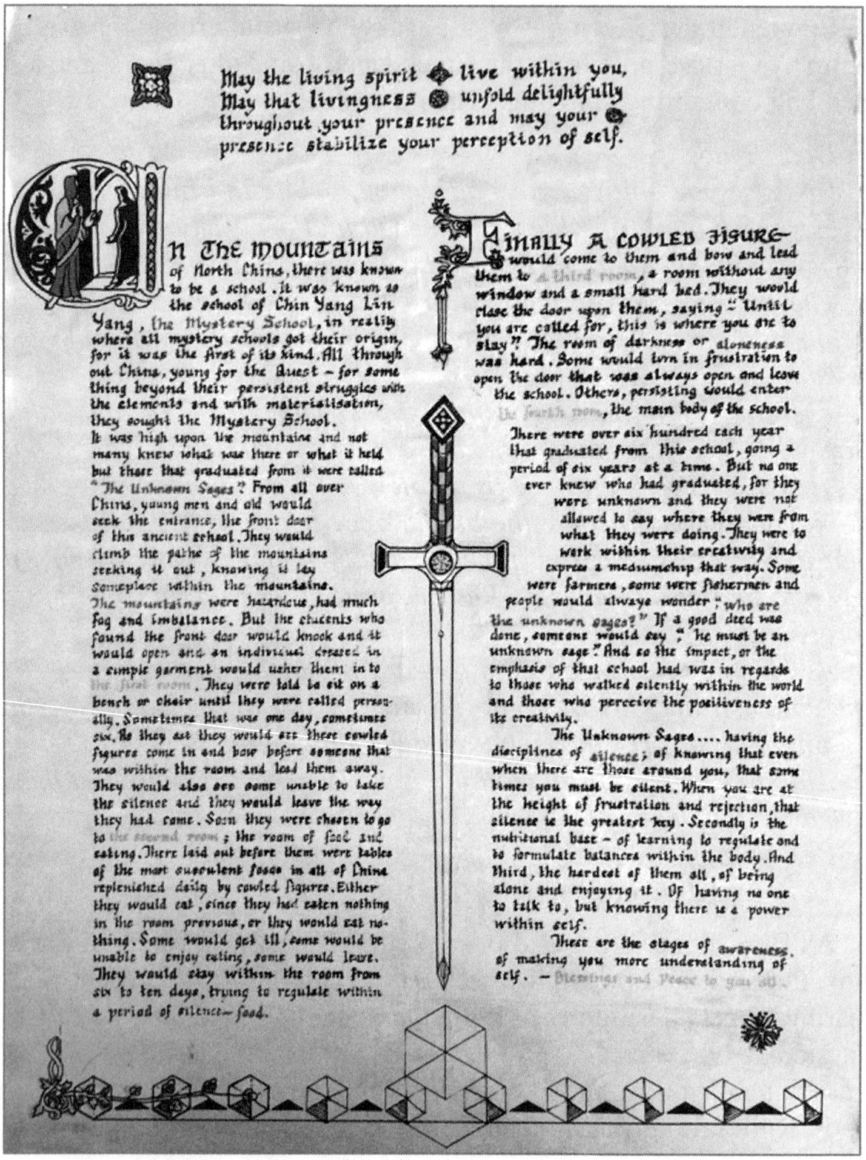

May the living spirit live within you,
May that livingness unfold delightfully
throughout your presence and may your
presence stabilize your perception of self.

IN THE MOUNTAINS of North China, there was known to be a school. It was known as the school of Chin Yang Lin Yang, the Mystery School, in reality where all mystery schools got their origin, for it was the first of its kind. All throughout China, young for the Quest – for something beyond their persistent struggles with the elements and with materialisation, they sought the Mystery School.

It was high upon the mountains and not many knew what was there or what it held but those that graduated from it were called "The Unknown Sages". From all over China, young men and old would seek the entrance, the front door of this ancient school. They would climb the paths of the mountains seeking it out, knowing it lay someplace within the mountains.

The mountains were hazardous, had much fog and imbalance. But the students who found the front door would knock and it would open and an individual dressed in a simple garment would usher them in to the first room. They were told to sit on a bench or chair until they were called personally. Sometimes that was one day, sometimes six. As they sat they would see these cowled figures come in and bow before someone that was within the room and lead them away. They would also see some unable to take the silence and they would leave the way they had come. Soon they were chosen to go to the second room; the room of food and eating. There laid out before them were tables of the most succulent foods in all of China replenished daily by cowled figures. Either they would eat, since they had eaten nothing in the room previous, or they would eat nothing. Some would get ill, some would be unable to enjoy eating, some would leave. They would stay within the room from six to ten days, trying to regulate within a period of silence – food.

FINALLY A COWLED FIGURE would come to them and bow and lead them to a third room, a room without any window and a small hard bed. They would close the door upon them, saying: "Until you are called for, this is where you are to stay". The room of darkness or aloneness was hard. Some would turn in frustration to open the door that was always open and leave the school. Others, persisting would enter the fourth room, the main body of the school.

There were over six hundred each year that graduated from this school, going a period of six years at a time. But no one ever knew who had graduated, for they were unknown and they were not allowed to say where they were from what they were doing. They were to work within their creativity and express a mediumship that way. Some were farmers, some were fishermen and people would always wonder; "who are the unknown sages?" If a good deed was done, someone would say; "he must be an unknown sage". And so the impact, or the emphasis of that school had was in regards to those who walked silently within the world and those who perceive the positiveness of its creativity.

The Unknown Sages.... having the disciplines of silence; of knowing that even when there are those around you, that sometimes you must be silent. When you are at the height of frustration and rejection, that silence is the greatest key. Secondly is the nutritional base – of learning to regulate and to formulate balances within the body. And third, the hardest of them all, of being alone and enjoying it. Of having no one to talk to, but knowing there is a power within self.

These are the stages of awareness, of making you more understanding of self. – Blessings and Peace to you all.

Teachings from the ancient Chinese Mystery School of Chin Yang Lin

Appendices

A crystal Pyramidion

The Great Pyramid's Golden Tip

The apex of the Great Pyramid at Giza was once adorned with a pyramidion (plural, pyramidia), a common practice of the Egyptians who often added a capstone upon structures such as pyramids and obelisks. During Egypt's Old Kingdom, pyramidia were generally made of diorite, granite or fine limestone. In the Middle Kingdom period through to the end of the pyramid-building era, they were built from granite. In the case of pyramid capstones, the pyramidion was often covered with gold or electrum (a naturally occurring alloy of gold and silver, with trace amounts of copper and other metals or gold) to reflect the rays of the sun. Middle Kingdom pyramidia were often inscribed with royal titles and religious symbols.

Very few pyramidia have survived into modern times. Most that remain are made of polished black granite and inscribed with the name of the pyramid's owner. Four pyramidia, the world's largest collection, are housed in the main hall of the Egyptian Museum in Cairo. Among them are the pyramidia from the so-called Black Pyramid of Amenemhat III at Dahshur and of the Pyramid of Khendjer at Saqqara.

The Egyptians associated such pyramidia with the Benben Stone. The Benben in Egyptian mythology is a stone with a conical shape and, according to some theorists, may be of extraterrestrial origin. It represented the cycle of the seasons and was a symbol of the Phoenix. As such, it was an important feature of the Temple of the Phoenix, which was within the precinct of the Great Sun Temple of Heliopolis.

In the mythology of ancient Egypt, there are several accounts of the creation of the world. One of these is centred on the god Atum who brought the universe into being. In the beginning, there was nothing but darkness and chaos. Subsequently, it was out of the primordial waters of Nu that the primordial hill, known as the Benben stone, arose, on top of which stood Atum. As the Benben stone rose from the primeval waters, it has been suggested that this word is associated with the verb 'weben,' which is the Egyptian hieroglyph for "to rise."

In another verion of the myth, the Benben stone was the primeval hill on which Atum first landed. The god looked around and realised that there was nothing around him but darkness and chaos. He was alone.

Desiring companionship, Atum began the work of creation. In some versions of the myth, Atum masturbated and through this act created Shu (the god of air) and Tefnut (the goddess of moisture). In other variations of the story, these deities were created by Atum's copulation with his own shadow.

Shu and Tefnut left Atum on the Benben stone and went away to create the rest of the world. After some time, Atum is said to have grown worried about his children. Removing his eye, he sent it in search of them. Shu and Tefnut returned with their father's eye, and Atum, seeing his children return, shed tears of joy. These teardrops, which fell on the Benben stone on which Atum was standing, transformed into human beings.

The Benben stone is also recorded to have been a sacred object that was once kept in the special shrine known as the "hwt benben," which translates as "House of the Benben." This sacred relic was in the innermost sanctuary of the temple in Heliopolis where Atum once served as its chief deity. The original cult object is said to have been lost at some point in history. Nevertheless, based on pictorial evidence, it has been suggested that this was an upright stone with a rounded top. Other solar temples would also have their own Benben stones. For example, the temple of Aten in El-Amarna that was built by the Pharaoh Akhenaten during the 14th century BC is recorded to have possessed a Benben stone, as did the 12th Dynasty Pyramid of Amenemhat III, which is today displayed in the Egyptian museum in Cairo.

Apart from being the name of a cult object, the Benben stone is also used to describe a type of ancient Egyptian architectural element, a characteristic that brings one to the connection between the Ancient Egyptian pyramidion and quartz crystal.

While most researchers believe that capstones were put in place to show off a Pharaoh's riches, others suggest that there was a deeper purpose at work. In this theory, the relatively tiny pyramidion compared with the length, breadth and height of the mighty edifice on which it sat became the key component of the entire structure. The material from which the pyramidion was made absorbed the sun's energies, thus enabling the capstone to serve as a cosmic key much like the key to a machine. In the case of the Great Pyramid, the whole structure was covered with polished limestone, which, enhanced by its golden capstone, shone at night like a terrestrial bright star visible from space.

According to the Egyptian authorities, there is no doubt about the matter. They claim that the Great Pyramid was built as a tomb for the pharaoh Cheops and the capstone was looted by thieves who also stole many other relics and treasures from the pyramids.

However, New Age theorists believe that the Great Pyramid was not built as a tomb and is far older than the 2,500 years put forward by the Egyptian authorities. Many believe that the structure is a machine and that it was its capstone that switched it on.

There appears to be little doubt that the Great Pyramid is encoded with many scientific and metaphysical laws and formulae. It has been suggested that one of the reasons for these incorporations is so that the Great Pyramid can accumulate and transmit cosmic energies. The idea is supported by the occurrence of "magical" numbers and series in its dimensions.

Those who are concerned with the challenging question of the Pyramid's precise measurements find themselves drawn to the matter of its apex. Peter Lemesurier[68] claimed that the dimensions of the Pyramid's internal spaces foretell the collapse of our present civilisation, an event that would be followed by a Messianic return and the birth of a new order. According to those that study Pyramid prophecy, this would be the time that the "stone that the builders rejected," the missing capstone of the Pyramid, will be restored to its apex.

This all-important capstone would have sat on the flat top of the pyramid, 480 feet above its base. In his 2016 work,[69] ancient metrology expert John Neal describes how the full height of the pyramid, reaching to its natural apex, would have been just over 481 feet. Like other pyramid capstones, its pyramidion would have repeated the form of the larger pyramid, making it a perfect scale model. In the case of the Great Pyramid, exactly 441/440th of its natural apex is missing, and this is because it is missing its pyramidion. 441/440 is an important ratio due the Earth's spin, which deforms it from the spherical. Consequently, it reduces the Earth's polar radius and expands its equatorial radius to make the mean radius of the Earth 441/440 of the polar radius. It is believed that the pyramidion would have had something to do with this ratio, possible adding 1/440 to reach the true apex of its geometry.

The late and great authority on ancient and sacred mysteries, John Michell, wrote that the numerical patterns within the structure's dimensions imply that its capstone consisted of not just one pyramidion

---

68 Lemesurier, P., *The Great Pyramid Decoded,* Element, 1996.

69 Neal, J., *All Done with Mirrors*, Secret Academy, 2016

but a series of diminishing size, each one forming the tip of the one underneath it. Michell speculated that the top one was fashioned out of solid gold, 5-inches in volume.

Yet, as Michell astutely pointed out, if this 5-inch gold capstone is to represent the whole structure in miniature, it must itself have had a separate tip. Michell believed that this tiny object could only have been some form of quartz crystal.

There are many traditions that describe how crystals were used in antiquity for attracting and transmitting cosmic energies. Edgar Cayce, the “Sleeping Prophet” of America, described his visions of Atlantis’ crystal technology which empowered the pre-Flood civilisation but which, finally, by its abuse precipitated the cataclsym. Other channeling sources have described the iniquitous process in the latter years of Atlantis in which newborn infants had a programmed quartz crystal implanted in the base of the spine, so that the State had the ability to control behaviour throughout the individual’s life.

The means by which the crystal pyramidion could have been held in place at the top of the Great Pyramid is suggested by the investigative findings of Moses Cotsworth.[70] He visited Egypt in 1900 to observe the shadows cast by the Great Pyramid at certain seasons. During the visit Cotsworth identified a strange Egyptian hieroglyph showing a truncated pyramid topped by a staff or *gnomon* as an apparatus for refining the shadow from a pyramid’s peak, thereby permitting measurements to be made of the length of the year. A metal rod of that description, set into the truncated pyramid, would also serve to house the parts of the capstone, securing them in place through holes drilled down their centres. A diamond or quartz crystal point on that rod, appearing at the apex of the golden tip, would cast the finest possible shadow and might also serve, like the “cat’s whisker” fine wire in a crystal set used to detect radio signals, to concentrate energies for the Pyramid’s principal cosmic function.

---

[70] Cotsworth, M., *The Need of a Rational Almanac*, Forgotten Books (reprint), 2018

The Sepher Yetzirah, The Book Of Formation

Chapter One

1. YAH, the Lord of Hosts, the living Elohim, King of the Universe, Omnipotent, the Merciful and Gracious God, Supreme and Extolled, Dweller in the Height whose habitation is Eternity, who is Sublime and Most-Holy, engraved His name and ordained (formed) and created the Universe in thirty-two mysterious paths (stages) of wisdom (science), by three Sepharim, namely, Numbers, Letters, and Sounds, which are in Him one and the same.

2. Ten Sephiroth (ten properties from the Ineffable One) and twenty-two letters are the Foundation of all things. Of these twenty-two letters three are called "Mothers," sewn "Double," and twelve "Simple."

3. The ten numbers (Sephiroth) out of Nothing are analogous to the ten fingers and the ten toes: five over against five. In the center between them is the covenant with the Only One God. In the spiritual world it is the covenant of the voice (the Word), and in the corporeal world the circumcision of the flesh (the rite of Abraham).

4. Ten are the numbers (of the Sephiroth) out of Nothing, ten--not nine; ten--not eleven. Comprehend this great, wisdom, understand this knowledge and be wise. Inquire into the mystery and ponder it. Examine all things by means of the ten Sephiroth. Restore the Word to Its Creator and lead the Creator back to His throne again. He is the only Formator and beside Him there is no other. His attributes are ten and are without limit.

5. The ten ineffable Sephiroth have ten infinitudes, which are as follows: The infinite beginning and the infinite end;

The infinite good and the infinite evil;

The infinite height and the infinite depth;

The infinite East and the infinite West; The infinite North and the infinite South; and over them is the Lord Superlatively One, the faithful King. He rules over all in all from His holy habitation for ages of ages.

6. The appearance of the ten spheres (Sephiroth) out of Nothing is as a flash of lightning or a sparkling flame, and they are without beginning or end. The Word of God is in them when they go forth and when they return. They run by His order like a whirlwind and prostrate themselves before His throne.

7. The ten Sephiroth have their end linked to their beginning and their beginning linked to their end, cojoined as the flame is wedded to the live coal, for the Lord is Superlatively One and to Him there is no second. Before One what can you count?

8. Concerning the number (10) of the spheres of existence (Sephiroth) out of Nothing, seal up your lips and guard your heart as you consider them, and if your month opens for utterance and your heart turns towards thought, control them, returning to silence. So it is written: "And the living creatures ran and returned." (Ezekiel i. 14.) And on this wise was the covenant made with us,

9. These are the ten emanations of number out of Nothing:

1st. The spirit of the living Elohim, blessed and more than blessed be the living Elohim of ages. His Voice, His Spirit, and His Word are the Holy Spirit.

2nd. He produced air from the spirit and in the air. He formed and established twenty-two sounds--the letters. Three of them were fundamental, or mothers; seven were double; and twelve were simple (single); but the spirit is the first one and above all.

3rd. Primordial water He extracted from the air. He formed therein twenty-two letters and established them out of mud and loam, making them like a border, putting them up like a wall, and surrounding them as with a rampart. He poured snow upon them and it became earth, as it reads: "He said to the snow be thou earth." (Job. xxxvii. 6.)

4th. Fire (ether) He drew forth from the water. He engraved and established by it the Throne of Glory. He fashioned the Seraphim, the Ophanim, and the Holy Living Creatures (Cherubim?), as His ministering angels; and with (of) these three He formed His habitation, as it reads: "Who made His angels spirits, His ministers a flaming fire."

5th. He selected three consonants (I, H, V) from the simple ones--a secret belonging to the three mothers, or first elements; א מ ש (A, M, Sh), air, water, fire (ether). He sealed them with His spirit and fashioned them into a Great Name and with this sealed the universe in six directions. He turned towards the above and sealed the height with י ה ו (I, H, V).

6th. He turned towards the below and sealed the depth withה י ו (H, I, V). 7th. He turned forward and sealed the East with ו י ה (V, I, H).

8th. He turned backward and sealed the West with ו ה י (V H, I).

9th. He turned to the right and sealed the South with י ו ה (I, V, H).

10th. He turned to the left and sealed the North with ה ו י (H, V, I).

NOTE. This arrangement of the letters of the Great Name is according to the Rev. Dr.

Isidor Kalisch.

10. These are the ten ineffable existences out of nothing; From the spirit of the Living God emanated air; from the air, water; from the water, fire (ether); from the fire, the height and the depth, the East and the West, the North and the South.

Chapter Two

1. There are twenty-two basic (sounds and) letters. Three are the first elements (water, air, fire), fundamentals, or mothers; seven are double letters; and twelve are simple letters. The three fundamental letters א מ ש have as their basis the balance. At one end of the scale are the virtues and at the other the vices, placed in equilibrium by the tongue. Of the fundamental letters מ (M) is mute like the water, ש (Sh) hissing like fire, א (A) a reconciling breath between them.

2. The twenty-two basic letters having been designed, appointed, and established by God, He combined, weighed, and exchanged them (each with the others), and formed by them all beings which are in existence, and all which will be formed in

time to come.

3. He established twenty-two basic letters, formed by the voice and impressed upon the air by the breath. He set them to be audibly uttered in five different parts of the human ץ ר ס ש ז, Dentals ת נ ל ט ד ,Linguals ;ק כ י ג ,Palatals ;ע ח ה א ,mouth: namely, Gutturals .ף מ ו ב ,Labials

4. He fixed the twenty-two basic letters in a ring (sphere) like a wall with two hundred and thirty-one gates, and turned the sphere forward and backward. Turned forward, the sphere signified good; when reversed, evil. Three letters may serve for an illustration: ע ג נ O, N, G), pleasure (joy), and nothing worse than (ע נ ג There is nothing better than (N, G, O), plague (sorrow).

5. How was it all accomplished? He combined, weighed, and changed: the א (A) with all ב A), and all again with (א the other letters in succession, and all the others again with (B); and so with the whole series of letters. Hence it follows that there are two hundred and thirty-one formations, or gates, through which the powers of the letters go forth; every creature and every language proceeded from One Name and the combinations of its letters.

6. He created a reality out of Nothing. He called the nonentity into existence and hewed colossal pillars from intangible air. This has been shown by the example of combining the letter א (A) with all the other letters, and all the other letters with א. By speaking He created every creature and every word by the power of One Name. As an illustration, consider the twenty-two elementary substances from the primitive substance of א. The production of every creature from the twenty-two letters is proof that they are in reality the twenty-two parts of one living body.

Chapter Three

1. The first three elements (the Mother letters, ש מ א) resemble a balance, in one scale virtue and in the other vice, placed in equilibrium by the tongue.

2. The three Mothers, ש מ א, enclose a great, wonderful, and unknown mystery, and are sealed by six wings (or elementary

circles), namely, air, water, fire--each divided into an active and a passive power. The Mothers, א מ ש, gave birth to the Fathers (the progenitors), and these gave birth to the generations.

3. God appointed and established three Mothers, א מ ש, combined, weighed, and exchanged them, forming by them three Mothers, in the universe, in the year, and in man (male and female).

4. The three Mothers, א מ ש, in the universe are: air, water, and fire. Heaven was created from the elementary fire (or ether) ש, the earth, comprising sea and land, from the elementary water, מ, and the atmospheric air from the elementary air, or spirit, א, which establishes the balance among them. Thus were all things produced.

5. The three Mothers, א מ ש, produce in the year heat, coldness, and the temperate state. Heat was created from fire, coldness from water, and the temperate state from air, which equilibrates them.

6. The three Mothers, א מ ש, produce in man (male and female) breast, abdomen, and head. The head was formed from the fire, ש; the abdomen from the water, מ; and the breast (thorax) from air, א, which places them in equilibrium.

7. God let the letter א (A) predominate in primordial air, crowned it, combined it with the other two, and sealed the air in the universe, the temperate state in the year, and the breast in man (male and female).

8. He let the letter מ (M) predominate in primordial water, crowned it, combined it with the other two, and sealed the earth in the universe (including land and sea), coldness in the year, and the abdomen in man (male and female).

9. He let the letter ש (Sh) predominate in primordial fire, crowned it, combined it with the other two, and sealed heaven in the universe, heat in the year, and the head of man (male and female).

Chapter Four

1. The seven double letters, ב ג ד כ פ ר ת (B, G, D, K, P, R, Th), have a duplicity of pronunciation: ד ד, כ כ, פ פ, ר ר, ת ת, (two

voices), aspirated and unaspirated, namely .They serve as a model of softness and hardness, strength and weakness=ג

2. The seven double letters symbolize wisdom, riches, fertility life, power, peace, and grace.

3. The seven double letters also signify the antitheses to which human life is exposed. The opposite of wisdom is foolishness; of riches, poverty; of fertility, sterility; of life, death; of power, servitude; of peace, war; and of beauty, deformity.

4. The seven double letters point out the six dimensions, height, depth, East and West, North and South, and the Holy Temple in the center, which sustains them all.

5. The double letters are seven and not six, they are seven and not eight; reflect upon this fact, search into it and reveal its hidden mystery and place the Creator on His throne again.

6. The seven double letters having been designed, established, purified, weighed, and exchanged by God, He formed of them seven planets in the universe, seven days in the Year, and seven gateways of the senses in man (male and female). From these seven He also produced seven heavens, seven earths, and seven Sabbaths. Therefore He loved seven more than any other number beneath His throne.

7. The seven planets in the universe are: Saturn, Jupiter, Mars, Sun, Venus, Mercury, and Moon. The seven days in the Year are the seven days of the week (possibly the seven creative days are meant). The seven gateways in man (male and female) are two eyes, two ears, two nostrils, and the mouth.

8. NOTE. Knut Stenring differs from other authorities in his arrangement of the planets and days of the week in the following seven stanzas. Kircher has still a different order. Rev. Dr. Isidor Kalisch, Wm. Wynn Westcott, and The Sacred Books and Early Literature of the East adopt the following arrangement.

<u>The Hebrew Letters according to the Sepher Yetzirah.</u>

In the central triangle are the three Mother Letters from which come forth the seven Double Letters--the planets and the heavens. Surrounding the black star are the signs of the zodiac symbolized by the twelve Simple Letters. In the midst of this star is the Invisible Throne of the Most Ancient of the Ancients--the Supreme Definitionless Creator.

1st. He caused the letter. ב (B) to predominate in wisdom, crowned it, combined each with the others, and formed by them the Moon in the universe, the first day in the year, and the right eye in man (male and female).

2nd. He caused the letter ג (G) to predominate in riches, crowned it, combined each with the others, and formed by them Mars in the universe, the second day in the year, and the right ear in man (male and female).

3rd. He caused the letter ד (D) to predominate infertility, crowned it, combined each with the others, and formed by them the Sun in the universe, the third day in the year, and the right nostril in man (male and female).

4th. He caused the letterכּ (K) to predominate in life, crowned it, combined each with the others, and formed by them Venus in the universe, the fourth day in the year, and the left eye in man (male and female).

5th. He caused the letter פ (P) to predominate in power, crowned it, combined each with the others, and formed by them Mercury in the universe, the fifth day in the year, and the left ear in man (male and female).

6th. He caused the letter ר (R) to predominate in peace, crowned it, combined each with the others, and formed by them Saturn in the universe, the sixth day in the year, and the left nostril in man (male and female).

7th. He caused the letter ת (Th) to predominate in grace, crowned it, combined each with the others, and formed by them Jupiter in the universe, the seventh day in the year, and the mouth of man (male and female).

9. With the seven double letters He also designed seven earths, seven heavens, seven continents, seven seas, seven rivers, seven deserts, seven days, seven weeks (from Passover to Pentecost), and in the midst of them His Holy Palace. There is a cycle of seven years and the seventh is the release year, and after seven release years is the Jubilee. For this reason God loves the number seven more than any other thing under the heavens.

10. In this manner God joined the seven double letters together. Two stones build two houses, three stones build six houses, four stones build twenty-four houses, five stones build 120 houses, six stones build 720 houses, and seven stones build 5,040 houses. Make a beginning according to this arrangement and reckon further than the mouth can express or the ear can hear.

Chapter Five

1. The twelve simple letters ה ו ז ח ט י ל נ ס ע צ ק (H, V, Z, Ch, T, I, L, N, S, O, Tz, Q) symbolize the twelve fundamental properties: speech, thought, movement, sight, hearing, work, coition, smell, sleep, anger, taste (or swallowing), and mirth.

2. The simple letters correspond to twelve directions: east height, northeast, east depth; south height, southeast, south depth; west height, southwest, west depth; north height, northwest, north depth. They diverge to all eternity and are the arms of the universe.

3. The simple letters having been designed, established, weighed, and exchanged by God, He produced by them twelve zodiacal signs in the universe, twelve months in the year, and twelve chief organs in ` human body (male and female).

4, The signs of the zodiac are: Aries, Taurus, Gemini, Cancer, Leo, Virgo, Libra, Scorpio, Sagittarius, Capricorn, Aquarius, and Pisces. The months of the year are: Nisan, liar, Sivan, Tammuz, Ab, Elul, Tisri, Marcheshvan, Kislev, Tebet, Sebat, and Adar. The organs of the human body are: two hands, two feet, two kidneys, gall, small intestine, liver, esophagus, stomach, and spleen.

1st. God caused the letter ה (H) to predominate in speech, crowned it, combined it with the others, and fashioned by them Aries (the Ram) in the universe, the month Nisan in the year, and the right foot of the human body (male and female).

2nd. He caused the letter ו (V) to predominate in thought, crowned it, combined it with the others, and fashioned by them Taurus (the Bull) in the universe, the month liar in the year, and the right kidney of the human body (male and female).

3rd. He caused the letter ז (Z) to predominate in movement,

crowned it, combined it with the others, and fashioned by them Gemini (the Twins) in the universe, the month Sivan in the year, and the left foot of the human body (male and female).

4th. He caused the letter ח (Ch) to predominate in sight, crowned it, combined it with the others, and fashioned by them Cancer (the Crab) in the universe, the month Tammuz in the year, and the right hand of the human body (male and female).

5th. He caused the letter ט (T) to predominate in hearing, crowned it, combined it with the others, and fashioned by them Leo (the Lion) in the universe, the month Ab in the year, and the left kidney of the human body (male and female).

6th. He caused the letter י(I) to predominate in work, crowned it, combined it with the others, and fashioned by them Virgo (the Virgin) in the universe, the month Elul in the year, and the left hand of the human body (male and female).

7th. He caused the letter ל (L) to predominate in coition, crowned it, combined it with the others, and fashioned by them Libra (the Balance) in the universe, the month Tisri in the year, and the gall of the human body (male and female).

8th. He caused the letter נ(N) to predominate in smell, crowned it, combined it with the others, and fashioned by them Scorpio (the Scorpion) in the universe, the month Marcheshvan in the year, and the small intestine in the human body (male and female).

9th. He caused the letter ס (S) to predominate in sleep, crowned it, combined it with the others, and fashioned by them Sagittarius (the Archer) in the universe, the month Kislev in the year, and the stomach in the human body (male and female).

10th. He caused the letter ע (O) to predominate in anger, crowned it, combined it with the others, and fashioned by them Capricorn (the Goat) in the universe, the month Tebet in the year, and the liver in the human body (male and female).

11th. He caused the letter צ (Tz) to predominate in taste (or swallowing), crowned it, combined it with the others, and fashioned by them Aquarius (the Water Bearer) in the universe, the month Sebat in the year, and the esophagus in the human body (male and female).

12th. He caused the letter ק (Q) to predominate in mirth,

crowned it, combined it with the others, and fashioned by them Pisces (the Fishes) in the universe, the month Adar in the year, and the spleen in the human body (male and female).

6. He made them as a conflict, He arranged them as provinces and drew them up like a wall. He armed them and set one against another as in warfare. (The Elohim did likewise in the other spheres.)

Chapter Six

1. There are three Mothers or first elements, א מ ש (A, M, Sh), from which emanated three Fathers (progenitors)--primordial (spiritual) air, water, and fire--from which issued the seven planets (heavens) with their angels, and the twelve oblique points (zodiac).

2. To prove this there are three faithful witnesses: the universe, the year, and man. There are the twelve, the balance, and the seven. Above is the Dragon, below is the world, and lastly the heart of man; and in the midst is God who regulates them all.

3. The first elements are air, water, and fire; the fire is above, the water is below, and a breath of air establishes balance between them. The token is: the fire carries the water. The letterמ (M) is mute; ש (Sh) is hissing like fire; there is א (A) among them, a breath of air which reconciles the two.

4. The Dragon (Tali) is in the universe like a king upon his throne; the celestial sphere is in the year like a king in his empire; and the heart is in the body of men like a king in warfare.

5. God also set the opposites against each other: the good against the evil, and the evil against the good. Good proceeds from good, evil from evil; the good purifies the bad, the bad the good. The good is reserved for the good, and the evil for the wicked.

6. There are three of which each stands by itself: one is in the affirmative (filled with good), one is in the negative (filled with evil), and the third equilibrates them.

7. There are seven divided three against three, and one in the midst of them (balance). Twelve stand in warfare: three produce love and three hatred; three are life-givers and three

are destroyers.

8. The three that cause love are the heart and the two ears; the three that produce hatred are the liver, the gall, and the tongues; the three life-givers are the two nostrils and the spleen; and the three destroyers are the mouth and the two lower openings of the body. Over all these rules God, the faithful king, from His holy habitation in all eternity. God is One above three, three are above seven, seven are above twelve, yet all are linked together.

9. There are twenty-two letters by which the I AM (YAH), the Lord of Hosts, Almighty and Eternal, designed and created by three Sepharim (Numbers, Letters, and Sounds) His universe, and formed by them all creatures and all those things that are yet to come.

10. When the Patriarch Abraham had comprehended the great truths, meditated upon them, and understood them perfectly, the Lord of the Universe (the Tetragrammaton) appeared to him, called him His friend, kissed him upon the head, and made with him a covenant. First, the covenant was between the ten fingers of his hands, which is the covenant of the tongue (spiritual); second, the covenant was between the ten toes of his feet, which is the covenant of circumcision (material); and God said of him, "Before Abraham bound the spirit of the twenty-two letters (the Thora) upon his tongue and God disclosed to him their secrets. God permitted the letters to be immersed in water, He burned them in the fire and imprinted them upon the winds. He distributed them among the seven planets and gave them to the twelve zodiacal signs

Ancient Greek stele, "Grave Naiskos of An Enthroned Woman With An Attendant," showing a woman who is appearing to raise the lid of a laptop, complete with USB-like ports. Things are never what they seem!

Bibliography

Ashe, G., *The Ancient Wisdom*, Macmillan, 1977.

Baring, A., and Cashford, J., *The Myth of the Goddess: Evolution of an Image,* Penguin, 1993.

Betegh, G., *Pythagoreans, Orphism and Greek Religion*, in Huffman 2014a, 149–166.

Blavatsky, H., *Isis Unveiled: A Master-Key to the Mysteries of Ancient and Modern Science and Theology*, Theosophical Publishing Company, 1877.

—, *The Secret Doctrine*, Theosophical Publishing Company, 1889.

Bond, F., *The Gate of Remembrance*, Oxford, Blackwell, 1919.

—, *The Company of Avalon*, Oxford, Blackwell, 1924.

Bond, F., and Lea, T., *Gematria, A Preliminary Investigation of the Cabala contained in the Coptic Gnostic Books and of a similar Gematria in the Greek text of the New Testament*, 1917.

Budge, E., *Gods of the Egyptians,* London: Methuen & Co, 1904.

Clarke, J., *Ten Great Religions*, Houghton Mifflin Company, 1881.

Elder, I., *Celt, Druid, and Culdee*, London, 1962.

Frazer, J. *The Golden Bough.* Macmillan and Co, 1890.

Godwin, J., *Rosicrucian Trilogy: Modern Translations of the Three Founding Documents*, *Fama Fraternitatis, 1644; Confessio Fraternitatis, 1615; The Chemical Wedding of Christian Rosenkreutz, 1616*, Weiser Books, 2016.

Godwin, J; McLean, A., *The Chemical Wedding of Christian Rosenkreutz*, Phanes Press, 1991.

Graddon, N., *Otto Rahn and the Quest for the Grail*, Kempton, Illinois, Adventures Unlimited Press, 2008.

—. *Pythagoras of Samos: First Philosopher and Magician of Numbers*, Adventures Unlimited Press, 2021.

Hall, Manley P. *The Secret Teachings of All Ages*, Los Angeles. The Philosophical Research Society, Inc., 1928.

—, *Orders of the Quest*, Philosophical Research Society, 1949.

—, *The Sacred Knowledge of the Qabalah*, Martino Publishing, CT, 2013.

—, *The Tarot*, Philosophical Research Society, Los Angeles, 1978.

Hartley, C., *The Western Mystery Tradition*, Aquarian Press, 1968.
Hartmann, F., *Secret Symbols of the Rosicrucians*, Boston Occult Publishing Co., 1888.
Heckethorn, C., *The Secret Societies of All Ages & Countries,* G. Redway, London, 1897.
Heydon, J., *The Rosie Cross Uncovered,* 1662.
Higgins, G., *Anacalypsis,* Longman, London, 1836.
—, *Celtic Druids,* R. Hunter, London, 1827.
Jennings, H., *The Rosicrucians, their Rites and Mysteries*, Volumes 1 and 2, 3rd edition, John C. Nimmo, London, 1887.
King, C., *Gnostics and Their Remains,* Bell and Dalby, 1864.
Le Plongeon, A., *The Origin of the Egyptians*, 1914.
Lemesurier, P., *The Great Pyramid Decoded*, Element Books, U.K., 1977.
Levi, E., *Dogme et Rituel de la Haute Magie*, Paris, 1854-1856.
Lomax, T., *A Complete History of the Druids: Their Origin, Manners, Customs, Powers, Temples, Rites and Superstitions*, 1810.
Lundy, J., *Monumental Christianity*, J.W. Bouton, 1876.
Maltwood, K., *A Guide to Glastonbury's Temple of the Stars*, The Women's Printing Society, Ltd., London, 1934.
—, *The Enchantments of Britain or King Arthur's Round Table of the Stars*, Victoria Printing and Publishing Co., 1944.
—, *King Arthur's Round Table of the Zodiac,* Victoria Printing and Publishing Co., 1946.
Matthews, C., *Celtic Spirituality*, Paulist Press, 1996.
Michell, J., *City of Revelation*, Abacus, 1973.
—, *Ancient Metrology*, Pentacle Books, Bristol, 1981.
—, *New Light on the Ancient Mystery of Glastonbury*, Thrift Books, 1990.
—, *The Dimensions of Paradise: Sacred Geometry, Ancient Science and the Heavenly Order on Earth*, Simon & Schuster, London, 2008.
—, *The Earth Spirit: Its Ways, Shrines and Mysteries*, Thames and Hudson, 1975.
—, *The New View Over Atlantis*, London. Thames and Hudson, 1983.
Michell, J. and Rhone, C., *Twelve Tribe Nation*, Inner Traditions, 1991.

Myer, I., *Qabalah—The Philosophical Writings of Solomon Ben Yehuda Ibn Gabirol*, 1888.

Neal, J., *Ancient Metrology*, vols. I-II, Squeeze Press, 2016-2017.

Pennick, N., *The Ancient Art of Geomancy*, Thames & Hudson, 1996.

Piggott, S., *The Druids*, Thames & Hudson, 1968.

Pike, A., *Morals and Dogma*, 1871.

Rahn, Otto, *Kreuzzug gegen den Gral,* Urban Verlag Freiburg i/Breisgau, 1933.

—, *Luzifers Hofgesind: Eine Reise zu den guten Gelstern Europas,* Schwarzhaupter Verlag, Leipzig, 1937.

Reiser, O., *This Holyest Erthe: The Glastonbury Zodiac and King Arthur's Camelot*, Perennial Books, London, 1974.

Rensselaer, Mrs John King, *The Devil's Picture Book: the History of Playing Cards*, 1890.

Roberts, A. (Ed.). *Glastonbury: Ancient Avalon, New Jerusalem*, Rider, 1978.

Ross, A., *Pagan Celtic Britain*, Academy Chicago Publishers, 1996.

Spence, L., *Druids: Their Origins and History*, Barnes & Noble, 1995.

—, *Myths & Legends of Babylonia & Assyria*, Harrap, 1916.

Smithen, L., *St Joseph of Arimathea at Glastonbury,* 1954.

Stone, E., *The Stones of Stonehenge*, Robert Scott, London, 1924.

Taylor, J., *The Great Pyramid: Why Was It Built, & Who Built It?* Longman, Green, Longman, and Roberts, London, 1859.

Taylor, T., *The Life of Pythagoras by Iamblichus*, translated from the Greek, Theosophical Publishing House, Los Angeles, 1905.

—, *Eleusinian and Bacchic Mysteries: a Dissertation*, Bouton, New York, 1891.

—, *The Mystical Hymns of Orpheus*, 1787.

Westcott, W., *Numbers: their Occult Power and Mystic Virtues*, Theosophical Publishing Society, 1890.

Waite, A., *The Real History of the Rosicrucians*, London, 1887.

Wells, H.G., *The Outline of History.* George Newnes, 1919-1920.

Wilder, A., *Philosophy and Ethics of the Zoroaster,* Theosophical Publishing Society, 2005.

Yates, F., *The Rosicrucian Enlightenment*, Routledge and Kegan Paul, London and Boston, 1972.

This book is dedicated to those who have junked the shackles of our mass-conscious world, love Mother Nature, and live happily, one day, one step at a time.

Get these fascinating books from your nearest bookstore or directly from: Adventures Unlimited Press

www.adventuresunlimitedpress.com

THE GODS IN THE FIELDS

Michael, Mary and Alice-Guardians of Enchanted Britain

By Nigel Graddon

We learn of Britain's special place in the origins of ancient wisdom and of the "Sun-Men" who taught it to a humanity in its infancy. Aspects of these teachings are found all along the St. Michael ley: at Glastonbury, the location of Merlin and Arthur's Avalon; in the design and layout of the extraordinary Somerset Zodiac of which Glastonbury is a major part; in the amazing stone circles and serpentine avenues at Avebury and nearby Silbury Hill: portals to unimaginable worlds of mystery and enchantment; Chapters include: Michael, Mary and Merlin; England's West Country; The Glastonbury Zodiac; Wiltshire; The Gods in the Fields; Michael, Mary and Alice; East of the Line; Table of Michael and Mary Locations; more.

280 Pages. 6x9 Paperback. Illustrated. $19.95. Code: GIF

CRYSTALS, MOTHER EARTH AND THE FORCES OF LIVING NATURE

By Nigel Graddon

Graddon presents a three-part narrative through the medium of crystal, "solidified light," according to the ancients. Part 1, Physical Crystal, describes the origins of the Universe and our Earth, and the gradual evolution of the mineral kingdom in its diverse forms, which find their highest vibrational power in the mysterious world of crystal. Part 2, Amazing Crystal, examines mind-blowing uses of crystal in the past and present.. Among its highlights are: in the past, the Great Pyramid's original crystal tip, the legend of the Rose Queen Goddess of Languedoc, Dr. Dee's scrying mirror and amethyst pendant, and the Black Stone and the Goddess; and exotic future applications such as Time Crystals and Quasicrystals. This is followed by an analysis of Mother Earth's living forces, including the legendary Crystal Skulls of Mesoamerica.

336 Pages. 6x9 Paperback. Illustrated. $19.95. Code: CMEF

THE MYSTERY OF U-33

By Nigel Graddon

The incredible story of the mystery U-Boats of WWII! Graddon first chronicles the story of the mysterious U-33 that landed in Scotland in 1940 and involved the top-secret Enigma device. He then looks at U-Boat special missions during and after WWII, including U-Boat trips to Antarctica; U-Boats with the curious cargos of liquid mercury; the journey of the Spear of Destiny via U-Boat; the "Black Subs" and more. Chapters and topics include: U-33: The Official Story; The First Questions; Survivors and Deceased; August 1985—the Story Breaks; The Carradale U-boat; The Tale of the Bank Event; In the Wake of U-33; Wrecks; The Greenock Lairs; The Mystery Men; "Brass Bounders at the Admiralty"; Captain's Log; Max Schiller through the Lens; Rudolf Hess; Otto Rahn; U-Boat Special Missions; Neu-Schwabenland; more.

351 Pages. 6x9 Paperback. Illustrated. $19.95. Code: MU33

JACK THE RIPPER'S NEW TESTAMENT
Occultism and Bible Mania in 1888
By Nigel Graddon

This book offers evidence, for the first time, that those responsible for the Whitechapel murders were members of a hit team associated with a centuries-old European occult confederacy dedicated to human sacrifice. This was corroborated in the private papers of a Monsignor who carried out intelligence work for Pope Pius X in the run-up to the outbreak of global conflict in 1914. The priest told of the existence of a Vatican-based cabal of assassins formed by the infamous Borgias that is in alliance with a Teuton occult group formed in the 9th century. It was from within this unholy alliance that assassins travelled to London to carry out the Ripper murders to "solve a sticky problem for the British Royal Family"

302 Pages. 6x9 Paperback. Illustrated. $19.95. Code: JRNT

OTTO RAHN & THE QUEST FOR THE HOLY GRAIL
The Amazing Life of the Real "Indiana Jones"
By Nigel Graddon

Otto Rahn, a Hessian language scholar, is said to have found runic Grail tablets in the Pyrenean grottoes, unearthed as a result of his work in decoding the hidden messages within the Grail masterwork *Parsifal*. The fabulous artifacts identified by Rahn were believed by Himmler to include the Grail Cup, the Spear of Destiny, the Tablets of Moses, the Ark of the Covenant, the Sword and Harp of David, the Sacred Candelabra and the Golden Urn of Manna. Some believe that Rahn was a Nazi guru who wielded immense influence within the Hitler regime, persuading them that the Grail was the Sacred Book of the Aryans, which, once obtained, would justify their extreme political theories.

450 pages. 6x9 Paperback. Illustrated. Index. $18.95. Code: ORQG

THE LANDING LIGHTS OF MAGONIA
UFOs, Aliens and the Fairy Kingdom
By Nigel Graddon

British UFO researcher Graddon takes us to that magical land of Magonia—the land of the Fairies—a place from which some people return while others go and never come back. Graddon on fairies, the wee folk, elves, fairy pathways, Welsh folklore, the Tuatha de Dannan, UFO occupants, the Little Blue Man of Studham, the implications of Mars, psychic connections with UFOs and fairies. He also recounts many of the strange tales of fairies, UFOs and Magonia. Chapters include: The Little Blue Man of Studham; The Wee Folk; UFOlk; What the Folk; Grimm Tales; The Welsh Triangle; The Implicate Order; Mars—an Atlantean Outpost; Psi-Fi; High Spirits; "Once Upon a Time…"; more.

270 Pages. 6x9 Paperback. Illustrated. $19.95. Code: LLOM

ALICE'S WONDERLAND
The Search For the Hidden Door
By Nigel Graddon

Graddon looks into the esoteric nature of Alice in Wonderland and the Hidden Door. Chapters on: Lost Worlds Shambhala; Agarttha; The Land of the Nradas; Asia Mysteriosa; India's Underworld Planets; Xibalba; Hyperborea; The Hole at the Pole; "Phantom Islands"; Atlantis; Parallel Worlds; "Etherea"; The Celtic Otherworld; Don Quixote and the Caves of Montesinos; The Elf Kingdom of Laurin; High Strangeness; Celluloid Worlds Purgatory; The Ninth Gate; Glastonbury Grove; Alice's Worlds Carroll; "Secunda"; Avalon; Alice and the Rosy Cross; more.

364 Pages. 6x9 Paperback. Illustrated. $19.95. Code: ALWR

SECRET MARS: The Alien Connection
By M. J. Craig

While scientists spend billions of dollars confirming that microbes live in the Martian soil, people sitting at home on their computers studying the Mars images are making far more astounding discoveries… they have found the possible archaeological remains of an extraterrestrial civilization. Hard to believe? Well, this challenging book invites you to take a look at the astounding pictures yourself and make up your own mind. *Secret Mars* presents over 160 incredible images taken by American and European spacecraft that reveal possible evidence of a civilization that once lived, and may still live, on the planet Mars… powerful evidence that scientists are ignoring! A visual and fascinating book!

352 Pages. 6x9 Paperback. Illustrated. $19.95. Code: SMAR

GODS AND SPACEMEN THROUGHOUT HISTORY
Did Ancient Aliens Visit Earth in the Past?
By W. Raymond Drake

From prehistory, flying saucers have been seen in our skies. As mankind sends probes beyond the fringes of our galaxy, we must ask ourselves: "Has all this happened before? Could extraterrestrials have landed on Earth centuries ago?" Drake spent many years digging through huge archives of material, looking for supposed anomalies that could support his scenarios of space aliens impacting human history. Chapters include: Spacemen; The Golden Age; Sons of the Gods; Lemuria; Atlantis; Ancient America; Aztecs and Incas; India; Tibet; China; Japan; Egypt; The Great Pyramid; Babylon; Israel; Greece; Italy; Ancient Rome; Scandinavia; Britain; Saxon Times; Norman Times; The Middle Ages; The Age of Reason; Today; Tomorrow; more.

280 Pages. 6x9 Paperback. Illustrated. $18.95. Code: GSTH

PYTHAGORAS OF SAMOS
First Philosopher and Magician of Numbers
By Nigel Graddon

This comprehensive account comprises both the historical and metaphysical aspects of Pythagoras' philosophy and teachings. In Part 1, the work draws on all known biographical sources as well as key extracts from the esoteric record to paint a fascinating picture of the Master's amazing life and work. Topics covered include the unique circumstances of Pythagoras' birth, his forty-year period of initiations into all the world's ancient mysteries, his remarkable meeting with a physician from the mysterious Etruscan community, Part 2 comprises, for the first time in a publicly available work, a metaphysical interpretation of Pythagoras' Science of Numbers.

294 Pages. 6x9 Paperback. Illustrated. $18.95. Code: PYOS

VIMANA:
Flying Machines of the Ancients
by David Hatcher Childress

According to early Sanskrit texts the ancients had several types of airships called vimanas. Like aircraft of today, vimanas were used to fly through the air from city to city; to conduct aerial surveys of uncharted lands; and as delivery vehicles for awesome weapons. David Hatcher Childress, popular *Lost Cities* author, takes us on an astounding investigation into tales of ancient flying machines. In his new book, packed with photos and diagrams, he consults ancient texts and modern stories and presents astonishing evidence that aircraft, similar to the ones we use today, were used thousands of years ago in India, Sumeria, China and other countries. Includes a 24-page color section.

408 Pages. 6x9 Paperback. Illustrated. $22.95. Code: VMA

PROJECT RAINBOW & THE PHILADELPHIA EXPERIMENT

By David Hatcher Childress

The story of the "Philadelphia Experiment" originated in late 1955 when Carl M. Allen sent an anonymous package marked "Happy Easter" containing a copy of Morris Jessup's book *The Case for the UFO: Unidentified Flying Objects* to the US Office of Naval Research. The book was filled with handwritten notes in its margins, written with three different shades of blue ink, appearing to detail a debate among three individuals. They commented on Jessup's ideas about the propulsion for flying saucers, discussed alien races, and expressed concern that Jessup was too close to discovering their technology. Jessup was then discovered with a hose wired to his exhaust pipe to bring the toxic fumes into his car. It was ruled a suicide. Was Jessup murdered as many people believe? Did the Defense Industrial Security Command (DISC), commanded by Wernher von Braun, have something to do with his death? Over 50 photographs and diagrams.

232 Pages. 6x9 Paperback. Illustrated. $22.00. Code: PRPE

EMPIRE OF SHIVA

By David Hatcher Childress

Childress brings us the evidence for a global civilization that worshipped the Hindu god Shiva—a civilization that is over 20,000 years old. They sought after gold and other metals, jade, obsidian, granite, diamonds and other gems. They also brought numerous plants and animals with them and utilized the many plants in new worlds including magic mushrooms, chocolate, vanilla, maize, potatoes, yams, coconuts and more. These Shiva worshippers came from across the Indian subcontinent, Tibet, Turkey and the Middle East, Southeast Asia, Indonesia, Pacific Islands, Mexico, Central America, Colombia, Peru, Madagascar, and other areas. They had huge fleets of oceangoing ships that traversed the Indian Ocean, Southeast Asia and the Pacific. When Shiva Ruled the World; Gobekli Tepe and Shiva; The Land of Shiva-Hiva; Shiva Lands of the Indian Ocean; The Cham-Khmer Shivites; Central America and Shiva; South America and Shiva; Mount Kailash, Tibet and Vimanas; The Endurance of Shiva; more. 16-page color section.

384 Pages. 6x9 Paperback. Illustrated. $22.00 Code: EOSV

IS EARTH REALLY SOLID?
The Evidence Re-Examined

By Oliver Milatovic

Geologist Oliver Milatovic takes a critical look at whether our Earth is actually a solid as claimed by most geologists, or is in fact partially hollow. He examines the creation of the Earth, other planets and our Moon. This far-reaching book takes on such topics as: The scientific method; Scientific laws, principles and effects; Common mistakes in applying the scientific method; Science as intellectual or logical endeavor; Science as a language; An outdated and obsolete paradigm is actually being used in modern science; Questioning the validity of the current model of Earth's interior; Seismological studies of Earth's interior; Errors and misinterpretations of seismological data; Gravity inside Earth; The myth of Earth having an iron core; and more. Revealing the true origin of the Earth and its interior, according to contemporary astronomical-astrophysical research, that falsifies the old paradigm; What is the real cause of geomagnetism and the magnetic field of celestial bodies?; more. The book is populated throughout by scores of illustrations and images.

480 Pages. 6x9 Paperback. Illustrated. $22.00. Code: IERS